H.D. and the Victorian Fin de Siècle

H.D. and the Victorian Fin de Siècle argues foremost that H.D. eluded the male modernist flight from Romantic "effeminacy" and "personality" by embracing the very cults of personality in the Decadent Romanticism of Oscar Wilde, A.C. Swinburne, Walter Pater, and D.G. Rossetti that her male contemporaries most deplored: the cult of the demonic femme fatale and of the "effeminate" Aesthete androgyne. H.D., Laity maintains, used these sexually aggressive masks to shape a female modernism that freely engaged female and male androgyny, homoeroticism, narcissism, and maternal eroticism.

For male modernist poets such as Pound and Eliot, Swinburne in particular personified the type of "effeminate" Romantic poet whose "unhealthy," "vague" language practices, Sapphic femmes fatales, and feminine Aesthetes demonstrated the need for a "masculinized" modernist poetics and poetry. Their ensuing doctrines of aesthetic distance and impersonality, Laity argues, attempted to "kill" the dissident subjectivities of the femme fatale and the male Aesthete mask that had dominated their youth. H.D., in contrast, evaded the repressive gender ideologies of male modernism by returning to these twin agents of dissident desires and their attendant "abject" body tropes, poetic forms, and experimental linguistic practices.

Focusing on the early *Sea Garden*, the plays and poetry of the 1920s, and her later epic, *Trilogy*, *H.D. and the Victorian Fin de Siècle* demonstrates H.D.'s shift from the homoerotic, "white," vanishing tropology of the male androgyne fashioned by Pater and Wilde to the "abject" monstrously sexual body of the Pre-Raphaelite and Decadent femme fatale.

(*continued after p. 215*)

H.D. and the Victorian Fin de Siècle

Gender, Modernism, Decadence

CASSANDRA LAITY

Drew University

CAMBRIDGE
UNIVERSITY PRESS

Published by the Press Syndicate of the University of Cambridge
The Pitt Building, Trumpington Street, Cambridge CB2 1RP
40 West 20th Street, New York, NY 10011-4211, USA
10 Stamford Road, Oakleigh, Melbourne 3166, Australia

First published 1996

Printed in the United States of America

Library of Congress Cataloging-in-Publication Data
Laity, Cassandra.
H.D. and the Victorian fin de siècle : gender, modernism,
decadence / Cassandra Laity.
p.   cm. – (Cambridge studies in American literature and
culture ; 104)
Includes bibliographical references.
ISBN 0-521-55414-4
1. H. D. (Hilda Doolittle), 1886–1961 – Knowledge – Literature.
2. Women and literature – United States – History – 20th century.
3. English literature – 19th century – History and criticism.
4. Decadence (Literary movement) – Great Britain.   5. Modernism
(Literature) – United States.   6. American poetry – English
influences.   7. Sex (Psychology) in literature.   8. Gender identity
in literature.   9. Aestheticism (Literature)   I. Title.
II. Series.
PS3507.0726Z77   1996
811'.52 – dc20   96-3827
                                                                    CIP

A catalog record for this book is available from the British Library.

ISBN 0-521-55414-4 Hardback

Contents

Acknowledgments

I owe my deepest gratitude to Susan Stanford Friedman and Rachel Blau DuPlessis whom I met ten years ago at the H.D. Centennial meetings in an atmosphere of excitement and promise that brought forth this book and many others. I am indebted to their groundbreaking work on H.D., gender, and other subjects, grateful for their unequaled generosity toward new scholars, and thankful for the intellectual exchange they continue to generate at all levels of the academy. Although I did not write my dissertation on H.D., I would also like to thank my professors at Michigan, especially Martha Vicinus, George Bornstein, and the late Earl Schulze whose teaching and mentorship contributed to this book (although I alone am responsible for its content).

This book has been enriched by the many academic communities and people I encountered at Dickinson College, Vanderbilt University, the University of Oregon, and elsewhere. I am particularly grateful for the friendship, encouragement, and intellectual commune I enjoyed with Sharon O'Brien, Susan Chase, Vereen Bell, Michael Kreyling, Phylis Frus, Claudia Ingram, Ann Ardis, Richard Dellamora, Eileen Gregory, Adalaide Morris, Louis Silverstein, and Diana Collecott. Here in New Jersey I am greatly indebted to Johan Noordsij for his wisdom and friendship during our conversation of many years. He has taught me much.

I wish to thank Josie Cook and the Interlibrary Loan Department at Drew University for supplying me with all the books and articles I needed at crucial stages of this project. Large sections of my writing were aided by timely grants from the Beinecke Library at Yale University (1987), a NEH for University Professors (1988), and a Mellon Assistant Professorship at Vanderbilt University (1987–1988).

Finally, Jim knows just how impossible this book and everything else would be without him.

Introduction
Dramatis Personae
The Aesthete Androgyne and the Femme Fatale

<hr>

This book argues foremost that H.D. eluded the male modernist flight from
Romantic "effeminacy" and "personality" by embracing the very cults of
personality in the British fin de siècle that her contemporaries most deplored: the cult of the demonic femme fatale and that of the Aesthete
androgyne. As I hope to demonstrate, Swinburne's decadent Hermaphroditus or the crystal man of Pater's androgynous, homoerotic Aestheticism
lies behind the mask of the "crystalline youth" H.D. adopted throughout
the 1920s in *Hippolytus Temporizes* and elsewhere,[1] while in her later work,
Swinburne's and Rossetti's Pre-Raphaelite femmes fatales inform *Trilogy's*
exploding, abject poetic of reviled Venuses – Venus herself, Lilith, Mary
Magdalene, and others.

My study first became organized around the figures of the Decadent
femme fatale and the male androgyne because their outlines were almost
always discernible behind male modernist denouncements of Romantic
personality in favor of modernist "impersonality," and by contrast, in the
active, desiring "I" of H.D.'s shifting feminine modernism. These sexually
dissident masks formed a convenient nexus for the ongoing debates about
sexuality and gender provoked by such historical or social phenomena as
the New Woman, the sexologists' theories of female inversion, and the
crisis in male sexual definition engendered by Oscar Wilde's infamous trials.[2] Moreover, in the gendered and competing schemes of Romantic influence configured by contrasting male and female agendas for modern
poetry, the fatal woman and the male Aesthete androgyne often enact the

paradigmatic repulsion/attraction to the maternal feminine that literary critics are currently finding inscribed throughout corresponding strains of male
and female modernisms.[3]

Although male theorizers of modernism such as Eliot, Yeats, and Pound
violently denounced these twin emblems of Romantic linguistic and sexual
"morbidity," H.D. was not alone among women writers in her identification with the Decadents' sexual/textual bodies of female desire and male
androgyny. Katherine Mansfield's early letters and journal entries reveal an
almost obsessive identification with the sexual ambiguities of Oscar Wilde
and a devotion to the Decadents that Sydney Janet Kaplan describes as
persistently "deeper than fashionability." Wilde's androgyny affirmed the
young woman's physical sense of herself as "child, woman and more than
half man." And Mansfield's exuberant recordings of Wilde's sexual aphorisms – "for we castrate our minds to the extent by which we deny our
bodies" – show us the young writer in the act of assembling a sexually
renegade authorial self.[4] Richard Dellamora rightly observes that Wildean
Aestheticism helped women writers "like [Katherine Mansfield]" "claim
for themselves both a power of utterance and a power over their bodies
and relationships."[5] Other women writers appear to have constructed a
patchwork feminine tradition that traced a line from Sappho through Decadent renderings of the lesbian femme fatale such as Swinburne's Sappho
in "Anactoria" or the titular persona of his autobiographical novel, *Lesbia
Brandon*. Renée Vivien's passionate, visceral, lesbian poetic of Decadent
goddesses – Venus of the Blind, Madonna of the Plague, the elusive Mai-
tresse of her love poetry – derive from her extensive reading in Swinburne.[6]
As Susan Gubar observes in her important "Sapphistries," Vivien regarded
Decadence as "fundamentally a lesbian literary tradition."[7]

The scope and pervasiveness of the transgressive discourses of "masculine desire" or demonic female eros in nineteenth-century literature,
poetry, and poetics have been demonstrated by Victorian scholars such as
Nina Auerbach, Richard Dellamora, Thaïs Morgan, Linda Dowling, and
others.[8] As Dellamora claims in his groundbreaking *Masculine Desire: The
Sexual Politics of Victorian Aestheticism*, although the category "homosexuality" was first introduced by medical literature (1870), the exploration of
new models for male love and gender identification "has a long, complex
development in the rhetoric of nineteenth-century poetry" from Shelley

through the poetry of the 1890s (*Masculine Desire* 1). Similarly, Alan Sinfield's *The Wilde Century: Effeminacy, Oscar Wilde and the Queer Moment,* cites "a line of nineteenth-century poets [who] cultivated" effeminacy in order to resist "patriarchal pressure" caused by diverse historical phenomena.[9] I would add that in addition to the representation of alternative masculinities, this developing, pervasive strain of Romanticism includes topoi for female narcissism, androgyny, homoeroticism, and role reversal. Further, like Sinfield's "Wilde century" and Dellamora's "Aestheticism," which encompass earlier aesthetic movements of the nineteenth century, my reference to the sexually transgressive poetic, which can be traced from early Romanticism through the 1890s as, variously, "Decadent Romanticism," "Decadence," or "the fin de siècle," is not limited to a single decade. Notably, each movement and its writers display important stylistic, philosophical, and historical differences; however, the experimentation with renegade sex/gender identities through similar masks, image complexes, poetic forms, and linguistic practices persists. For example, Pre-Raphaelitism, Aestheticism, and Decadence each deploy the white or crystal boy androgyne, the scarlet femme fatale, language practices deemed "effeminate" by their critics (from Robert Buchanon to T.S. Eliot), neo-Platonic theories of sex, gender, or spiritual "sameness," as well as other Greek encodings of dissident desires.

I will argue that the Decadent topoi of the femme fatale and the male androgyne and their attendant tropes, forms, and linguistic practices in works by the Pre-Raphaelites, Swinburne, Pater, and Wilde created a "feminine" tradition for modernist women poets who, unlike twentieth-century women novelists, did not claim to think back through their mothers, the strong women poets of the past. Unable or unwilling to recognize a tradition of women poets in the nineteenth century,[10] H.D. and others used the Decadents to fashion a modernist poetic of female desire. In the next generation of male poets, theories of modern poetry authored by Eliot, Pound, Yeats, and others repeatedly raise the specters of the femme fatale and the Aesthete to warn against the "hedonism" they believed had plunged Romanticism into decadence and decay. Women modernists such as H.D., however, responded differently to the powerful feminine subjectivities of their early reading that were presently driving their male contemporaries toward a foreboding masculinization of poetry. The ready agents of a sexually transgressive poetic – the fatal woman and the Aesthete androgyne – therefore articulated a fluid range of forbidden sexualities, including androgyny, homoeroticism, and role reversal, not available in the modernist poetic of male desire, which, as critics such as Susan Stanford Friedman, Rachel Blau DuPlessis, and Shari Benstock have demonstrated, prompted the twentieth-century woman writer to evolve alternative modernisms.[11] As I hope to demonstrate, the dual textual bodies of Decadent transgressive desire, with their attendant grotesque body tropes, disruptive language practices, and sympathetic theories of love and sexuality, effectively countered the major male modernists' anti-Romantic theories of impersonality. These doctrines, at their most conservative, insisted on normative male masks, purgative conceptions of the female image, masculinist theories of love and desire, and closed, self-referential linguistic theories.

From the early *Sea Garden*, H.D.'s poetic narratives of desire shuttle between the erotic masks of the Greek androgyne and the Sapphic femme fatale she had inherited from the Decadent Victorian Hellenists. By contrast, I argue in Chapter One, male modernist essays proposing the virtues of aesthetic impersonality frequently burned in effigy the femme fatale and the "effeminate" Aesthete, revealing what appeared to be a submerged crisis over the issue of sexual masking (my phrase) – the erotic orientation of the poetic "I." Reacting against the very real threat of a poetic legacy that valorized the feminine "I," male theorizers of early modernism socially constructed the Decadent past as a ruinous form of feminine writing emblematized by the seductive siren song of the femme fatale or the sexually ambiguous male Aesthete. Eliot's and Yeats's myths of their poetic development told of their narrow escape from the designing Romantic foremother or "effeminate" forefather whose sorcery had reduced them to mawkish Aesthetes in their impressionable youths. Kermode's *Romantic Image* unwittingly affirms that modernist theories of imagination subsequently sought to purge the monstrous femme fatale of her pathological "excess," reducing her to the passive, remote, and seamless image emblematized by the dancer.[12] Similarly, as we shall see, certain tenets of Yeats's, Pound's, and Eliot's theories of personae or masking ritually stripped away the Aesthete masks worn by their formerly "effeminate" selves. Indeed, if, as Eve Kosofsky Sedgwick and other critics claim, the gendered fallout from Wilde's trials triggered a general crisis of sexual definition and introduced new epistemological categories such as "the [male] homosexual," into representation, the male aesthete that had sparked debate in the nineteenth century became a renewed site of anxiety and subversion in the twentieth. Pound's staging of his own Aesthete persona's death in *Hugh Selwyn Mauberley* as representative of his theory of personae, for example, suggests that in addition to the battle of the sexes, the crisis of homo/heterosexual definition Sedgwick ascribes to Oscar Wilde's trials was strongly affecting the next generation of poets, who were already guilty by association. The ensuing male modernist war on Romantic personality often seemed aimed at snuffing out dissident subjectivities (indeed, Joseph Bristow notes that the word "personality," which Wilde "repeatedly turned to in his trials – both elud[ed] and yet signal[ed] the object of homosexual attraction").[13] The ensuing silencing system may have worked effectively against many women writing, but others were compelled toward these eroticized sites of gender trouble.[14] H.D.'s Decadent revisions helped her, therefore, to create a myth of womanhood counter to the myth of manhood represented by male modernist anti-Romantic programs for poetry.

I argue in Chapter One from a selection of essays, memoirs, letters, and other anti-Romantic prose documents produced by H.D.'s male contemporaries Yeats, Eliot, and Pound, that such writings often comprised masculinist "scripts"[15] for modernism. H.D.'s prose and poetic canon, however, appears frequently to vie for possession of the literary future through her inverse allegiance to the presiding geniuses of the feminine past. Thus (contrary to Harold Bloom's Oedipal model of father–son combat), Yeats's, Eliot's, and Pound's anti-Romantic scripts for poetic modernisms construct their Romantic precursors as insidiously possessive, fatal foremothers or forefathers whose influence threatened to feminize both their psyches and their art by entrapping them in the servile, effeminate position of the Aesthete.[16] By contrast, H.D.'s histories of her poetic development reach backward toward reconnection with the early Romantic, feminine, self. Although H.D. did not write essays detailing the dos and don'ts of modernism, her reviews, memoirs, letters, notes, and particularly H.D.'s several fictional autobiographies, provide a career-long gendered narrative of her modernist poetics. In *HER*,[17] H.D.'s 1920s' fictional history of her sexual and aesthetic beginnings, poems from Swinburne introduce the young woman poet to the boyishly androgynous sister/mother love that will articulate her discovery both of her bisexuality and poetic vocation. H.D.'s second, revised, mid-1940s' myth of Romantic origins, her autobiographical novel set in Pre-Raphaelite London, "White Rose and the Red," imaginatively reestablishes modernist continuity with the Victorian cult of womanhood by recasting her male contemporaries as members of the Pre-Raphaelite Brotherhood and H.D. as Elizabeth Siddal – prototype of the Decadent mother muse.[18] Following my preliminary discussion of the sex/gender politics inscribed in male modernist, anti-Romantic theories of mask and Image, I explore H.D.'s early deployment of Decadent masks and images in Chapter Two. The remainder of the book traces the course of H.D.'s changing Decadent revisionism throughout her career.

Reinforced, perhaps, by the high visibility of the femme fatale and the Aesthete androgyne in the early programs for male modernism she witnessed at first hand, H.D.'s dissenting poetic of disruptive body troping, sexual masking, and linguistic practices persistently returns to the twin Decadent agents of forbidden desire she first encountered in her early passion for Swinburne, Rossetti, Morris, and others. H.D.'s writings of the feminine body do not therefore engage the seamless, passively sentient icons for sexual/linguistic "unity" often prescribed by male modernism, but effectively defer and disfigure the modernists' most conservative Image/objects of desire by deploying both the evasive, white, vanishing tropology Pater, Wilde, and others had fashioned from the androgynous male ideal of Greek statuary, and the abject, monstrously sexual body of the Pre-Raphaelite femme fatale.

I will demonstrate in Chapter Three that the early H.D., like many other women writers, used a set of codes for the Decadent boy body such as "whiteness," "*diaphaneitè*" (transparency), intricacy, and artifice to configure the female body. Later, as I argue in Chapters Five through Seven, H.D. turned to the more visceral, grotesque, and abject femme fatale of poems such as Swinburne's "Anactoria" for refigurations of the mother muse. Further, H.D. avoided her male contemporaries' oppositional, gender-coded masks of love and sexuality through recourse to Decadent maskings based on sex/gender "sameness" found in the Romantic "Platonic" convention of incestuous brother–sister doublings, homoerotic boy–man dyads, and mother–son relations. In addition, the Decadent personae of a shape-changing, sexually renegade "author" who encompasses (his) diverse sexual personae – the Faustines, Venuses, Hyacinths, and so on of dramatic collections such as Wilde's *Poems* or Swinburne's *Poems and Ballads* – offered an example of "split" sexual masking. In H.D.'s volumes of erotic monologues such as *Hymen* (1921) or *Heliodora* (1924), the phantasm of a shaping power, "H.D.," explores a range of emotions and desires, from the maternal eroticism of "Demeter" to the male–male homoeroticism of her "Hyacinth." Related to this, the Aesthete's and fatal woman's poetic vehicles – Decadent quest romance or heretic Victorian monologue – offered an established form for the sexual history that would organize H.D.'s searching narratives of feminine desire in poetry, prose, and long poems such as *Hippolytus Temporizes, HER, Trilogy,* and *Helen in Egypt.*

However, H.D.'s feminist revisions of Decadent Romanticism required an extremely careful maneuvering through the straits of the feminist revisionary process. Passive acquiescence to Decadent influence could be dangerous to both the feminist text and the female psyche. Despite his sexually transgressive poetics, the Aesthete poet's possession of a male body, his operation within a male discourse, and his differing power relation to the conventional poetic of male desire gave rise to a set of narrative strategies whose sometime misogyny rendered the woman writer invisible or worse. Internalizing Decadent misogyny or the consciously perverse "religion of vice" might therefore expose the woman writer to the very censure and self-abasement she sought to escape. Sydney Kaplan expresses unease with the young Mansfield's total self-immersion in the persona of the Wildean Aesthete, who "even in his supposed androgyny" remains a "male" figure ("K.M.'s London" pp. 166, 167). Perhaps the implicit denial of her own female body as well as terror of Wildean "perversity" led to Mansfield's agonized letter of homosexual panic in which she denounced her affairs with women as having been initiated under Wilde's demonic influence. She wrote, "Wilde acted so strongly and terribly upon me that I was constantly subject to exactly the same fits of madness as those which caused his ruin and his mental decay."[19] Similarly, co-option by the corrupt femme fatale could be equally devastating: Lillian Faderman goes so far as to attribute Renée Vivien's lurid death by starvation to her identification with Swinburne's Lesbia Brandon, among other Decadent sadomasochistic images of the "doomed lesbian."[20]

Albeit for feminist purposes, H.D.'s early poetry unwittingly embraces the "homosocial"[21] misogyny implicit in some Aesthetic appropriations of the boy–man Greek mentoring system, which define women's love as base, animalistic, and inferior to the higher love between men. Shakespeare's sonnets to the "foul" Dark Lady and the Fair Youth demonstrate the misogynist pitfalls of this classical construct, which produced in Victorian Hellenists such as Pater a similar split between the coarsely material, vampire femme fatale (Mona Lisa) and the pure boy priest (Marius the Epicurean, the crystal man of his essays, and others) he modeled after the white masculine ideal of Greek male statuary.[22] Accordingly, as early as H.D.'s *Sea Garden* (1916), white, shimmering, and chiseled landscape/bodies of androgyny provide space and respite from stifling, overripe Venusbergs of oppressive desire. By the poetic monologues ("Hyacinth"), verse plays (*Hippolytus Temporizes*), and prose (*Hedylus*) of the 1920s, H.D.'s sexual poetic appears largely to revolve around a full-blown dichotomy between the white Aesthete androgyne or his Artemisian counterpart and the corrupt, scarlet femme fatale. Although the early H.D. used the typically Paterian aversion toward the femme fatale – frequently to great effect – in order to pronounce against the conventionally feminine sexuality she perceived as polarizing the sexes and disallowing erotic/spiritual "sameness," H.D.'s poetic of male androgyny threatened to self-destruct in the 1930s, as Susan Friedman and others have demonstrated.[23]

H.D.'s primary Romantic vehicle for sexual "sameness," the Aesthete androgyne of Victorian Hellenism, eventually exacted a heavy price from the woman poet: While H.D.'s inscriptions of a feminine desire or language in the white, vanishing body of the male androgyne cleared a space for erotic/linguistic play, they simultaneously denied the woman poet the empowering difference of her female body. From the 1930s onward, H.D. cast off her primary mask of boy-androgyne, summoning the power of the abject, the horrific, and often violent tropology of the femme fatale, which would force the maternal feminine body/text into representation.

H.D.'s shift from the mask of the male Aesthete to that of the femme fatale appears to be prompted by the changing purposes, scope, and orientation toward the feminine of the experienced (and battle-scarred) H.D. Harold Bloom, George Bornstein, and others map the phases of Romantic influence demarcating the careers of male moderns such as Yeats, Eliot, and Stevens.[24] Similarly, H.D.'s rejection of the male Aesthete persona for the mask of the Pre-Raphaelite femme fatale (prototype of the Decadent fatal woman) demonstrates two distinct revolutions in her Decadent revisionism reflecting the shifting sex/gender concerns and psychodynamics unique to the career of a woman writer. Accordingly, I argue in the second half of the book, H.D. generated a second Romantic myth of origins and a later agenda for female modernism in her Pre-Raphaelite novels, supplanting the earlier *HER*. In the meantime, I hope to demonstrate, H.D. became aesthetically reattuned to the persona of the siren (of literature and film) during her immersion in Violet Hunt's biography of Elizabeth Siddal, *Wife of Rossetti,* and during her simultaneous involvement with director Kenneth MacPherson and avant-garde cinema in the early 1930s. A few years later, H.D.'s pivotal psychoanalysis with Freud reconciled her to both her bisexuality and her search for the mother/lover[25]: H.D.'s new figuration of the mother muse as the flagrantly sexual femme fatale informs her unpublished Pre-Raphaelite novel, "White Rose and the Red" (composed 1947–8). A more inclusive, cultural and female-identified modernist agenda is set forth in this fictional autobiography of the prototypical femme fatale – Elizabeth Siddal – which regroups H.D.'s male contemporaries in the composite personae of Aldington-Rossetti, Pound-Swinburne, and Lawrence-Morris around the nineteenth-century cult of womanhood represented by Siddal-H.D. Immersed in the Pre-Raphaelites, H.D. herself professed of her earlier work, "I had actually adjusted my opera-glasses the wrong way round, to the Greek scene," and referred to her current fascination with the Pre-Raphaelite "legend" as a "new direction." She tellingly described the Pre-Raphaelite novels she wrote during the mid-1940s as the "prose phase" that necessarily preceded "the poetry."[26]

I conclude the book with an analysis of the abject femme fatale in H.D.'s major, late poem, *Trilogy.* Drawing upon disruptive theories of body troping such as Julia Kristeva's notion of abjection (*Powers of Horror*), Monique Wittig's writings of the lesbian body (*The Lesbian Body*), and Mikhail Bakhtin's discussion of "the grotesque image of the body" (*Rabelais and His World*), I approach H.D.'s epic as a poem of the explosive and exploded body that revels in the monstrous femmes fatales she encountered in Pre-Raphaelite art – Mary Magdalene, Lilith, Venus, and others.[27] Unlike Eliot's listless collection of misfits in an earlier male epic of poetic modernism, *The Waste Land,* H.D.'s "straggling company" of war-torn artist dejects, city dwellers, and prophets are propelled across the divide of epochs toward a new linguistic/erotic modernity molded from Decadent "bodies that mat(t)er."[28]

The study of sexually transgressive Decadence and its impact on modernist women (and men) writers has just begun. The numerous, thoroughgoing books on male modernism and the influence of nineteenth-century poetry by Harold Bloom, George Bornstein, Frank Kermode, James Longenbach, and others focus rather on modernist continuities with the more sexually conventional theories and theorists of early Romanticism and Victorianism.[29] Similarly, some attention has been given to the influence of the early Romantic imagination on women writers such as Emily Dickinson or Willa Cather.[30] Contemporary feminist inquiries into the possible impact of the sexually renegade Decadents on modernist women writers began in major surveys of the many influences shaping the modernisms of several twentieth-century women writers, such as Susan Gubars and Sandra Gilbert's *No Man's Land,* vols. I and II, and Shari Benstock's *Women of the Left Bank.* References to Baudelairean or Swinburnian Decadence have appeared most often in literary studies of Renée Vivien and Natalie Barney. Sydney Kaplan's *Katherine Mansfield and the Origins of Modernist Fiction* dwells on Mansfield's relation to Oscar Wilde as part of a larger mapping of literary origins.[31] In addition to these works, *H.D. and the Victorian Fin de Siècle* has benefited from recent works by Victorian scholars such as Richard Dellamora, Jonathan Dollimore, Thaïs Morgan, Linda Dowling, and others, which are uncovering the poetic discourses of sexual/linguistic transgression referred to as "Decadence."[32] My critique of male modernism has also been much aided by reassessments of the political implications (although not the sex/gender implications) of the modernist poetics of impersonality formulated by Eliot and Pound. These include Lyndall Gordon's two literary biographies of Eliot, *Eliot's Early Years* and *Eliot's New Life,* Gail McDonald's *Learning to be Modern,* Andrew Ross's *The Failure of Modernism,* and Louis Menand's *Discovering Modernism.* I am also indebted to Elizabeth Butler Cullingford's pathbreaking study of Yeats and gender in *Gender and History in Yeats's Love Poetry.*[33]

My purpose in this book, to conduct a sustained exploration into the Decadent revisionism of one modernist woman poet within the larger context of competing male and female modernisms, has given me the freedom to concentrate on the course of an entire career. However, the scope of this book prevented me from exploring in depth the many women writers I encountered in my research – Willa Cather, Violet Hunt, Virginia Woolf, among them – whose fascination with the transgressive poetics of Oscar Wilde, Swinburne, the Pre-Raphaelites, and others demands further, specialized study.

For
Sally Wheelock Brayton
Jim Hala
and
Zachary Laity Hala

Chapter One

The Rhetoric of Anti-Romanticism
Gendered Genealogies of Male Modernism

Most recent critical commentaries on Eliot, Yeats, and Pound acknowledge their sometime conservative if not misogynist attitudes toward women.[1] However, the complex of literary, historical, and psychosocial events underlying the hypermasculine rhetoric of the modernist poetic enterprise is just beginning to receive attention. Gail McDonald's pathbreaking *Learning to Be Modern* discusses at length Eliot's and Pound's project to "masculinize" the modern image of the poet and his work, although she subordinates the sex/gender issue to the (equally important) matter of class. Identifying the male modernists' compulsion to separate themselves from scribbling women and dandified men with the fall of the (American) "feminized" gentry and the emerging "culture of professionalism," McDonald focuses on the ensuing class war that made it imperative for the male modern poet (and scholar) to remodel himself after "serious, hardworking, professional men who made substantive contributions to the real world." " 'Women,' " McDonald notes, "was code for whatever stood in the way of serious, productive creation" (McDonald 62, 64, 87). In this chapter I suggest that Eliot's, Pound's, and Yeats's highly public "masculinization" of poetic modernism also constituted a response to the crisis of sex/gender identification that critics have attributed variously to Oscar Wilde's infamous trials, the proliferation of women writers, the New Woman, and other twentieth-century social or historical phenomena drawing attention to the epistemology of "sex."[2]

The mainstream poets' professed agenda for modernism appears to have

shared the male modernist novelists' prohibition against sexual or androgynous female images such as the femme fatale – a taboo that Gilbert and
Gubar attribute to the rise of the New Woman – and against the newly
introduced type of "the homosexual" modeled after Oscar Wilde and his
association with "leisure, privilege and high culture" in the aftermath of
his trials.[3] Indeed, perhaps the most urgent polemic against "effeminacy"
issued from the poets who had lionized the late-Victorian Romantics in
their youth and now faced the task of erasing the feminine Aesthete from
modern memory and reinventing a more acceptable sex/gender image of
the poet and his poetics. As Yeats records in his *Autobiographies,* although
the *literati* had originally viewed Oscar Wilde as a "triumphant figure,"
their approbation turned to expressions of contempt (which Yeats did not
share) following the revelations made by his trials. Yeats notes Lionel Johnson's obvious "bitterness" and quotes from a letter in which Johnson fu-
riously denounces Wilde's treachery and imposture: "He got a 'sense of
triumph and power, at every dinner table he dominated, from the knowledge that he was guilty of that sin which, more than any other possible to
man, would turn all those people against him if they but knew.' "[4] Yeats
recalls that Aubrey Beardsley was dismissed from his art editorship at *The
Yellow Book* – although he disliked Wilde and possessed "no sexual abnor-
mality" – because of the public outrage over his illustrations for Wilde's
Salome (Auto 216). Pound's and Eliot's reaction against the feminized gentry, therefore, may also be interpreted as a form of sexual panic on the part
of the successors of Oscar Wilde, whose guilty verdict had unmasked the
feminine, aristocratic, and insouciant pose of the Aesthete poet as sexually
deviant. Before discussing in detail the gendered theories of mask and Image inherent in the early male modernist poetic program, it would be useful
to survey the masculinist rhetoric that pervaded male modernist anti-
Romanticism in general.

Even a cursory glance at the misogynist rhetoric that attended the male
modernists' anti-Romantic program for a renovated modernism suggests
familiar dismissals of effeminate men's and women's writing: The charges
leveled against the past include sentimentalism, effeminacy, escapism, lack
of discipline, emotionalism, self-indulgence, confessionalism, and more.
T.E. Hulme's famous manifesto, "Romanticism and Classicism," divided
literary history into strict gender categories. The Romanticism of Swin-

burne, Byron, and Shelley was defined as "feminine," "damp," and "vague"; Classicism, which formed the model for Imagism, "dry," "hard," "virile," and "exact."[5] Irving Babbitt, who first made the distinction between Romanticism and Classicism,[6] and authored seminal attacks on the decadent and subversive tendencies of Romanticism, strongly influenced the anti-Romantic and misogynist rhetoric of his pupil, T.S. Eliot.[7] The tension between a masculinist humanism and an effeminate romanticism is discernible in Eliot's famous definition of the Romantic "dissociation" of "thought" and "feeling"[8] – which he specifically assigned to the "feminine type" of writing – and the "unified sensibility" he defined as implicitly masculine. Eliot grouped "Mr. Joyce" among the "strongest" writers who "make their feeling into an articulate external world." Virginia Woolf, by contrast, demonstrated a "more feminine type," which "makes its art by feeling, and by contemplating the feeling rather than the object": "The charm of Mrs. Woolf's shorter pieces consists in the immense disparity between the object and the train of feeling which it has set in motion."[9] Ezra Pound, to whom H.D. had been briefly engaged, colorfully extended the modernist critique of Romantic writing to a gender-biased construct of literary history. Pound included Dante and the French symbolists under the masculine designation, flamboyantly disclaiming "the softness of the 'nineties' " for which "I have different degrees of antipathy or even contempt."[10] Elsewhere he criticized the "theatricals" of the Victorian Romantics for "pestering the reader with frills and festoons of language" (LE 270). And during his middle period, Yeats dismissed his earlier "womanish introspection" and temporarily abandoned the Romantic feminine lyric forms he had employed.[11] Other modernists frequently linked Romanticism with women writers in dismissals of both. T.E. Hulme blamed the present decayed state of Romanticism for giving license to the self-indulgent sentimentality, confessionalism, and flowery imagery of women writers:

> The carcass is dead and all the flies are upon it. Imitative poetry springs up like weeds, and women whimper and whine of you and I alas, and roses, roses, roses, all the way. It [Romanticism] becomes the expression of sentimentality rather than of virile thought.[12]

Similarly, H.D.'s then husband Richard Aldington, in his review of a novel by Violet Hunt in The Egoist, maintained that women writers were "incapable" of the "indirect" method of writing, and could only imitate the confessional mode that he equated with Rousseauan Romanticism, thus relegating them to the "great second class" of writers.[13] Finally, explicit or implicit rejections of feminine writing frequently characterized Pound's and Eliot's praise for the masculine virtues of science, intellectual rigor, unity, objectivity, and concreteness.

This chapter examines those places in the male modernists' rhetorical crusade against Romanticism where aspects of the new poetic program (modernism) are proposed as correctives to the linguistic and sexual "perversities" of the past. I suggest that the current male anxiety about sex/gender identification is apparent in the masculinist predisposition of certain modernist doctrines of poetic identity, language, and the female body formulated in opposition to Romantic effeminacy. These incidences of gender trouble occur in various anti-Romantic expositions on modernist "impersonality," the sex/gender designation of the poet's mask, and on the Image/object – both as it applies to representations of the female beloved and as a theory of metaphor containing gendered notions of language.

The first section on modernist masking specifically concerns those presentations of Yeats's masks, Eliot's objective correlative, and Pound's personae that erect a version of the Romantic hero/poet – a Mauberley, a Hamlet, a Shelley, or the youthful poet himself – and proceed to demonstrate how its particular operations will counteract the subject's effeminacy. Such theories of poetic sexual identity often conjure perverse typologies of both the Romantic effeminate Aesthete and the appropriating femme fatale enacting what the modernists appear to have regarded as the typically Romantic, sexually/textually ruinous pathologies of son–mother fixation, or, more covertly, male–male desire. Here the objective correlative, the mask, or the persona serves as a literary acid test, affording the poet or critic a means to divine the symptoms of Romantic effeminacy, if not provide the curative. Related to this, I will argue that the male modernists' social construction of Romanticism as both a deadly "foremother" and a sexually ambiguous forefather departs from Bloom's Freudian model of father–son combat and more closely resembles Chodorow's theory of male identity formation whereby the son necessarily severs his symbiotic connection with the mother and "the feminine world."[14] In Section II of this chapter, The Sexual Politics of the Image/Object, I examine conceptions of the female image, typified by New Critic Frank Kermode's *Romantic Image,* that profess to displace the femme fatale in favor of a more passive, "aesthetic" female body. I also explore anti-Romantic linguistic theories of the Image/object claiming to inhibit evasive signification – which feminist criticism has come to associate with women's writing[15] – and to promote a more exacting, masculinist correspondence between "word" and "thing."

In this chapter I am also concerned with the ways in which the masculinist doctrine of impersonality paradoxically summoned the presences of the femme fatale and the male aesthete it was intended to suppress. As Judith Butler suggests in *Bodies That Matter,* if, according to Lacan's and Foucault's shared notion "that regulatory power produces the subjects [and sexualities] it controls," then "the 'threat' that compels the assumption of masculine and feminine attributes" is the feminized male and the masculinist woman (*Bodies* 102, 103). It has become a critical commonplace that modernist impersonality defined itself mainly through opposition to the errors of Romanticism. Peopled therefore by "these [erroneous] figures of hell" (*Bodies* 103), modernist poetics not only alerted women writers to the subversive sexual personae of Romanticism but also unwittingly created a pervasive myth of the sexual woman and the androgynous man.

Finally, my mapping of the gendered narratives of male poetic modernism is selective, and is not intended as an exhaustive study of these complex and often contradictory theories. Very few scholarly examinations of gender and male poetic modernism in Eliot and Pound have yet appeared.[16] My main purpose is to demonstrate that certain tenets of male modernism excluded women writers such as H.D. (and sexually dissident male writers) and defined a strain of male modernist poetics from a female modernism that embraced the masks, images, and linguistic practices of Decadent Romanticism.

However, this proposed model for a "male" anti-Romantic modernism and a "female" Romantic modernism should not be regarded as monolithic. Quoting Sandra Gilbert's sharp division between the "male modernist," who seeks the "consolation of orthodoxy," and the "female modernist," who wishes to "restore the primordial chaos of transvestism," Jessica Feldman notes in *Gender on the Divide: The Dandy in Modernist Literature,* "men, as well as women, have . . . sought the chaos of transvestism."[17] Feldman proposes that the nineteenth-century (French) dandy forms "an icon of modernism."[18] Indeed, Pound never abandoned his Whistlerian affectations, and biographer Peter Ackroyd notes that several of Eliot's friends remarked his peculiarly Decadent practice of wearing cadaver-green face powder at private parties.[19] The hypermasculine slogans of male modernist anti-Romanticism often bore no relation to male modernist poetic practice, which was frequently steeped in the "female" and androgynous poetics they outwardly deplored. As Elizabeth Butler Cullingford demonstrates in her study of Yeats's feminism (*Gender and History in Yeats's Love Poetry*), even as the rhetoric of Yeats's poetics lapses into misogynist posturings (Cullingford 8), his love poetry reveals a lifelong experimentation with gender roles and sexuality. Similarly, if all gender is performative, Eliot and Pound's prose often gave conflicting performances, assuming masks of strident virility in their most public pronouncements, while more privately, they "cross-dressed." The modernists' most vociferous pronouncements against "effeminate" Romanticism enacted Chodorow's psychosocial model of male rebellion against the feminine. However, as I will discuss later, Eliot, Pound, and Yeats experienced a strong concurrent pull toward "feminine" Romanticism. Both Eliot and Pound more privately constructed a self-identifying, male homoerotic paradigm of Romantic influence closely resembling the sympathetic, "pre-Oedipal" exchange. Indeed, to women writers such as H.D., modernist anti-Romanticism must have seemed a bewildering about-face, intensifying their sense of exclusion and alienation from the heady intellectual commune of earlier years.

I The Mask: The Ritualized Death of the Aesthete Poet

The male modernists' campaign to reinvest the poet with a masculine identity is apparent in the published, personal accounts of their own narrow escapes from the influence of a devouring feminine Romanticism into an autonomous modernism. Throughout his career, Eliot in particular appears to have suffered from a profound erotic ambivalence toward Romanticism. Eliot most often denounced his former Romanticism as a sexually ambiguous "feminine" influence. In his essay, "On the Development of Taste," a late case history of his Romantic origins (1933), Eliot's description of his former thralldom suggests at once both matriphobic and homophobic recoil from excessive self-identification with an all-encompassing fatal foremother or a seducing forefather – neither of which resembles Harold Bloom's father–son combat within the Freudian family romance. Eliot's delineation of his fall into Romanticism begins rhapsodically,

> It [the discovery of the Romantics] was like a sudden conversion; the world appeared anew, painted with bright, delicious and painful colors. Thereupon I took the usual adolescent course with Byron, Shelley, Keats, Rossetti, [and] Swinburne.

and becomes increasingly disenchanted,

> I take this period to have persisted until my nineteenth or twentieth year. . . . Like the first period of childhood, it is one beyond which I dare say some people never advance. . . . At this period, the poem, or the poetry of a single poet, invades the youthful consciousness and assumes complete possession for a time. We do not really see it as something with an existence outside ourselves: much as in our youthful experiences of love, we do not so much see the person as infer the existence of some outside object which sets in motion these new and delightful feelings in which we are absorbed. The frequent result is an outburst of scribbling which we may call imitation. . . . It is not a deliberate choice of a poet to mimic, but writing under a kind of daemonic possession by one poet.[20]

Eliot's characterization of his early Romantic intimacy both as a "daemonic possession" and as an "invasion" places the young poet in a suggestively erotic, feminine, victimized relation to the Romantic foremother/forefather. Under the influence of Romanticism, the young Eliot finds himself absorbed by self-indulgent, erotic fantasy (resembling the experience of first love) in which the other exists as an extension of his own ego. Eliot associates Romanticism with "the first period of childhood" as a passive and implicitly female-identified phase of uncontrolled passions and self-absorption. Eliot cautions that Romantic influence should be nothing more than an adolescent phase of erotic and linguistic experimentation that the young poet properly renounces in his passage to a mature (modernist) manhood: "It [the Romantic period of adolescence] is, no doubt, a period of keen enjoyment; but we must not confuse the intensity of the poetic experience in adolescence with the intense experience of poetry" (*TUPTUC* 33).

Although, as Elizabeth Cullingford argues, Yeats was unable to sustain the mask of manhood he undertook during his middle period, Yeats's masculinist reconstruction of the phases of his personal and poetic development, which critics such as Ellmann and Bornstein have accurately traced in his *Memoirs,* the *Autobiographies,* prose essays, and letters, begins with an account of the early Yeats as an effeminate Romantic.[21] Dominated and consumed by his obsession for a masterful woman both in life (Maud Gonne) and art, the Aesthete poet wrote poems of "longing and complaint" to the nineteenth-century femme fatale who ruled his imagination. Yeats would describe his early poetry as effeminate and escapist–"a flight into fairyland . . . and a summons to that flight" (*Letters* 90) – and as overshadowed by a "sentimental sadness" and "womanish introspection" (*Letters* 434). Yeats's depiction of his early Romantic imagination incorporated the common modernist conception of Romanticism as a dangerous, erotic, and potentially unmanning Venusberg that leads the poet more and more deeply into his own solipsistic fantasies and away from the virile forces of sexual energy, will, and intellect. T.E. Hulme warned against the seduction of Romanticism, which he compared to "a drug": "Accustomed to this strange light, you can never live without it" (*Speculations* 127). Similarly, Yeats cautioned George Russell against a nineties' Aestheticism he described as that "region of brooding emotions . . . which kill the spirit and the will, ecstasy and joy equally, [and whose dwellers] speak to me with sweet insinuating feminine voices" (*Letters* 434). Under the spell of Romanticism's siren song, the early Yeats felt powerless and "alone amid the obscure impressions of the senses"; he produced a fragmented and "sterile" art "full of decorative landscape and stilllife." After the turn of the century, Yeats called for "more manful energy" and executed his "movement downward upon life."[22]

Neither of the foregoing narratives of Yeats's and Eliot's struggle to overthrow Romantic influence recall the Bloomian Oedipal combat: Rather, both male modernists appear to be resisting the pre-Oedipal attachment to an eroticized precursor whose hold over the young man must be broken. Nancy Chodorow's woman-centered model for the formation of male gender identity offers a more plausible psychoanalytic theory for the male modernists' struggle to defend against the "feminine" past. Chodorow's description of the socialization process that forces the boy to forge a male identity through severing his pre-Oedipal attachment to the mother is reflected in both Eliot's and Yeats's accounts of their break from the adolescent phase of an effeminate Romanticism and their consequent willful re-creation of themselves as masculine and mature modernists. Further, the frequently hazy designation of modernism as that which is not-Romantic and therefore effeminate writing, suggests the psychodynamics of Chodorow's model whereby the son struggles "to distinguish and differentiate" himself from "the feminine world" represented by his mother in order to acquire a masculinity he defines abstractly as "that which is not feminine and/or connected to women" (Chodorow 174). Eliot's lifelong yearning toward the self-identifying (pre-Oedipal) relation he associated with Romanticism is demonstrated by an essay written during his most anti-Romantic phase: "Reflections on Contemporary Poetry" (1919) celebrates rather than condemns the sympathetic, "feminine" bond between the younger poet and his literary first love.[23] (Significantly, "Tradition and the Individual Talent" and "Reflections" were published in the same year, but the latter was suppressed in favor of the more oppositional scheme of the now-famous essay.) Although the openly homoerotic male–male scheme of influence demonstrated by "Reflections" does not identify the beloved "dead author[s]" who initiated the younger poet's erotic awakening, the passage quoted earlier from his essay "On the Development of Taste" and other case histories of Eliot's poetic origins suggest that the Romantics provoked Eliot's own youthful "conversion" experience.

Indeed, the passage from "On the Development of Taste" and "Reflections on Contemporary Poetry" would seem to demonstrate the emotional extremes of sexual panic and homoerotic ardor toward the same event – the sudden onset of the younger poet's first romance with the literary past. Like "The Development of Taste," "Reflections" equates the poet's "first [literary] passion" with his development as a poet and a man: "It is possible to say that there is a close analogy between the sort of experience which develops a man and the sort of experience which develops a writer" ("Reflections" 39). In both essays, "the experience" issues from the younger poet's impulsive engagement with an older master in a mystical, erotic exchange. We recall that Eliot's early Romantic reading had struck him "like a sudden conversion," "the world appeared anew, painted with bright, delicious and painful colors" (*TUPTUC* 33). Similarly, in "Reflections," Eliot's youthful poet is "overcome," "seized" by "a peculiar personal intimacy," a "first passion," for the dead poet precursor that brings him to "crisis" and changes him, perhaps, "within a few weeks" ("Reflections" 39). However, unlike "On the Development of Taste," where the young Eliot's desire for poetic, creative sympathy involves him in delusion, "Reflections" depicts the equally susceptible younger poet's entrance into "a genuine love affair" that is "ineffaceable." If, in "On the Development of Taste," personal autonomy and poetic power depend on escape from feminizing self-identification with the Romantic precursor, the "feminine," male–male, erotic merger of "Reflections" ushers the young poet into artistry, sexuality, and personhood. He is "broadened," "quickened," and metamorphosed "from a bundle of second-hand sentiments into a person": "We are changed," Eliot concludes, "and our work is the work of the changed man" ("Reflections" 39). The striking contrast between the essays suggests Eliot's acute ambivalence toward his intimacy with the Romantic past and, further, his split personality, between the public spokesperson for a "virile" modernism and the more androgynous poet courting sexual/spiritual "sameness."

Given Eliot's oscillation between combative and sympathetic models of (Romantic) influence, it is not surprising, therefore, that Eliot's scourge against Romantic sameness, "Hamlet and His Problems" (1919) (*SE* 121–6), appeared in the same year as "Reflections." I hope to demonstrate that in "Hamlet and His Problems" Eliot's famous objective correlative constitutes the missing literary device that condemns the Shakespeare of both *Hamlet* and the sonnets to the related effeminate Romantic debilities of son–mother fixation and, Eliot suggests, male–male homoeroticism. Defined as the antidote to Romanticism and contextualized mainly in terms of the mother–son psychological narrative of Hamlet, Eliot's objective correlative takes on the problematics of male sexual identity. Eliot's Hamlet would seem to represent the archetypal arrested Romantic who cannot detach himself from the demonic mother and remains mired in his obsession with her.

As Eliot acknowledges in the first paragraphs, his essay is conceived in reaction against the most "dangerous" of critics – frustrated Romantic poets who focus vicariously on the psychology of the protagonist – of which Coleridge and the German Romantic Goethe are exemplars: "Such a mind had Goethe, who made of Hamlet a Werther; and such had Coleridge who made of Hamlet a Coleridge." Eliot's essay may be read as a direct response to Coleridge's Hamlet – an attempt to kill Coleridge's Romantic conception of Hamlet. For while Eliot contends that the play should be approached historically, his essay fixes both on the psychology of Hamlet and specifically on a Coleridgean Hamlet whose excessive inwardness and effeminacy he blames for the play's "artistic failure" (SE 123). (Coleridge was responsible for the enduring notion of Hamlet as a romantic hero, and Coleridge himself declared that "Hamlet . . . was the character in the intuition and exposition of which I first made my turn for philosophical criticism. . . .")[24] Eliot's and Coleridge's contrasting attitudes toward the Oedipal script of Hamlet demonstrate the gendered polarities of Romanticism and modernism. Coleridge's Romanticism urges the semiotic modality of the pre-Oedipal attachment to the mother, while Eliot's modernism promotes severance with the mother and accession into the Symbolic Law of the father. Coleridge consistently praises what Kristeva would term the more "semiotic" (feminine) modalities of Hamlet's language: He is struck by "the language of sensation" in Scene One "among men who feared no charge of effeminacy. . . ." He is particularly impressed by Hamlet's "aversion to externals," "[his] habit of brooding over the world within him and the prodigality of [his] beautiful words. . . ."[25]

By contrast, Eliot views Hamlet as an unregenerate Romantic, immersed in his paralyzing "feelings" toward his mother. Eliot repeatedly pronounces "the essential emotion of the play" to be "the feeling of a son toward a guilty mother" (SE 124) – a "feeling" that he describes as so "inexpressibly horrible" that he wonders "under compulsion of what experience" Shakespeare undertook the theme of Hamlet (SE 126). Throughout the essay, Eliot suggests that, lacking the intervention of an objective correlative, Hamlet's theme of mother–son eros remains unredeemably "pathological": "The intense feeling, ecstatic or terrible, without an object or exceeding its object, is something which every person of sensibility has known; it is doubtless a subject of study for pathologists. It often occurs in adolescence . . ." (*SE* 126). We recall that Eliot contrasted Joyce's successful objectification of "feeling" into an articulate external world" with Woolf's "feminine type" of writing, which "makes its art by feeling and by contemplating the feeling rather than the object." The creator of *Hamlet* may therefore be said to have been overwhelmed by the Romantic, adolescent, "feminine type" of literary imagination. Indeed, Eliot concludes that "Shakespeare tackled a problem which proved too much for him . . ." (*SE* 126).

Further, Eliot's vague allusion to the perversity of the sonnets would seem to target Shakespeare's appeal to male–male love. Eliot accuses Shakespeare of beclouding the text of *Hamlet* with the implicit perversions of his sonnets: "*Hamlet,* like the sonnets, is full of some stuff that the writer could not drag to light, contemplate or manipulate into art. And when we search for this feeling, we find it, as in the sonnets, very difficult to localize." This insidious "stuff," Eliot asserts, contrasts with Shakespeare's exposition of other themes (in *Othello,* etc.) that are "intelligible, self-complete, in the sunlight." Eliot's rhetoric of sexual morality – "light" and "dark" – impugns Shakespeare's sometime sexual deviance, further underscored by Eliot's (probably) unconscious indirect reference to the fair youth and dark lady who play out various illicit sexualities, including homoeroticism, in the shifting love/sex triangles of the sonnets.[26]

Elsewhere Nancy Gish demonstrates Eliot's critical and editorial tendency to submerge sex/gender sameness in favor of "universal" themes. Paradoxically, Eliot reviews Djuna Barnes's *Nightwood* favorably, insisting that Barnes's lesbian/gay novel is "not a psychopathic study," although "the miseries that people suffer through their particular abnormalities . . . are visible on the surface." Rather, the novel is a success because "the deeper design is that of the human misery and bondage which is universal." Gish notes further that Eliot's editorial cuts in the text focus largely on Doctor O'Connor's speeches "about his transvestism and homosexual experience."[27]

Unlike the characters of *Nightwood*, whose difference, Eliot asserts, is only the occasion for a novel of human suffering, Eliot's *Hamlet*, then, remains a psychopathic study, refusing to relinquish the Romantic affectation of lingering on sex/gender sameness. Hamlet's "problems" are thus the theme of the play left unmitigated by the universalizing operations of the objective correlative, which might have supplied "a set of objects, a situation, a chain of events, which shall be the formula of that *particular* emotion; such that when the external facts are given, the emotion is immediately evoked" (*SE* 125).

Like Eliot's selective objective correlative in "Hamlet and his Problems," Pound's multiform theory of personae enabled him to act out the literary homocide of his former Aesthete mask. Pound's assassination of his Romantic self in *Hugh Selwyn Mauberley* is frequently cited as a prime example of his dictum to cast off multifarious personae in "each poem." Pound himself described the volume in which *Mauberley* appears, *Personae*,[28] as the testing ground for his new theory: "I began the search for the real in a book called *Personae*, casting off, as it were, complete masks of the self in each poem."[29] Further, Pound's decision to adapt his theory of personae probably crystallized before he began composing *Mauberley* (1919). In that poem, Pound killed, buried, and inscribed the epitaph for his Aesthete self, thus – like the Eliot of "On the Development of Taste" – laying waste to a Romantic past he conceived as dangerously "effeminate." Further, Pound's ritual execution of his Aesthete personae also targeted, among other things, Romantic "sameness," and specifically the neo-Platonic philosophy of self-identification with a male or female "twin soul."

In *Mauberley*, Pound includes the effeminate Aesthete and his mother/sister twin among nongenerative forms of sexuality such as (male) homosexuality, which McDonald remarks of the *Cantos*, Pound "condemned in some of the most vitriolic language in American poetry" (24). Pound's Mauberley is the flaccid, self-absorbed Aesthete, "capable" only of "maudlin confession, / Irresponse to human aggression. . . . Lifting the faint susurrus / Of his subjective hosannah." Turning against his early enthusiasm for the Pre-Raphaelite twin soul (to be discussed shortly), Pound now pictured a listless, barren, and ravaged Elizabeth Siddal, absorbed by "sterile" languor, with a "half-ruin'd face" and wasted body, "thin as brook water," and with a "vacant gaze" (92). As Ronald Bush observes in *The Gender of Modernism*, Pound returned to a conventional conception of woman as "a chaos" controlled by male principles of form and order, an image that rejects Romantic twinning for the inequality implied by the nature/culture binary of gender stereotypes (Scott 353).

Pound brashly routed out the Aesthete in favor of more "virile" personae such as Walt Whitman and other impersonations of the American ideal of masculine arrogance and dynamism. In "Patria Mia," Pound's manifesto for an American Renaissance, he praised the "eager, careless . . . animal vigor" of American manhood over "the melancholy, the sullenness, the unhealth of the London mass."[30] Ridiculing the progressive debates about sexuality in Britain, Pound proclaimed his aversion to male sexual "pathologies," jibing,

> In England . . . if any man be abnormal or impotent . . . if he be in one of a number of known ways pathological, he sets to writing books on the matter and to founding cults and collecting proselytes. And he seems to expect society to reform itself according to his idiosyncrasies. (SP 41)

Pound's public demolition of the sexually ambiguous Victorian Aesthete was shared by the Vorticist movement in general. Indeed, the Vorticists initially believed that the war would complete their work of detonating the Decadent past among other things. They regularly used war terminology to describe their project: "A *Risorgimento*," Pound wrote, "implies a whole volley of liberations . . ." (SP 112). Gaudier-Brzeska wrote in a "Vortex" he sent before he was killed in battle, "THIS WAR IS A GREAT REMEDY."[31] The Victorian age was among the Vorticists' favorite targets. The following poem, printed in the Vorticist journal of the same name, *Blast,* and written by Wyndham Lewis, reveals the Vorticists' collective desire to explode the stuffy, unmanly, and sexually idiosyncratic Victorians:

> BLAST
> years 1837 to 1900 . . .
> BLAST their weeping whiskers – hirsute
> RHETORIC of EUNUCH and STYLIST –
> SENTIMENTAL HYGIENICS
> ROUSSEAUISMS (wild Nature cranks)
> FRATERNIZING WITH MONKEYS . . . [32]

However, Like Eliot, Pound would never fully sever his initial identification with the Aesthetes or his longing for the spiritual kinship he associated with Romanticism. H.D. recalled that the young Pound shared her passion for Swinburne and introduced her to Rossetti and Morris.

Although H.D.'s *HER* deliberately played down Pound's role in her own Romantic phase of poetic development, H.D.'s later memoir of Pound (*End to Torment*, composed in 1927)[33] resurrects an exuberantly Romantic young Pound who resembled the red-haired Swinburne, "read me [Morris's] 'The Haystack in the Floods' with passionate emotion" (23), and "literally shouted Morris's 'The Gilliflower of Gold' " (22). Pound's collected love poems to his fiancée, H.D., *Hilda's Book* (published in *End to Torment*) is unabashedly influenced by the Victorian Romantics they read to each other and particularly by Swinburne. The young Pound unquestioningly shared the Romantic, Dantean conception of the beloved as a twin soul. In "La Donzella Beata" from *Hilda's Book*, the lover addresses his beloved (H.D.) as "Soul/caught in the rose hued mesh / of o'er fair earthly flesh" (70).

Like Eliot, the later anti-Romantic Pound discreetly expressed his craving for a generative, sympathetic bond with the poetic past. Gail McDonald explores Pound's notion of "Apostolic Succession"[34] as a male–male erotic/creative continuum whereby the younger apprentice and his master (past or present) "metaphorically" engage in "a sexual relationship" (McDonald 24). McDonald demonstrates Pound's turn "to the imagery of mystic enlightenment and sexual ecstacy" in his elaborations on the male–male sympathetic relation of poetic influence (24).[35] In "Psychology and Troubadours," a chapter added to *The Spirit of Romance* in 1932, Pound cites the all-male Chivalric love cults of the Troubadours to illustrate the passion arising from an elite, male–male mentorship: "Beyond a certain border, surely we come to this place where the ecstasy is not a whirl or a madness of the senses, but a glow arising from the exact nature of the perception."[36] McDonald notes the "speculative and uncharacteristically tentative" tone of the essay – "I have no particular conclusion to impose upon the reader" – and we recall that Eliot was reticent about "Reflections," in which the younger poet is similarly "quickened" by the "genuine affair" between himself and his dead masters (McDonald 24).

Significantly, Pound specifically employs the phrase "Apostolic Succession" to describe his ineffaceable bond to the Romantics and Victorians. In a passage from the aptly titled "How I Began" (1913),[37] Pound shares Eliot's compassion for poetic influence as "profound [literary] kinship." Citing Yeats as mediator between himself and the Romantic tradition from

Shelley to the "men of the nineties," Pound reflects, "Besides knowing living artists, I have come in touch with the tradition of the dead. . . . [there is much worth] in this sort of Apostolic Succession, . . . for people whose minds have been enriched by contact with men of genius retain the effects of it."[38] As James Longenbach comments on this passage depicting Pound's spiritual communion with the Romantic tradition: "In England, [Pound] recovered the dead by meeting the living who retained the past in their very selves. Yeats became Pound's guide through a poetic underworld inhabited by Rhymers, Pre-Raphaelites, Victorians, Shelley and Keats."[39] And while Pound publicly scorned Swinburne as the worst example of Romantic effeminacy (to be discussed later), in a 1910 letter to Margaret Cravens he revealed his worship of the poet he included among his early masters, ". . . I have gone back to my Swinburne with new eyes – at least to the poems in the 'Laus Veneris' edition. . . . [these poems give us] the *great* Swinburne, the high priest, the lifter of the hearts of men."[40]

Like Pound's personae and Eliot's objective correlative, Yeats's oppositional theory of the "anti-self" ("all / That I have handled least, least looked upon") (*VP* 367) served similarly as a gender-corrective device at times. Among its many functions, the anti-self possessed the power to lessen or counteract Romantic "morbidity," effeminacy, and mother–son symbiosis – particularly during the intervals when Yeats sought to depose the "womanish introspection" of his early poetry and the Aesthetic movement.

Richard Ellmann's *The Man and the Masks* (1948) is probably largely responsible for the still relevant schematization of Yeats's poetics into successive feminine and masculine phases intimately connected to a crisis of sex/gender identification in his life (which Ellmann links, among other things, to Maud Gonne's marriage) and the ensuing antidotal doctrine of masks. Ellmann first singled out Yeats's letter to George Russell (1904) in which Yeats deems his early poetry "unmanly" and prone to a "womanish introspection" as a crucial turning point in Yeats's career – "Yeats's fullest statement of his change of heart" – and as the catalyst behind his implicitly "masculine" conception of the antiself: "The theory of the mask bulked large in his work," Ellmann comments, "giving the opposing self a symbolic form."[41]

Cullingford attributes Yeats's midlife manly posturing, in his letter to Russell and elsewhere, to his work in the theater and to his readings in

Nietzsche (1903): "Nietzsche's insistence upon hardness and 'virility' suggested to Yeats that the railings of his own early poetry could be analyzed in terms of gender" (Cullingford 78). Although Nietzsche certainly provided Yeats and many of his contemporaries with a vocabulary of gendered binaries during his middle phase, the emphasis on a virile "hardness" resounded throughout Anglo-American modernism from T. E. Hulme, to Pound, the Imagists, and Eliot.[42] I would add to Ellmann's and Cullingford's speculations about Yeats's "manly" phase that the sexual panic sweeping through the modernist movement in the wake of Wilde's trials and other incidences of gender trouble contributed to Yeats's personal crisis and alerted him to the gender implications of his early work. Yeats would never wholly abandon his ties to Decadence and its valorization of "the feminine"; however, his gendered theories of masking temporarily shared the modernists' scorn for the effeminate mask of the Aesthete androgyne.

Although Yeats collected letters of sympathy for Wilde during his trials,[43] he was not entirely immune to the backlash against Wilde among his contemporaries. Yeats claimed that he had not expected Wilde to act on the fantasies that had "taken a tragic turn," later confessing that he had originally mistaken Wilde's "words" for "play" (*Auto* 189), and he implicitly condemned Wilde's persona as suggestive of "something pretty, feminine, and insincere."[44] Yeats's disenchantment with the Aesthete pose and his gendered doctrine of the opposing self was reflected in his attitude toward the tragic generation, whom he now pictured as glutted Aesthetes yearning for the simplicity of a more manly era:

> The typical young poet of our day is an aesthete with a surfeit, searching sadly for his lost Philistinism, his heart full of an unsatisfied hunger for the commonplace. He is an Alastor[-poet] tired of his woods and longing for beer and skittles.[45]

Like Eliot's objective correlative in "Hamlet and His Problems," the "antiself" Yeats would prescribe to prune the Romantic excesses of the "aesthete with a surfeit" implied an agenda to masculinize the image of the poet.

Yeats's scheme of sexual masking advocated the split with his Romantic foremother by displacing his former Shelleyan doctrine of sympathetic attachment to a mother/sister twin with an image of the beloved as anti-self.

George Bornstein traces Yeats's disenchantment with the Shelleyan neo-Platonic cult of "exclusive devotion" to a female "likeness of the self" in the early part of the twentieth century and his subsequent re-creation of the beloved as an "anti-self" who "forms an exact contrary rather than the Shelleyan counterpart of his normal self."[46] Yeats's rejection of the feminine included the type of the femme fatale and the mother–son erotic narrative of the Romantic quest romance.

Like Eliot and Pound, Yeats's early conception of the beloved derived from Rossetti and the Pre-Raphaelites, while his philosophy of love was shaped by the Shelleyan quest for a twin spirit in quest romances such as *Alastor:* "My head was full of the mysterious women of Rossetti . . . which seem always waiting for some Alastor[-poet] at the end of a long journey."[47] Behind Yeats's running account of Wilde's "downfall" in the *Autobiographies,* Yeats continually returned to the saga of the Rhymers's implicitly unhealthy Aesthetic cult of the femme fatale: "woman herself was still in our eyes . . . romantic and mysterious, still the priestess of her shrine, our emotions remembering the *Lilith* and the *Sybilla Palmifera* of Rossetti" (*Auto* 201).

Cullingford's argument that, during his "manly" phase, Yeats rejected the feminine romantic lyric that often inscribes social constructions of love and sexuality "with . . . roots in historical and material circumstances" applies to the Romantic quest romance form as well (Cullingford 78, 4). Based on the androgynous Aesthete's search for his sexual and spiritual double, Romantic quest romance embedded ideologies of sexual "sameness," maternal eros, homoeroticism, and androgyny that were antithetical to the modernists' program to reform the effeminate image of the poet. In Yeats's essay on "The Philosophy of Shelley's Poetry" (1900) (*E&I* 65–95) particularly, the sexual history of the quest romance became synonymous with the hazards of Romantic twinning, which Yeats reinterpreted as the projection of the Aesthete poet's morbid, onanistic fantasies or a sexual trap laid by the ever-elusive femme fatale. Yeats now singled out Shelley's *Alastor* and Keats's *Endymion* as exemplary plots of the damaging sister/mother love that had submerged the Aesthetes of his generation in sexual deprivation and malaise.

Questioning the motives behind his own early quest romance, *The Wanderings of Oisin,* in "The Circus Animals' Desertion" (1939), Yeats portrayed the poem as a collection of "themes" of "the embittered heart" and its young author as "starved for the bosom of his [Oisin's] fairy bride" (*VP* 629). In *Autobiographies,* Yeats blamed Keats's *Endymion* for inaugurating his era's cult of the temptress, which fragmented the (male) poet's mind, rendering his imagery supersensuous and sterile (*Auto* 209). In his essay on Shelley, Keats's *Endymion's* quest for the moon goddess Cynthia came to represent the Aesthetes' emasculation by the maternal "woman star" of unfulfilled desire. And in the same essay, Yeats pictured Shelley, "who hated life," as "lost in a ceaseless reverie, in some chapel of the Star of infinite desire" (*E&I* 91, 93, 94). Finally, in *A Vision,* Yeats placed the poets he associated with the quest for the fatal woman, Baudelaire and Ernest Dowson, at the Thirteenth Phase of the "The Sensuous Man," where "sensuality without the mixture of any other element" stimulates linguistic morbidity: "There is almost always a preoccupation with those metaphors and symbols [that are] most strange or most morbid." Here "happy love is rare" and "the woman" and "every beloved object" "becomes harder to find" (*Vision* 129, 130).

However, as Elizabeth Cullingford has demonstrated, Yeats never relinquished his attraction toward "the feminine" he often associated with Victorian Romanticism. Curiously, even within Yeats's oppositional theory of the beloved as "anti-self," the beloved took on the aspect of virile antitypes such as the warrior queen or the New Woman – as I have written elsewhere[48] – revealing a more androgynous notion of what his contemporaries meant by the "masculinization" of poetry. Like Eliot and Pound, Yeats also appears to have retained his early fascination with (Romantic) spiritual/ erotic sameness. Cullingford revalues the early Romantic, feminine phase of Yeats's career and uncovers a third phase in Yeats's later years when his identification with the feminine reemerged as a fascination with lesbianism, female androgyny, and "the woman in me" (Cullingford 269).[49]

Finally, although Richard Aldington was not among the leading theorizers of modernism, the other male modernist closest to H.D. was as irreverent as Pound in his public pronouncements against Romanticism. In one of several essays defining Imagism, Aldington condemned the "slop" and "sentimentality" of Romanticism, adding: "Have you seen those unfinished poems by Shelley which go something like this: 'O Mary dear, that you were here / with your tumtyttum and clear, and your tumtytymty bosom/ like tumty ivy-blossom,' and c.?" His (temporary) fierce, anti-Romantic pose, like Pound's, would register in H.D.'s fictional autobiographies as the brutish, oppositional sensibility spawned by the modern age. Indeed, H.D.'s anti-Romantic Aldington- and Pound-figures form grim representations of the "virile" modernist personae I have traced through Yeats's, Eliot's, and Pound's early theories.

Aldington's rough dismissals of Romanticism appear to have struck H.D. deeply and in her fictional autobiographies form part of a nexus of wartime obliterations, including the "charnel house" of World War I, the brute cynicism of modern aesthetics, and the random desperation of wartime promiscuity. Indeed, as we shall see, H.D.'s fictionalizations of the early modern period frequently depict Aldington's desperate wartime transformation from gentle poet to harsh cynic and womanizer by way of his embittered anti-Romanticism. In *Asphodel*, for example, H.D.'s autobiographical heroine, Hermione, hopelessly tries to connect with the former poet (based on Richard Aldington) during his brief leave from the front by reciting the lines from the Romantics he once loved:

> She wanted to reach out and the time was short, . . . what was he now reading? Did he read nowadays? She never now could ask him, he was sure to flaunt the old things at her, bruise and tear her with some frivolous, silly or destructive jibe, make fun of something sacred, something deep down that she hadn't known she cared for til he took it, turned it inside out, spat on it. *Swiftly walk o'er the western wave*, for instance though she didn't care for Shelley. . . . What had happened? What was done, was now lost? (*Asphodel* 135)

When Hermione lights on an admittedly morbid (mis)quote from Landor, "There are no fields of asphodel this side of the grave," Darrington responds predictably, "Damn, you might have thought of something cheerful" (137).

II   *The Sexual Politics of the Image/Object*

Gendered theories of (male) modernist masking had addressed the sexual orientation of the poet on the perceiving end of the relationship between author and object of desire. Doctrines of the Image, however, began with the *object* on the assumption that the right Image/object, like the archetype, would provoke the right sensation in the perceiver and thus assure the transmission of "the properly aesthetic emotion" (*Speculations* 136). Deviant texts, metaphors, words, or bodies that might inspire or correspond to desires outside the "universal" (white, male, heterosexual) category were therefore precluded by such assertions as Eliot's "speech varies [but] all our eyes are the same" (*SE* 343), "the first condition of right thought is right sensation" (*SE* 126), or Pound's mathematical formulations of the image as "a sort of inspired mathematics which gives us equations . . . for the human emotions."[50] Commenting in general on the weakness of the Imagists' essentialist definition of "sensation," Louis Menand reflects, "any argument that bases itself on the primacy of sensation quickly reaches the end of its tether, since it is, after all, trying to prove the importance of things whose virtues are not immediately apparent to everyone" (Menand 36). The following discussion concerns gendered, modernist approaches to the Image, first as a linguistic body and second as a female body, which purport to claim the Image/object from the unhealthy, abject, "state" of Romantic words and women.

Eliot's and Pound's famous indictments of Swinburne's evasive signification in formulations of the Imagist doctrine targeted Romantic linguistic indeterminacy as the corrupting agent in the relationship between poet and object. The restoration of poetry to "a healthy state," both poets imply, thus depends on a poetic language that fixes a strict, one-to-one correspondence between the word and its referent; and as Shari Benstock suggests, such definitions of Imagism imposed a phallogocentric notion of language (Benstock 327, 328).

Eliot maintained that Swinburne's poetry was neither "morbid," "erotic," nor "destructive" (*SE* 25), elsewhere describing the Decadents' "religion of vice" as "not more than a game of children dressing up and playing at being grownups" (*SE* 65). However, despite his attempt to trivialize the transgressive desire of Romantic writing, Eliot's sexual repugnance is discernible in the rhetoric of his attack on Swinburne's language, which still concludes that Swinburne is sick:

It is in fact the word that gives him the thrill, not the object. When you take to pieces any verse of Swinburne, you find always that the object was not there – only the word . . . [Swinburne's] morbidity is not of human feeling but of language. Language in a healthy state presents the object, is so close to the object that the two are identified.

They are identified in the verse of Swinburne solely because the object has ceased to exist, because the meaning is merely the hallucination of meaning, because language, uprooted, has adapted itself to an independent life of atmospheric nourishment. . . . (*SE* 284, 285)

Eliot's Swinburne is distracted by a pornographic fetishization of words – "the word gives him the thrill not the object." Having relinquished his semiotic power, Swinburne's uprooted language gives way to a perverse free-play, at once morally condemning both author and text to "morbid-ity" – a code word for sexual decadence. (We recall that Yeats also associated Decadent sexuality with linguistic morbidity: The Decadent po-ets Baudelaire and Dowson are placed at his Phase Thirteen in *A Vision,* where "sensuality [exists] without the mixture of any other element" and "there is almost always a preoccupation with those metaphors and symbols [that are] most strange and most morbid" (129, 130). Unable to foster the strict relationship between word and thing that characterized certain early modern theories of the Image, Swinburne's misplaced sexuality becomes an effect of his seductive words. Language in a "healthy state," Eliot im-plies, aims straight for the object of its desire (like "an arrow," Menand glosses (35), suggesting the phallic association).

Pound's similar criticism of Swinburne's language raises the specter of the dominating femme fatale as the presiding genius of his misplaced sex-uality/textuality. Pound asserts that in Swinburne, "the word-selecting, word-castigating faculty was nearly absent. Unusual and gorgeous words attracted him." Evoking the wreck of Romanticism's siren song, Pound warns against such a surrender to "unusual" and "gorgeous words": "This is of all sorts of writing the most dangerous to an author, and the uncon-scious collapse into this sort of writing has wrecked more poets in our time than perhaps all other faults put together" (*LE* 293, 294).

Wallace Stevens wrote in *Adagia* that "not all objects are equal," sug-gesting the relative power of Aesthetic objects to call forth the complexity of emotional/aesthetic experience.[51] The critical attention given to the im-age of the beautiful woman in the modernism of Yeats, Stevens, Pound, Joyce, and others suggests that the female muse remained the object of choice both for male modernism and the New Criticism. Frank Kermode's *Romantic Image* identifies the dancer or the beautiful "woman in movement" as among the paradigmatic images of modern thought (Kermode 57). Kermode's essay persuasively demonstrates the pervasiveness of the female Romantic Image in modernist poetry from Imagism and Vorticism through Yeats's famous "body swayed to music." Paradoxically, however, Kermode's theory of Romantic continuity between the fatal woman and the dancer reinscribes the modernist prohibition against the brazenly sexual, "pathological" image of the femme fatale. The succeeding image of the impersonal and passive dancer possesses none of her precursor's sexual power, but exists merely as "the cue" for the presumed male author's "passion" (56).

However, Judith Butler's argument that wherever the "two figures of abjection" – the masculinist woman and the feminized man – are prohibited "by law," they loom large on the symbolic horizon, might be applied to modernist anti-Romantic suppressions of the aggressively sexual femme fatale (*Bodies* 104). Kermode's essay perhaps best exemplifies the troubling return of the abject or horrific fatal woman produced by male modernist (and New Critical) restrictions against her. Kermode's argument that the modernist detour from Romantic personality successfully "extracted chemically pure" (63) the poetics of the Romantic female Image, leaving her passively sentient and dancing "in her narrow luminous circle" (58), paradoxically illustrates the "constituting effect of regulatory power" (*Bodies* 22).

It must be remembered that Kermode, like the New Critics in general, draws upon the most conservative sexual discourses of the modernists. Thus, Kermode's assertion that the Yeatsian dancer represents the "central icon" "of Yeats and of the whole [modern] tradition" (89) oversimplifies the sex/gender complexities of both Yeats and modernism, choosing from among Yeats's most traditional female tropes.[52] (Cullingford categorizes Yeats's rejection of the "shrill" educated female for the passive, unthinking female body as "a regression in Yeats' acceptance of changing gender roles" (136).)

Kermode's argument is based on the (male) modernist gender-biased division between the "aesthetic" and the "personal." The dancer, an object of normative male desire, is equated with the "aesthetic," while the fatal woman's implication in other forms of desire is dismissed as an incidental, intrusive "pathology" on the part of the author. Thus, Rossetti's Decadent female Images are, for example, partly blamed on "the vagaries of his [Rossetti's] emotional life" (61). The impersonal female image is safely desexualized − "unimpassioned, wise in its whole body" − while she "attracts unbounded passion" in the normative male observer/poet (62). The dancer never looks back: Kermode cites "Michael Robartes and the Dancer" in affirming that the "wisdom" apportioned to the female Image herself emerges only from the discipline of "the looking-glass" (52) − visual self-study readies her for the poet's male gaze. Impersonal art is therefore synonymous with the correspondence between the artist's male desire and his necessarily inert female image.

The centerpiece of Kermode's essay is his somewhat lengthy lyrical appreciation of the modernist dancer he pictures at an imagined stage center of modernist tradition, turning "in her narrow luminous circle, still but moving, dead but alive" (59). Kermode's Image openly borrows from Yeats's dancing Herodiade, performing "seemingly alone in her narrow moving luminous circle," which Yeats used to illustrate the self-referentiality of art ("separate from everything heterogeneous and casual, from all character and circumstance") (*Auto* 215). Indeed, the spectacle presented by these almost identical male texts of two remote bodies − the authorial figure gazing, the woman turning − might be taken as a representative scene of male poetic modernism at its most conservative.

However, although Kermode easily demonstrates a continuity between the Pre-Raphaelite cult of the "dead [female] face" and Yeats's expressionless "thinking body," the essay struggles with the more difficult task of explaining where and how the dancer lost her "pathological" aspect in the transition from Romantic to modern. And for the postmodern reader, the Medusan body of Kermode's essay recalcitrantly refuses to observe this separation, pushing the boundaries of Kermode's admittedly ambiguous thesis. Bakhtin's definition of the normative "canonized body," which reaffirms the existent social order in contrast to the revolutionary "grotesque" (in "The Grotesque Image of the Body") provides a useful model for exploring the disturbing return of the banished femme fatale in Kermode's essay.

In keeping with Bakhtin's description of "classic and naturalist images" of the body, Yeats's and Kermode's "dancer" is contained within a smooth, sanitized shell. She is Bakhtin's seamless, entirely "finished, completed and strictly limited body" of social convention (Bakhtin 320). Elsewhere Kermode quotes affirmatively Yeats's objection to an artist friend whose interest "in unshapeliness [and] deviations from the perfect type," discouraged the "compact between the artist and society" (Kermode 57). Both Yeats and Kermode visualize their turning dancer behind an invisible shield that prevents any interaction – sexual or otherwise – with the male writer. She is a concise example of Bakhtin's canonized body, a "self sufficient" body limited only to the events of "the individual closed sphere" (Bakhtin 327). Locked in the dull round of a measured albeit "moving" and "luminous" field, Yeats's dancer suggests the bounded perfection of Bakhtin's self-enclosed body of the new canon, "[in which] all attributes of the unfinished world are carefully removed, as well as all the signs of inner life" (Bakhtin 320).

But Kermode's New Critical text cannot suppress the unruly narrative of the unlawful Decadent body. Although he states that "the [female] emblem can exist in isolation from its pathological aspect" (67), I am not convinced by his assertion that the placement of Pater's passage on Mona Lisa in Yeats's *Oxford Book of Modern Verse* "at once" lifts her "out of the stale ecstasies of 'decadent' appreciation," making of her "an emblem of both the *paysage intérieure* and the concreteness of modern poetry" (58). The reverse would seem to be true in the gender narrative of Kermode's essay. The Medusan body, rather, wreaks havoc on Kermode's placid scene of poet and dancer. Her introduction into the essay as a prohibited figure through various references to the Decadent femme fatale's punishing, "tainted 'Medusan' beauty," such as Kermode's approving quote from Huysmans – "[she is] the beast, monstrously irresponsible, who poisons everything she touches, like Helen of old" (68) – at once interjects the spreading image of the torrential, grotesque body, forcing a sexual/textual confrontation between male author and female monster. Kermode struggles uncomfortably with the refractory femme fatale, confessing, "It must be admitted that the full-blown dancer emblem owes much to 'decadent' sources," and, "it is impossible to separate the face [of the femme fatale] from the dancer, and the complex of ideas they embody certainly includes some that belong to pathology rather than to aesthetics" (68, 61). "But

for ease of exposition," Kermode dodges, "some pretence of such a separation must be made" (61). Kermode concludes by begging the question,
"For the most part I omit considerations of pathology . . ." (61). Kermode's discomfort might emerge from a sense that his gendered narrative
of modernism only affirms those gendered narratives of modernism that
sought to quell anxiety rather than elucidate the complicated psychodynamics of the Romantic Image he clearly apprehends but prefers not to
confront.

Androgynous men and unnaturally raucous women ran wild throughout
male modernist prose and poetry. Like H.D., as we shall see in the next
chapter, the early Yeats was fascinated with Swinburne's Decadent lesbian
femme fatale, "Faustine" (*Auto* 200); and the wild, fantastical, fatal women
he left behind in his early poetry resurfaced in his androgynous warrior
queens, and again at the end of his life in the lusty deject, Crazy Jane.
Eliot's self-conscious dandies and "fragmented" creative souls may be said
to resemble the effeminate outlaws of his theories – Hamlet, Shelley, Swinburne, his own adolescent self – more than the vague and contradictory
mask of the impersonal poet urged by his anti-Romantic slogans. And
although Eliot was chosen as the spokesman for what was then perceived
as the plight of a generation, critics such as Lyndall Gordon discover looming types of the romantic agon and the fatal woman in the personal narratives of his poetry. Louis Menand, perhaps, most eloquently describes the
superimposition of Pater's fatal, vampiric, La Gioconda on the "one
woman" that comprises all the women of Eliot's *Waste Land*. While Men-
and views the *Waste Land*'s composite images of Pater's Mona Lisa as emblematic of "the evolutionary history of consciousness," her overwhelming
presence also suggests that having been "foreclosed or banished from the
proper domain of 'sex' " (*Bodies* 23), the type of the Romantic femme
fatale is the female body that matters in Eliot's *Waste Land*:

> [She] appears first in the epigraph as the ancient Sybil who cannot die, and
> again, perhaps, in "The Burial of the Dead," as "Belladonna, the Lady of
> the Rocks" ("She is older than the rocks among which she sits . . ." runs
> Pater's description). She is the woman in "The Game of Chess" surrounded

by "her strange synthetic perfumes" and on whose dressing-room walls hang the "withered stumps of time" – the artistic record of the mythical past (". . . and all this has been to her but as the sound of lyres and flutes, and lives only in the delicacy with which it has moulded the changing lineaments, and tinged the eyelids and the hands"). And she appears, finally, in "The Fire Sermon," where she draws "her long black hair out tight," while

> . . . bats with baby faces in the violet light
> Whistled, and beat their wings
> And crawled head downward down a blackened wall

(". . . like the vampire, she has been dead many times and learned the secrets of the grave"). (Menand 81, 82)

Cullingford's argument that Yeats's adherence to the love poem and particularly the flexible, "feminine" lyric genre enabled him, at times, to escape male modernist misogyny and inscribe new definitions of love and sexuality applies, perhaps, more urgently to the modernist woman poet. The next chapter, on H.D.'s early masks and images, forms a counterpoint, in some respects, to the preceding discussion of oppositional male modernist gender narratives. I begin with H.D.'s *HER,* a fictional autobiography in which the young woman writer experiences her first stirrings of sexual and writerly identity under the empathic influence of Swinburne's Decadent lyrics and monologues from the *Poems and Ballads.* Unlike Eliot's and Yeats's Romantic myths of poetic origins, which appear to defend against an enthralling Romantic foremother, H.D.'s fictional case history (*HER*) reestablishes connections with the Swinburnian foremother whose poetry valorizes the feminine, the maternal, the homoerotic, and the androgynous sexuality/textuality. In *HER,* Swinburne's songs of forbidden love give the young heroine access to transgressive erotic and poetic "masks" – the male androgyne and the femme fatale among them – that thwart the modernist poetic of male desire.

Having explored H.D.'s Decadent Romantic masks and her countermyth of poetic development in *HER* (composed 1926, 1927), I return to H.D.'s Imagist volume *Sea Garden* (1916) to examine the ways in which H.D. both breaks the male modernist Image equation between "word" and "thing" and writes a "feminine" Imagism by drawing specifically upon the evasive signification and the landscape/floral imagery of Decadent love poetry. Finally, I discuss H.D.'s subsequent turn to the Decadent monologue or lyric form and its attendant masks of the femme fatale and the boy-androgyne.

Chapter Two

H.D.'s Early Decadent Masks and Images

HER; Sea Garden

I H.D.'s Romantic Myth of Origins

In the same year that Eliot published his objections to the Romantic dissociation of sensibility ("The Metaphysical Poets"), H.D. completed her first fictional biography, *Paint It Today* (1921), in which her narrator presumed that the "stream" of literary history had diverted to the Victorian Romantics that formed the modernists' early reading:

> I drift with the stream, since I believe the stream now to be drifting toward some ultimate land, . . . made up of the early visions of all the early poets we read when we were sixteen, whom we outgrew when we were twenty and whom we find again in our peaceful thirties. (*Paint It* 69)

Far from dissociating herself from the Wildean Aesthete, H.D.'s aspiring poet heroine in her fictional autobiography, *Asphodel* (composed 1921–22), regards the Aesthetes, headed by Wilde, as a parental tradition of sexually transgressive artists. Hermione begs her women lover to live with her in London by sentimentally invoking the Aesthete community and their code of "Greeks and flowers":

> "We are children of the Rossettis, of Burne Jones, of Swinburne. We were in the thoughts of Wilde when he spoke late at night . . . to a young man called Gilbert. They talked of Greeks and flowers. . . . We belong here. (*Asphodel* 53, 54)

And, as early as 1916, H.D. had evoked Romantic visionary landscape in her proposed agenda for modern poetry as the central image of a forged reconciliation between the Romantic past and the war-torn present. H.D.'s 1916 review of Yeats's *Responsibilities* called for a modern poetry that would follow the example of Yeats's dual Victorian and modern heritage:

> It seems that Mr. Yeats' responsibility . . . has only just begun . . . For it seems in moments of despair that we have no past, no future. But Mr. Yeats has both. Can we not spiritually join our forces, and . . . reinvoke some golden city, sterner than dream-cities, and wrought more firm. . . . [1]

Later, in the 1940s, when H.D. expanded her lifelong fascination with Swinburne to include the Pre-Raphaelites, Morris, and Rossetti, she openly acknowledged her own "sense of continuity" with the Victorian Romantics. Commenting in "H.D. by Delia Alton" on her recent unpublished novel set in the Pre-Raphaelite period, "White Rose and the Red," H.D. indicated a familial rather than adversarial relation to her Romantic past:

> the [Pre-Raphaelite] artists of the *Rose* . . . seem near, familiar, *familiars* almost. . . . perhaps because of my early devotion to their legend. I know more about them or sometimes seem to know more about the Rossetti-Morris circle than I do of my own contemporaries. . . . It is the sense of continuity that inspires me. ("Delia Alton" 194, 195)

H.D.'s persistent need for connection rather than rupture with the Romantic past departed significantly from her male contemporaries' insistent rejection of the effeminate late Romantics.

It has often been noted that unlike Yeats, Eliot, and Pound, H.D. did not express her agenda for modernism in the form of critical essays. Some critics attribute H.D.'s silence in print to her indifference to the narrow Imagist doctrine that her own art surpassed. Others have suggested that H.D. was disinterested in the Imagist doctrine that launched early modernism. Lawrence Rainey goes so far as to accuse H.D. of scorning an "active or genuine dialogue with her contemporaries," whose "unprecedented production of critical-theoretical writings [articulated] the historical, formal, or ideological grounds for the modernist experiment."[2] As I have attempted to demonstrate, H.D. was implicitly barred from the anti-Romantic, gender-biased discourse that characterized the prevailing program for modernism. H.D.'s letters to Amy Lowell in 1916 (Beinecke Library) during the preparation of the Imagist anthology reveal that she actively participated in the compilation of the anthology and was well aware of the tenets of Imagism. Further, the preceding excerpt from H.D.'s review of Yeats's *Responsibilities* indicates that insofar as she could, H.D. not only entered into a dialogue with a lesser known "Pound" who shared her conception of Yeats as a living spiritual and creative connection to the Romantics, but attempted to form an agenda for modernism from this legacy. H.D.'s later conception of the Pre-Raphaelites as "familiars," a term that suggests both a mystical and familial bond with the literary past, resembles Eliot's reverent "profound kinship" with his precursor in the little known "Reflections on Contemporary Poetry." Like most of H.D.'s work, these utterances from Eliot and Pound do not jibe with the popular, hypermasculine agenda for modernism.

However, H.D. did voice her formulations for the future of poetry in her private, unpublished notes on writing, in her unpublished reviews, memoirs, and the unpublished prose fiction of the twenties. In such works H.D.'s career-long dialogue with Decadent Romanticism simultaneously incorporates a debate with the anti-Romantic, male modernist enterprise. Works such as *HER* – a fictional representation of H.D.'s early poetic development – trace a woman modernist writer's response to the Romantic past, creating an alternative case history to the personal "scripts" shared by such male modernists as Yeats and Eliot. Indeed H.D.'s fictionalized autobiographies of her poetic origins reverse the order of Yeats's and Eliot's highly publicized personal histories, which moved from the early suffocating attachment to a "female" Romanticism toward severance from the past and the assumption of an autonomous "male" modernism. By contrast, H.D.'s young women poets begin at the ending[3] of the prevailing masculinist narrative of modernism. These female genealogies of modern poets begin with the split from Romanticism and its attendant erasure of female identity, and proceed to work backward toward recovery of a former Romantic self that experienced a primary and frequently homoerotic bond with a sister/mother muse. H.D.'s heroines thereby extricate themselves from the strict sex/gender codes that polarize the sexes and efface the woman poet in the London literary circle. In narratives such as *HER* and *Paint It Today,* the adolescent Romantic self, under the influence of Swinburne's *Poems and Ballads* in particular, discovers poetic and prophetic power through a homoerotic bond with a mother/sister love who is boyishly androgynous. Chodorow's theory that boys perceive masculinity in opposition to "the feminine world," while girls acquire female identity through maintaining a continuity and connection with the mother, describes the psychodynamics behind the contrasting schemes of poetic influence developed by H.D. and the major male modernists (Chodorow 174). While Yeats's and Eliot's program for a "virile" modernism depends on separation from the Romantic foremother, H.D.'s young poet heroines achieve creative autonomy through connection to a reconstructed "feminine" tradition.

Unlike the scripts of her male contemporaries, H.D.'s fictionalized histories of her involvement in the Imagist circle, *Asphodel* and *Paint It Today*, therefore describe the break with Romanticism and the subsequent transition to a modernist poetic as a painful indoctrination into a predatory, patriarchal sexual politics H.D. associated by turns with World War I, the "modern [aesthetic] cult of brutality,"[4] and her own confining role as muse to Lawrence, Aldington, and Pound. In *Asphodel*, the sequel to *HER*, and *Paint It Today*, the poetry of Swinburne is frequently evoked to signify the poetic tradition that has been lost or crushed by the brutish sensibility of war and the modern age: Hermione laments the wartime devastation of the "true" poetic tradition she associates with Pater's Mona Lisa and Swinburne's "Itylus": "Prose and poetry and the Mona Lisa and her eye lids are a little weary and sister my sister, O fleet sweet swallow were all smudged out as Pompeii and its marbles had been buried beneath obscene filth of lava, embers, smouldering ash and hideous smoke and poisonous gas" (118). H.D. began composing fiction in 1917, hoping to regain what she called her "artist personality" by writing through the emotional "tangle" that obscured her poetic powers following the related crises of World War I, the breakup of her marriage, and her disenchantment with the London literary circle.[5]

HER

HER fictionalizes the events that occurred following H.D.'s withdrawal from Bryn Mawr in her sophomore year, focusing on her simultaneous relationships with Frances Gregg and Ezra Pound, to whom she was briefly engaged. Recently expelled from college, and painfully aware of her failure to "conform to [her family's] expectations" (4), Hermione initially rebels against familial constraints in her engagement to the unconventional young rebel poet, George Lowndes, only to find herself further circumscribed as the "decorative" object of his patronizing affections and clumsy sexual overtures. However, Fayne Rabb (based on Frances Gregg), the sister/ mother love she meets through a mutual friend, provides the way out of the morass: Both the marginal nature of Hermione's newly discovered forbidden sexual identity and the intense, self-identifying nature of her love enable Hermione to escape her position as object into "another country" where her powers might fully emerge.[6] Swinburne's formidable presence in the narrative, however – inscribed by Hermione's almost obsessive litany of quotations from his poetry and references to the Decadent Romantic himself – has yet to be fully explored.

Rachel Blau DuPlessis and Susan Stanford Friedman first considered *HER* in the context of 1920s lesbian novels such as Radclyffe Hall's *The Well of Loneliness* ("Two Loves" 208). Recent feminist scholarship has attributed the rise of the lesbian novel in the 1920s to the debates about female sexuality provoked by sex reformers such as Havelock Ellis. H.D. and Bryher knew Havelock Ellis and read with interest his theories about lesbian sexuality. However, one cannot overlook the widespread influence of Swinburne, Oscar Wilde, and others on the modern poets and specifically on H.D., Pound, and Frances Gregg, who apparently read Swinburne to themselves and each other during the years described in *HER* as obsessively as the text indicates. Although the sexologists certainly prompted much of the public and literary debates about female sexuality in the 1920s, once sparked, modernist women writers such as H.D. turned back to the literary tradition that first introduced them to the subject of variant sexualities and that, unlike the psychoanalytic literature, was authored by poets who admitted (to various degrees) to their own deviance.

Further, the Decadents' songs of forbidden love provided a storehouse of images and masks, such as the Aesthete androgyne and the femme fatale, that could help shape a modernist poetic of female desire. H.D.'s early reading in Swinburne's *Poems and Ballads* would have introduced her to lyric explorations of maternal eros, androgyny, lesbianism, male homoeroticism, and other forbidden subjects which avoid taking one moral stance, but represent a range of attributes and debates about deviant and illicit sexualities.[7] In reply to the moral outrage that immediately followed the publication of *Poems and Ballads*, Swinburne described his individual "studies of passion or sensation" as "dramatic, many faced, multifarious."[8] Indeed, the volume offers several conflicting stories of deviant sexual behavior or gender identification. For example, two poems that H.D. quotes in *Paint It Today*, "Hermaphroditus" and "Fragoletta," present contrasting views toward the dual sexualities of the androgyne.[9] In the former, the hermaphrodite is portrayed as a sterile, deprived creature whose dual gender identities cancel each other out:

> Love stands upon thy left hand and thy right,
> Yet by no sunset and by no moonrise
> Shall make thee man and ease a woman's sighs,
> Or make thee woman for a man's delight.

But "Hermaphroditus" is immediately succeeded by an ode to androgyny, "Fragoletta," in which the beautiful boy/girl is a "double rose of Love's," rendered more desirable by his (he is male) double sexualities (*P&B* I, 90, 92). In *Paint It Today* (65) H.D. used the lines just quoted to project her own ambiguity toward her bisexuality. Swinburne may have been the first to articulate for H.D. the debate about her "two loves separate" that resonated throughout her career.

Swinburne's erotic *Poems and Ballads* serve not only to affirm and encode Hermione's lesbian identity, but to articulate a spectrum of desires and gender disruptions not available to H.D. in the high modernist discourse of the 1920s. Swinburne's hymns to the Sapphic femme fatale or the male androgyne offered to H.D. and other women writers the example of an open sexual narrative, while simultaneously maintaining the fiction of a rebel "author" whose unruly psychosexuality comprises the various songs of his deviant personae. The Decadent Aesthete "author" slips easily between the sex/gender bounds of Sappho's violent lament for Anactoria or the implicitly male homoerotic ode to the blushing transparencies of Fragoletta's androgynous body. Desire flows unimpeded around and through the work's collection of masks for transgressive mood, passion, or agency. As we shall see, the sexual narrative of *HER* and its particular mesh of desires, conflicts, and anxieties is encoded through the Decadent personae of the boy androgyne and Swinburne's lesbian femme fatale, "Faustine."

The novel might therefore represent one modernist woman poet's attempt to dislocate herself from the prevailing poetic of male desire and to forge a female poetic from the Decadent Romantic past.[10] Through Swinburne's multiple explorations of desire, Hermione steps outside the narrow linguistic and sexual conventions imposed upon her by the young male poet, George Lowndes, based, significantly on Ezra Pound – an early but already oppressive version of the modernist poet and theorizer Pound was to become. From the opening pages of the novel, in which Hermione describes her predicament, she feels herself "clutch toward something that had no name yet" (8). Significantly Hermione's impulse toward freedom remains nameless until the insistent beat of Swinburne's words inside her head attunes her to those movements of desire, language, and prophecy that form the radical, homoerotic discourse of the novel – a discourse that persists even after Fayne Rabb herself briefly abandons the "sister-love" for George Lowndes. Swinburne's explorations of androgyny, homoeroticism, narcissism, and maternal eroticism shape the successive erotic personae Hermione projects on Fayne Rabb, who is at once the boy child, "Itylus," the "sister swallow," and the narcissistic "sister" of Swinburne's "Before the Mirror." Through her Decadent heritage, therefore, Hermione disrupts the poetic of male desire and becomes the speaking subject of her emerging poetic powers. The complex weave of Swinburne's poems that winds through the narrative recreates a countermodernist myth of womanhood, drawing on those Romantic linguistic practices, forms of desire, and theories of imagination that H.D.'s modernist contemporaries had pronounced "effeminate" and "morbid."

Quotations from five of Swinburne's poems recur throughout *HER*, including "Faustine," "Itylus," "Before the Mirror," and "The Triumph of Time" from *Poems and Ballads* and lines from the opening of Swinburne's play, *Atalanta in Calydon*, "When the hounds of spring. . . ." The most frequently quoted lines derive from "Itylus" (*P&B* I, 61–3), and particularly the line, "sister, my sister, O fleet, sweet swallow," which dominates the narrative of *HER*, inscribing the homoerotic and sympathetic love between Hermione and Fayne, as well as the prophetic and poetic dimensions that emerge from the sister/mother love. H.D.'s use of the poem derives in part from Swinburne's feminist revision of the Procne/Philomel myth, in which he places the emphasis on the bond between the sisters – Procne slays her own son, Itylus, in order to revenge her husband's rape and mutilation of her sister, Philomel.[11] While Philomel's romantic call to the "sister swallow" evokes homoeroticism, H.D.'s more overtly lesbian interpretation of the poem led her to misquote Swinburne's line, "The heart's division divideth us" as "The world's division divideth us" (p. 124 and passim), suggesting the heterosexism that denies lesbian love. Indeed, Swinburne's "Itylus" must stand as H.D.'s chief Romantic precursor poem: The lines resonate throughout her career, from *HER* to the later *Helen in Egypt*, always signifying the search for the kindred spirit love that was to distinguish H.D.'s philosophy of love. The refrain from "Itylus" hovers spectrally behind the narrative of *HER* from Hermione's first apprehension of the sexual and spiritual awakening inaugurated by Fayne. Thereafter, Hermione's chanting of "Itylus" forms a prelude to the lovers' erotic and prophetic sessions in her workroom, where "prophetess faced prophetess" (146). The lines of the poem haunt the physical as well as spiritual union of the lovers in Hermione's workroom; lying across the body of the sleeping Fayne, Hermione imagines their hearts beating to the rhythm of the poem: "*O sister my sister O fleet sweet swallow* ran rhythm of her head and *hast thou the heart to be glad thereof yet* beat rhythm of a heart that beat and beat . . ." (180).

The homoeroticism implied by the opening lines of "Itylus" forms part of a spectrum of desires and gender disruptions articulated by Swinburne's poems, including narcissism, androgyny, and maternal eroticism. Hermione's manipulation of Swinburne's shifting erotic/familial bonds frees her from the patriarchal sexual/textual politics represented by George Lowndes to discover the complexities of signification and thus, her poetic vocation. Swinburne's overtly narcissistic "Before the Mirror" (*P&B* I, 146–9) forms yet another strand in the matrix of forbidden desires that inscribe Hermione's love for Fayne. Swinburne's poem is dedicated to Whistler, and inspired by his painting, "The Little White Girl," in which a young girl in white leans languidly against a mantle whose mirror reflects her dreamy expression. Swinburne used Whistler's painting to create a romantic and erotic portrait of female narcissism; but he also suggests the Romantic neo-Platonic doubling that H.D.'s male contemporaries professed to shun along with the Aesthete mask. H.D. quotes most frequently from the lines that suggest a spiritual twinning between the girl and her ghostly sister image: "Art thou the ghost, my sister, / White sister there, / Am I the ghost, who knows?" (147). These lines recur frequently in conjunction with the opening lines of "Itylus," contributing to an evolving myth of womanhood whereby Hermione taps her spiritual, erotic, and poetic powers through intimate self-identification with a "twin-self sister" (16). The homoeroticism and narcissism of "Itylus" ("O sister") and "Before the mirror" are joined by the maternal eroticism of Fayne's shifting identity as slain boy child, "Itylus." Significantly, Hermione forgets Fayne's name following their initial meeting and fails to recognize the import of Fayne's appearance in her life until she has "named" her "Itylus." By "naming" Fayne with Swinburne's "Itylus," Hermione evokes a spectrum of forbidden desires associated with the Decadent Romantic, desires remaining nameless in the dominant discourse, and simultaneously discovers the infinite possibilities of language. As the slain boy child, Fayne is not only the lost sister, but the lost child in the shifting erotic/familial bonds that characterize Hermione's relation to Fayne. Further, Fayne's cross-gender identities as twin sister and the boy Itylus add to the several masks of androgyny that Hermione projects on her beloved: Fayne becomes successively the beautiful boy Pygmalion, the huntress Artemis, a "boy hunter," and the boy Itylus.

Although H.D. does not refer in *HER* to Swinburne's actual poetic explorations of androgyny, "Hermaphroditus," and "Fragoletta," as I mentioned earlier, she quotes Swinburne's reference to the boy/girl Fragoletta as a "double rose of Love's" in *Paint It Today* to evoke the double and more fluid sexualities of the androgyne and the bisexual. Hermione's articulation of her own and Fayne's double sexual identities in the "naming" of Fayne as the boy Itylus releases her from her object position in the discourse of male desire and gives Hermione access to the multiple, polysemous power of words. Hermione's discovery of her bisexuality, a "name" for Fayne, occurs, appropriately, while she endures the "obliterating" kisses of George Lowndes. Musing on his earlier quotation from Swinburne's *Atalanta,* she reflects: "The kisses of George smudged out her clear geometric thought but his words have given her something . . . *the brown bright nightingale amorous . . . is half assuaged for . . . for . . .* her name is *Itylus*" (emphasis H.D.'s). In the same meditation, Hermione lights upon her "heritage": "Words may be my heritage. . . . mythopoeic mind (mine) will disprove science. . . . She could not say how or when she saw this; she knew it related back to an odd girl . . ." (73, 76). Hermione's simultaneous discovery of the "mythopoeic mind," the multiple meanings of "words," and the plurality of her forbidden desires demonstrates the sexual/textual configuration Eliot and Pound deplored in Swinburne's "morbid," evasive signification that failed to yoke the word to its referent. One might also accuse the text of *HER* itself – a lesbian novel written in deliberately disjunctive and associative prose – of such Swinburnian effeminacy.

However, H.D.'s construction of a "female" tradition in her countermyth of Romantic origins poses problems for the individual female talent not encountered by her male contemporaries. While male poets constructed an opposition between a pathological and inferior Romantic poetics and an autonomous, vigorous modernism, both assumed a place in the tradition. By contrast, Hermione experiences an aggravated form of "anxiety of authorship" as she wavers between a feminine identity that would entirely silence her, or a marginal Decadent poetic identity that threatens, in the second half of the novel, to self-destruct. Hermione's use of Swinburne does not ensure that she will continue to write poems. Indeed, in assuming the Romantic forbidden and effeminate poetic, she risks the ostracism and censure of her male contemporaries, and equally if not more destructive, her own internalization of the Decadent discourse that would efface her powers. While Hermione is initially successful in finding a way out of the silencing system imposed by George Lowndes through her transformation of Swinburne, she is finally defeated and driven to madness by the relentless resurfacing of the "decadence" inscribed in the persona of the femme fatale.

THE FEMME FATALE AND THE BOY ANDROGYNE

Despite female images such as Swinburne's White Girl, *HER*'s celebratory poetic of sister love, like many of the homoerotic pairings in H.D.'s early work, is constructed largely from male images of boy androgyny, referring centrally to Itylus, the boy child who both names and externalizes *HER*'s maternal, homoerotic poetics of transgression. As I will discuss further in Chapter Three, among H.D.'s borrowings from the Victorian Hellenists were codings for male–male desire, such as the color white, which derived from nude Greek statuary.[12] H.D.'s evocations of "white light," particularly in the juxtaposition of stars or frost against natural images, frequently distinguish the synthesis between intellectual energy and passion she attributed to her boy androgynes and their Artemisian twins in the early poetry and prose. In *HER,* the color code for male–male homoerotic desire is associated specifically with Swinburne's "white sister" and Itylus. Moreover, there is evidence that H.D. and Frances Gregg found masks for their early love in the (male) hermaphroditic bodies of Swinburne's and Wilde's poems. On the flyleaf, back pages, and title pages of H.D.'s first copy of *Sea Garden,* Frances Gregg carefully inscribed several love poems to H.D., including a Swinburnian ode to H.D.'s androgynous beauty entitled after Swinburne's poem, "Hermaphroditus."[13] As we shall see, H.D. draws upon the sensuous passion for Greek statuary that had become a code for male homoeroticism in Swinburne, Pater, and Wilde throughout her early work. H.D. herself treasured the small, childlike statue of the *Hermaphrodite* she visited whenever she was in Rome and well knew it had inspired Swinburne's poem. In *Paint It Today,* H.D.'s heroine sees an image of her prewar, premarried self in the "gentle breathing" figure of the *Hermaphrodite,* "modelled in strange, soft, honey-colored stone" (65). And, although the early H.D. internalized the prohibition against the femme fatale as emblematic of an appropriating and "decadent" sexuality in *HER, Sea Garden,* and elsewhere, the fatal woman was clearly a body that mattered very much to H.D. throughout her long career.

Two abject Swinburnian phantasms thus encode the sexual encounter toward the end of the novel as the white, marble boy/girl of works such as "Hermaphroditus" and (H.D. imagines) "Itylus" gives place to the "decadent" demonic femme fatale, "Faustine"; and Hermione begins to doubt the integrity of the visionary and erotic powers she had discovered in Fayne. Both Hermione's and Fayne's reentrance into the heterosexist discourse that surrounds them is signaled by their shifting attitude toward Swinburne, who once articulated the nonhierarchical, androgynous sister love, and now speaks the erotic perversities of a religion of vice. Swinburne and George Lowndes thus appear temporarily in collusion; both agreed that Fayne and Hermione should be "burned as witches."

During *HER'*s pivotal kiss scene, lines from "Faustine" (P&B I, 119–

26) relate the erotically cruel encounter between Fayne and Hermione (162–4), transforming Fayne from white boy child to lesbian vampire Faustine. The poem's description of the sadistic empress's face on the Roman coin – "*Curled lips long since half kissed away. . . . long ere they coined in Roman gold, your face, Faustine*" – vies in the narrative with the white boy androgyne, represented by the specter of a boy statue's "luminous" "marble nakedness" (162). The sexual narrative thus poses an untroubled, white eroticism against the fatal woman's suggestively sadistic strain of sensuality: Fayne's "empress mouth made its down-twist, made its up-twist that scarred the line of the face . . ." (162). Fayne puts "into her low voice the sort of scorn that went with *curled lips long since half kissed away*" (163); but as suddenly, "the mouth was straight now, . . . [and] marble lifted from marble and showed a boy" (163). However, Faustine's ultimate dominion over the sexual narrative is apparent in the self-conscious decadence encoding the actual kiss between Fayne and Hermione – enacted as a ritualized celebration of vice complete with the gothic props of swirling "wine-colored" curtains and the obsessive incantation of "Faustine":

> I feel the fringe of some fantastic wine-colored parting curtains. Curtains part as I look into the eyes of Fayne Rabb. . . . curtains parted, curtains filled the air with heavy swooping purple. Lips long since half kissed away. Curled lips long since half kissed away. . . . Long ere they coined in Roman gold your face – your face – your face – your face – your face – Faustine. (163, 164)

Immediately following the kiss, Hermione looks up into Fayne's face, which is "too white," and feels as if they "had fallen into a deep well and were looking up" (164). While the scene effectively conveys the powerful eroticism that is lacking in Hermione's clumsy encounters with George Lowndes (and as I suggest later, in the lifeless "whiteness" of the boy statuary), the image of the well conjures up another form of confinement, perhaps more dangerous. H.D. deliberately evokes the "decadent" side of Swinburne to demonstrate the rupture of the sister love that climaxes in Fayne's betrayal of Hermione with George Lowndes. Shortly after the kiss, Fayne asks Hermione pointedly, "Isn't Swinburne decadent?" To Her's confused reply asking, "In what sense exactly decadent, Fayne?" Fayne cryptically pronounces their relationship "indecent" and "immoral": "Oh innocence holy and untouched and most immoral. Innocence like thine is totally indecent" (164). Fayne's new assessment of their intimacy and her subsequent repetition of George Lowndes's words, "He said you and I ought to be burnt for witchcraft," signals her betrayal with George Lowndes (165). Shortly afterward, Hermione's assimilation into the heterosexist discourse is complete when she concludes, "She knew that they should be burnt for witchcraft. . . . she knew that George was right" (165). Significantly, Lowndes also turns the very words from Swinburne that affirmed her sister love into a shocking pronouncement against what he perceives as a perverse, but titillating (to him) narcissism – "*Art thou a ghost my sister? Narcissa, are you a water lily?*" (208).

H.D. continues to manipulate the sometime Janus face of Decadence to convey Hermione's struggle to place her newfound desires and prophetic power as either perverse, isolating, and therefore annihilating, or as liberating. Abandoned by both Fayne and George, Hermione descends into mental and physical illness. In the climactic mad scene of the novel, Hermione's disassociated stream of thoughts and images debate whether she should go on "arguing" or conform to the consensus that would pronounce her and Fayne "decadent." While she repeatedly calls to Fayne through Swinburne's "Before the Mirror" – "my sister there" – Hermione just as abruptly switches back into the discourse of her family, fiancé, and the betraying Fayne, warning herself, "Remember always that Swinburne being decadent, there's no use arguing . . ." (208) (ellipsis H.D.'s).

However, as Deborah Kelly Kloepfer suggests, Hermione's outpouring of associative images and wild questionings paradoxically transport her back to psychic health and wrest her from the heterosexist discourse. At the conclusion of the novel Hermione awakens from madness into her love for the "white sister." The frost/star complex of Decadent male–male desire reemerges in the narrative as Her's walk through a winter landscape returns her to the lost boy child, and to her own poetic identity:

> Winter branches etched above her head caught reverberation of ice breaking. . . . Then her thought widened and the tension snapped as swiftly. . . . It's like Fayne exactly.

> When she said Fayne a white hand took Her. . . . Her saw Her as a star shining white against winter daylight. (225)

41

With the composition of *HER* in 1927, H.D. constructed a female Romantic myth of origins from Decadent monologue or lyric songs of deviant desire. However, H.D.'s first Imagist volume, *Sea Garden* (1916), reveals that the early fascination with the Decadent love poem she expressed in *HER* was genuine. Decadent Romanticism suffuses the imagery and sexual narrative of her early poetry to form an Imagism of different desires.

II   The Decadent Image

Referring in general to the limitations of Imagism in a letter to Charlotte Mew, May Sinclair unintentionally described its potential restriction on a poetics of female desire: "In writing to R[ichard] A[ldington], I said, 'some of you will have an emotion that the "Image" will not carry; then where are you?' " (qtd. in Guest 29–30). Prohibited, by modernist "impersonality," from the narrative strategies that might allow for a female "I," women poets could avoid the issue of desire in a nonsexual poetic of gender-neutral images, or search out images and poetic strategies that subverted the assumed masculinist eros behind the Image. Linguistically, as Shari Benstock argues, women Imagists such as H.D. also needed to " 'unhinge' [the male modernists'] forged alliance between signifier and signified, opening and unsettling the image construct and realigning the relationship between subject and object . . ." (Benstock 328). The poetic project for many women writers therefore became the search for metaphoric or narrative structures and modes of signification that would implant alternate forms of desire and sensation in the Image.

I hope to demonstrate that H.D.'s Imagism undermines masculinist theories of impersonality by way of the metaphoric landscape/bodies and language for transgressive desire she gleaned from the sexually diverse "Greece" of Victorian Hellenists such as Pater, Wilde, and Swinburne. *Sea Garden*'s white, chiseled, or brazenly colored and marred sea flowers, its decadent overflowered Venusbergs, and evasive (Swinburnian) linguistic practices thus form a narrative of competing sexualities and "unnatural" desires that deliberately implicate the authorial "I" behind the volume.

Indeed, much later, Douglas Bush's *Mythology and the Romantic Tradition* lambasted H.D.'s Imagism for its Decadent Aestheticism:

> H.D. is a poet of escape. Her refuge is a dream-world of ideal beauty which she calls Greece. . . . The fact is that the hard bright shell of H.D.'s poetry partly conceals a soft romantic nostalgia, which, however altered and feminized, is that of the Victorian Hellenists.[14]

Bush concludes that H.D. was more "escapist" than the Pre-Raphaelites, "who testify their consciousness . . . of a world outside themselves," and relegates H.D.'s "paradise" to the Greece of "Pater and Wilde."

The "Greece" constructed by the Victorian Hellenists as a haven for male–male desire and associated with the image complex of "light," "whiteness," and sculpture (Jenkyns 147–53) resembles the "crystalline" Imagism for which H.D. gained early fame. H.D. herself would make casual comparisons between her early style and the play of light on marble statuary at the Louvre (where she first saw the statue of the *Hermaphrodite*): "My idea of Paris," she wrote in 1936, "is a sort of holy, holy pilgrimage to the Louvre to see the lights and shadows on the marbles and wings of marble. All very early H.D."[15] And Louis Untermeyer is among those critics who praised H.D. for her possession of "the sculptor's power" to both animate and fix the image. Unintentionally evoking the Aesthete's sculptured emblem for male transgressive desire (which I discuss further in Chapter Three), Untermeyer remarked H.D.'s fusion of "warm blood and chill stone." "Her marble palpitates," he comments. Others, perhaps reacting subliminally to H.D.'s use of the Aesthetes' "unnatural" imagery, attacked H.D.'s Imagism for its cold artificiality and perversion – some describing *Sea Garden* as the work of a "frozen Lesbian."[16]

Finally, the narrative structure of *Sea Garden* appears to draw upon the Decadent Romantic convention of lyric, monologue, and quest-romance forms in which antithetical eroticized landscapes frequently enact a drama of imprisonment and escape – usually in the sensuous trap of the Venusberg and an alternately regenerating landscape of psychic and erotic power.[17] H.D. would have encountered the dialectical landscapes in such poems as Swinburne's "Laus Veneris," which contrasts the knight's thralldom to a dark Venus in "beds . . . full of perfume and sad sound" with his imagined escape to the cleansing wash of the sea, "where tides of grass break into foam of flowers" (*P&B* I, 18).[18] H.D.'s instructions to Amy Lowell regarding the ordering of her poems for Lowell's 1916 Imagist anthology indicate that she grouped her poems in sequential phases of passion. H.D. repeatedly requested that the "sea-pieces" "make for one sustained mood" and asked that another group of poems be followed by "Midday" "in crescendo."[19] *Sea Garden,* which H.D. had recently prepared for publication, reflects the same sensitivity to counterpoint: The late-summer gardens of poems such as "Garden" and "Orchard" are consistently spliced with the opposing white, rocky seascapes and glittering sea flowers of works such as "Pursuit," "Sea Gods," and "Sea-Violet." H.D.'s use of the dialectical landscapes of the Decadent Romantic sexual history shifts the discourse of her Imagism from the brief, impersonal word picture to a revisionist tale of desire – a tale that argues for the redefinition and revaluing of the forms and states of desire in its narrative progression from the static, self-defeating eroticism of the Venusberg to the exuberant sensuality of the glimmering, often artificial sea garden. Although the H.D. of *Sea Garden* appears to be using the abject landscape/body of the femme fatale as a "regulatory ideal" (*Bodies* 22), she bans the Venusberg in order to point up the merits of yet another figure of abjection – the male, homoerotic white, sculpted sea-garden/body of Decadent Aestheticism. H.D. thus omits the normative second term of the binary that would compel heterosexuality, dwelling entirely among realms of different desires. Indeed, *Sea Garden*'s hymns to the floral, white or brashly colored artifice of the sea garden and the contrasting cloying, overripe, dense, and decaying natural gardens might in fact describe a series of songs to the Decadent bodies of the white, marble boy androgyne and the Venusian femme fatale H.D. admired in "Fragoletta" and "Faustine" of Swinburne's *Poems and Ballads.*

The early H.D.'s appropriation of the Venusberg as the lower paradise of erotic love probably derives both from her male contemporaries' anti-Romanticism and from Decadents such as Pater, who celebrates the pure spirituality of the crystal boy androgyne above the "scarlet" corruption of woman's love ("that white light, purged from the angry bloodlike stains of . . . passion") (Pater in "Winckelmann" 213. Usually overripe, over-flowered, and located in an enclosed space – a garden, bower, or glade – the Venusberg conceals a deadly trap behind its apparently safe, sensuous refuge. Its dense, enclosed atmosphere proves stifling rather than protective.

Frequently the lush vegetation suggests the cloying sweetness of decay. Despite its sensuous promise, the love bower is actually sterile and blighting in its all-consuming torpor, which anesthetizes its victims, overpowering all generative impulses, including sensual desire. H.D.'s debt to poets such as Baudelaire and the Decadent garden in general for the paralyzing effect of a consuming desire is most apparent in *Sea Garden*'s "The Gift," in which the speaker (whose gender may be female) suffers under the influence of a sensuous dark Venus and her attendant garden. The poem is worth quoting at length.

. . .

Your garden sloped to the beach,
myrtle overran the paths,
honey and amber flecked each leaf,
the citron-lily head
one among many –
weighed there, over sweet

The myrrh-hyacinth
spread across low slopes,
violets streaked black ridges
through the grass.

The house, too, was like this,
over painted, overlovely –
. . . [20]

The obsessive urgency of the speaker's tone and her/his entrapment in an oversweet garden whose hectic colors "streaked," "flecked," and "spread" in a bizarre design evoke the deadly Decadent Venusberg. The poem's later references to "black violets" and "strangling" (18) myrrh-lilies adds to the catalogue of *fleurs du mal* which describe the devastating effect of a perverse passion. The series of deadly, oversweet, and overripe paradises occurring throughout *Sea Garden* include the more imagistic, briefly sketched gardens of "Sheltered Garden," "Garden," and "Orchard." Although the "I" throughout *Sea Garden* is ungendered, she/he perceives the overflowered paradise as a sensuous trap. "I have had enough. / I gasp for breath," cries the speaker in "Sheltered Garden," oppressed by the enclosure of "border-pinks, clove-pinks, wax lilies, / herbs, sweet-cress / . . . border on border

45

of scented pinks" (*CP* 19). In poems such as "Orchard," the hot, overripe, late summer/autumnal paradises with their "grapes, red purple . . . dripping with wine" evoke the cloying sweetness of the Decadent paradise (*CP* 29). The atmosphere of the garden, like the Venusberg, suggests stasis and torpor: "This beauty, / . . . without strength chokes out life"; "fruit cannot drop / through this thick air" (*CP* 20, 25). H.D.'s speakers long to break out of their psychic, erotic paralysis and escape to the heady freedom of the alternate stormy landscape:

> O to blot out this garden
> to forget, to find a new beauty
> in some terrible
> wind-tortured place. (*CP* 21)

In addition to the Venusberg of Swinburne's "Laus Veneris," whose "gateways smoke with fume of flowers" (18), the *Poems and Ballads* include several variations of the Decadent, erotic death-paradise. The late summer love bowers of Swinburne's "The Two Dreams," for example, suggest the erotic and psychological torpor of an illicit love that recalls H.D.'s "beauty without strength":

> Even this green place the summer caught them in
> Seemed half deflowered and sick with beaten leaves
>
> . . .
>
> The trees' weight burdening the strengthless air. (*P&B* I, 291)

Semiotically, H.D.'s lower paradises articulate a similar servitude to the normative object world that informed the sexual/textual politics of early modernism. Objects correspond to their names in poems such as "Sheltered Garden" or "The Gift," in which the landscape comprises a list of flowers, scents, and colors marking off in tedious detail the self-referential, closed world of the Image. The speaker of "Sheltered Garden" monotonously "names" the flowers that surround her/him – "border-pinks, clove-pinks, wax-lilies, / herbs, sweet-cress" – in an exhaustive catalogue of like things. Meaning is firmly fixed and redundant in the sheltered garden, where "every way ends, every road, / every foot-path leads at last / to the hill-crest" or to "the same slope" (*CP* 19). In the second half of the poem, the speaker imagines a violent attack on the garden – scattering, hurling, snapping its contents, and leaving "half-trees, torn, twisted / but showing the fight was valiant" (*CP* 20). The thematic destruction of the garden introduces the volume's preoccupation with the activity of disruption and displacement, which H.D. celebrates in the alternate landscapes of psychic and erotic power.

The spare, expansive territory of glinting rock terraces and scarred sea flowers forms the opposing landscape/body of exuberant sensuality and release. H.D.'s heady chases through wild territory in poems such as "Pursuit" and "Sea Gods," clear space for unwritten forms of desire and suggest the influence of Swinburne's poetics of the trace. Leslie Brisman's analysis of Swinburne's semiotics interprets Swinburne's refusal to refer to the object world as "a sign of the world being more than a collection of persons and objects: the gap between words and objects defines the domain of the gods."[21] Adalaide Morris perceives a similar compliance between H.D.'s visionary aesthetic in *Sea Garden* and her poetic of absence in which "each intense natural fact is the trace of a spiritual force." "Like a skilled tracker," Morris continues, "the poet [of *Sea Garden*] moves from sign to sign in rapt, sagacious pursuit." As Morris reminds us, H.D.'s 1916 review of John Fletcher's *Goblins and Pagodas* indicates that H.D. herself aspired beyond the confines of "direct representation": H.D. concedes that Fletcher "uses the direct image, it is true," but praises his attempt at a "more difficult . . . and richer form of art: not that of direct presentation, but that of suggestion."[22]

I would add to these assessments of H.D.'s and Swinburne's poetics of absence that the gaps also point toward an as yet unwritten world of desire. As Brisman observes, Eliot and Pound had aptly described Swinburne's evasive signification. Swinburne's linguistic indeterminacy may also be identified with a displaced and deferred desire/language – "the word gives him the thrill not the object." H.D.'s chase poems similarly elude the object in pursuit of an undelineated form of desire.

The speaker in "Pursuit" (*CP* 11, 12) reconstructs the passage of an elusive "you," presumably a god or spirit, through a series of visual disruptions in the landscape. Heel prints, snapped stalks, trampled leaves, mark the path of the unseen spirit who supposedly "whirled," "doubled" back, "fell," and finally disappeared into the arms of an imagined "wood daemon." Although the poem ends in loss – "I can find no trace of you" –

the unrealized world of erotic gratification (union with the "you") is temporarily reconstructed by the speaker's ardent pursuit of signs. The carefully drawn details of the landscape – its larch cones, wild hyacinth, slender trees, and underbrush – do not function as "concrete" Images and metaphors, but rather trace the movement of desire as evidence of its existence. Jerome McGann describes Swinburne's poetics of absence similarly: "[The] object [of language in Swinburne] is characteristically what Swinburne and Mallarmé both referred to as the effect of a thing rather than the thing itself."[23] In H.D.'s "Pursuit," meaning is merely "the hallucination of meaning": The poem's subject, erotic desire, emerges as the speaker passionately enacts the activity of signification, in which, according to Derrida, "by the movement of its drift . . . the emancipation of the sign constitutes in return the desire of presence." Similarly, in "Sea Gods," the longed-for god exists in the imagined traces of her/his presence:

> You will draw back,
> and the ripple on the sand-shelf
> will be witness of your track
>
> . . .
>
> you will come
> you will come
> you will answer our taut hearts
> . . . (CP 30)

Perhaps H.D.'s strongest debt to Decadent Aestheticism is apparent in the mangled, brittle, yet triumphant sea flowers that earned her the reputation for a sculpted, crystalline (or "frozen" and perverse) Imagism. The creator of Sea Garden may be said to share the Aesthetic imagination of Pater's autobiographical "poet" in Imaginary Portraits, whose strange fascination with an old building's display of metal-screen work, twisted with "fantastic grace into wreaths of flames or flowers" inspires a poetry noted for its "peculiar character as of flowers in metal."[24] H.D.'s "Sea Poppies," distorted, metallic, and glittering, are similarly "peculiar":

> Amber husk
> fluted with gold,
> fruit on the sand
> marked with a rich grain

treasure
spilled near the shrub-pines
to bleach on the boulders:

your stalk has caught root
among wet pebbles
and drift flung by the sea
and grated shells
and split conch-shells.

Beautiful, wide-spread
fire upon leaf,
what meadow yields
as fragrant a leaf
as your bright leaf? (*CP* 21)

Further, the deliberately perverse eroticism of H.D.'s oddly beautiful sea flowers appears to derive both from the "rare rank flowers" of the Decadents' *fleurs du mal* and from Swinburne's stoic, passionately celibate sea gardens. The burning, overexposed, "wide-spread" poppy recalls Swinburne's sea daisies, which emerge in startling relief from the purposeful vagueness of his language to create a stark and concrete form of Imagism:

But clear are these things; the grass and the sand,
Where, sure as the eyes reach, ever at hand,
With lips wide open and face burnt blind,
The strong sea-daisies feast on the sun. (*P&B* I, 41)[25]

Much later, H.D.'s notes for her unpublished Pre-Raphaelite novel, "White Rose and the Red," draw attention to Swinburne's childhood love of the sea and the "cruelty and beauty" of his mythology of the elements. She notes, "Buffeted by sea, swimming, bruises, struggle, salt-sting caused young S. sensuous pleasure. Cruelty & beauty in S., as in the sea. S. stoic in face of elements. His own mythology. . . ."[26] And, just as H.D.'s sea poppy eclipses the meadow flower, Swinburne's "foam-flowers endure when the rose-blossoms wither" (*P&B* II, 29).

The antithesis between the overripe, hot garden flower and the sea flower is a commonplace in Baudelaire, Swinburne, Poe, and others. In

Swinburne's elegy to his master, Baudelaire, "Ave Atque Vale," he asks the poet, "Shall I strew on thee. . . . quiet sea-flower moulded by the sea, / . . . Or wilt thou rather, as on earth before, / Half-faded fiery blossoms, pale with heat / And full of bitter summer . . . ?" (*P&B* II, 71). Further, however, H.D.'s sea flowers resemble the Decadent flower that flourishes in an artificial or hostile "clime." Although briny and "clean," they retain the suggestion of erotic power, defiance, and difference of the more lurid "strange flowers" in Swinburne, Poe, and Baudelaire. Swinburne's "Ave Atque Vale" also contrasts the natural flowers – "simplest growth of meadow-sweet or sorrel" with the French symbolists' bouquet of "leaf-buds poisonous, / Bare to thy subtler eye, but for none other / Blowing by night in some unbreathed-in clime" (*P&B* II, 71, 72, 73). And, despite its demonic sensuality, Theophile Gautier's provocative description of Poe's Decadent gardens in his foreword to Baudelaire's *Fleurs du Mal* suggests the brazen sexuality of H.D.'s sea flowers:

> These plants, with their strangely cut foliage . . . have a sinister and powerful beauty. You feel them dangerous in spite of their charm; they have . . . an awareness of immense power or irresistible seductiveness.[27]

(H.D. confessed in a later letter to Aldington that she was "infatuated" with Poe in school although she was reproved for admiring such a "morbid" poet.[28]) The triumphant female sexuality of Gautier's description distinguishes H.D.'s "beautiful, wide-spread" sea poppies, her suggestively aroused sea iris, whose "brittle flower" and "rigid myrrh bud" is "salt and stinging," and the sea rose that drips "acrid fragrance in a leaf." Decadent exoticism and artificiality characterize the harsh, frequently gilded exteriors of H.D.'s sea flowers, cut by the sand to a "hard edge," "fluted with gold," "cut in rock," or brilliantly colored with "spilt dye."

Finally, although *Sea Garden*'s flowers are deliberately left ungendered, they do suggest an "unnatural" androgyny: Like Swinburne's boyish huntress in *Atalanta in Calydon*, H.D.'s sea flower is a sexual misfit, "not like the natural flower of things / That grows and bears and brings forth fruit and dies" (*Atalanta* II, 634–5). Indeed, H.D.'s sea violet might be invoking the androgynous white sister (Frances Gregg)[29] of *HER* – "a star shining white against winter daylight":

Violet
your grasp is frail
on the edge of the sand-hill,
but you catch the light –
frost, a star edges with its fire. (*CP* 26)

If "not all objects are equal" in the literary imagination, H.D.'s Images
were judged by her contemporaries as novel – but shallow. Measured
against the more recognizable poetic of male desire, H.D.'s powerfully
erotic sea flowers appeared flat and dull. Contemporaries such as F. S. Flint
and Harold Monro admired H.D.'s obvious craft and the oddity of her
scarred, uprooted sea flowers; but both agreed, in the special number of
the *Egoist* on Imagism, that H.D.'s art lacked imagination.[30] Harold Monro
complained in "The Imagists Discussed" that H.D. relied too heavily on
"one image" (79) and F. S. Flint ("The Poetry of H.D.") detected a "tendency to pare and cut too far," and a "consequent . . . bareness and je-
juneness" (73). Behind such trivializations of H.D.'s work lurked
misogynist preconceptions about the "preciousness" of women's writing.
Monro conceded that H.D. was the "truest 'Imagist' of the group," but
implied that her "feminine" art could have little influence on the more
vigorously masculine Imagists such as himself:

> [Imagism's] future work will scarcely develop along the lines of her ex-
> ample. Her poems have a slight flavor of brine; they are as fragile as sea-
> shells. If I came too near them I should be afraid of crushing them into the
> sand with my clumsy feet. ("The Imagists Discussed" 79)

Richard Aldington added to the Imagists' devaluations of *Sea Garden*'s poetic experiments his somewhat condescending advisement against H.D.'s
spoiling the "novelty" of her volume in "another such garland" of "exquisite, unique sea-flowers."[31]

III   Toward the Dramatic Lyric and the Mask of Male–Male Desire

Following the publication of *Sea Garden* (1916) and the inevitable dissolution of the Imagist movement, H.D. experienced both a personal and

aesthetic crisis that appeared to turn on the issue of impersonality. Her male mentors' trivializations of H.D.'s work, combined with the recent crises of war and her shattered marriage, threatened to erode the active poetic "identity" H.D. required to write poetry. No longer content to conceal the conflicts she had begun to explore in *Sea Garden* behind the doctrine of impersonality, H.D. searched almost desperately[32] for a form that would authorize the woman writer as the speaking subject of her art.

The theme of depersonalization recurs throughout H.D.'s prose and letters of the period. H.D.'s objections to the self-conscious "cleverness," "originality," and brutality of postwar, post-Imagist modernists such as the Vorticists and James Joyce echo Edith Sitwell's more direct pronouncements against the prevailing "hatred of personality."[33] In her letters to Amy Lowell and Aldington (1917–18), H.D. confessed that she felt supplanted by the cultivated "cynicism" of the postwar modernists. "The *L[ittle] R[eview]* leaves us quite faint with its cynicism," she wrote to Lowell, "but I really can't judge – They all make me sad with their cynicism." H.D. professed an almost involuntary aversion to the antics of James Joyce, which she perceived as "diabolical strength," "great power but all turned to the wrong purpose." "(I fear I must confess it)," she wrote in another letter to Lowell, "I have grown too unutterably sick of all this modern cult of brutality." To both Aldington and Lowell, H.D. complained of feeling "deracinée," not "dans le movement," "old fashioned."[34] In her personal life, H.D. experienced the self-effacing "modern cult of brutality" as the predatory sexual politics of wartime promiscuity that culminated in her loss of Richard Aldington to the conventionally "feminine" but shallow Dorothy Yorke. Both her failed marriage and her male mentors' trivialization of H.D.'s work forced her to confront the irreconcilable split between her roles as muse and woman artist.[35] Unable to resolve the conflict or to fulfill either role, H.D. silently withdrew from the social network of modernist writers. H.D.'s successive poetic and fictional versions of the war years recount her self-imposed exile from the Lawrentian exaltation of "sex experience" that pervaded the London literary circle. In *Bid Me to Live*, H.D.'s autobiographical heroine, Julia, condemned the self-annihilating "war-consciousness" of Rico's (based on D. H. Lawrence) polarizing "man-is-man," "woman-is-woman" aesthetic as a "love cry, death-cry for [our] generation."[36]

Like *HER,* H.D.'s other fictional autobiographies, *Paint It Today* and *Asphodel,* repeatedly singled out the Decadent dramatic lyric as a means toward reconstructing a female sexual and poetic "identity." In *Paint It Today,* for example, H.D.'s artist heroine specifically advocates the personal song of the Decadent Romantic lyric over the impersonal and implicitly masculine "epic pictures" Eliot might have praised for their objectification of "feeling" into an "articulate external world":

> Large, epic pictures bored her. . . . She wanted the songs that cut like a swallow wing the high, untainted ether, not the tragic legions of set lines that fell like black armies with terrific force and mechanical set action. (11)

Here, H.D. perhaps urges a female agenda for modern poetry through her heroine Midget's endorsement of the lyric form – the "swallow wing" with its deliberate evocation of Swinburne's "Itylus." Midget's dismissal of "large epic pictures" for their "terrific force and mechanical set action" echoed H.D.'s accusations against the "modern cult of brutality" and specifically against Joyce's "diabolical strength" and "great power all turned to the wrong purpose." Elsewhere in *Paint It Today,* Midget laments her postwar estrangement from the earlier Romantic sexual and poetic self that fused the sister muse with the "swallow" song of Swinburne's "Itylus": Attempting to recall that former self from the devastations of war, her disastrous marriage, and the aesthetic cult of brutality, Midget writes piteously to Josepha (based on Frances Gregg).

> Is poetry enchantment? Have people forgotten what poetry is? You used to know what poetry is? Do you remember how you made me say "Swallow" [sic] to you? . . . Do you remember "the wild birds take flight and follow and find the sun?" (55–6)

And in *Asphodel,* Hermione articulates the loss of her integrated self to World War I through successive quotes from Swinburne's "Itylus," "Hymn to Proserpine," and the opening lyric of *Atalanta:*

> O sister, my sister, the hounds of spring are on winter's traces, will you yet take all Galilean but this thou shalt not take . . . they were burned beneath lava, smoke, ashes, dust, death, years, obliteration . . . Self of self was so buried. . . . Who was she? Where was she? (125)

The Decadent Victorian monologue's device of the mask or persona, particularly in its most confessional manifestations, offered H.D. more range than the Image to voice a modernism of the margins. Inhabited by a male or female speaker who, according to Robert Langbaum, expressed "extraordinary moral positions and extraordinary emotions," the Decadent dramatic monologue often strove to adapt heretical or pathological stances toward sexual or social convention.[37] Indeed Swinburne laid the blame on the pathology of the dramatic monologue in his public defense against the moral outrage provoked by the *Poems and Ballads*. Carol T. Christ describes Swinburne's monologue as "deliberately revisionary": "Swinburne often casts his poems in such a way that they ask the reader to entertain the revision they pose" (Christ 29, 30). Swinburne's deployment of deviant personae in his various songs of the self therefore provided H.D. with a model for the dramatic monologues of *Hymen* (1921) and *Heliodora* (1924), which explore various phases of emotion or desire through a Greek mask.

"HYACINTH"

The following discussion of H.D.'s "Hyacinth" (*CP* 201–6) introduces the exploration of H.D.'s male masking that will occupy the next two chapters.[38] "Hyacinth" best illustrates H.D.'s evolution from the deliberately unidentified sexualities of *Sea Garden* H.D. derived from Victorian lyric, monologue, and quest-romance forms, toward the Decadent dramatic lyric itself, which often named and framed the abject personae of the femme fatale and the male Aesthete androgyne. The poem's celebration of the homoerotic boy–man continuum of the Hyacinth myth over the baser charms of the "russet" femme fatale characterizes H.D.'s early adaptation of the effeminate male mask in order to "argue" for a homoerotic muse and against the traditionally "feminine" role.[39] While the homoerotic myth of the poem may encode H.D.'s relationship with Bryher, there is evidence to suggest that H.D. assumes a male mask in the poem's erotic man–boy configuration to project the spiritual bond she believed she had shared with Aldington – a sympathetic bond that was painfully severed by his preference for the shallow and sexually vital temptress, Dorothy Yorke. Before exploring the biographical dimensions of "Hyacinth," however, I begin with an examination of "Hyacinth's" sexual personae and their association with the unnamed Romantic landscapes of *Sea Garden*.

In "Hyacinth," the Venusberg and the antithetical "white" landscape reconstruct Apollo's conflict between a predatory heterosexuality and the memory of his inspiring homoerotic love for the boy Hyacinth, whom he accidentally slew in a discus contest. Apollo's monologue moves from his rejection of the debilitating lower paradise inhabited by the temptress to an imaginative projection of the purgative mountain haunt where he will remain faithful to the boy's memory. From the opening of the poem, in which Apollo reveals his preference for Hyacinth to the outraged seductress, Apollo's enraptured meditation on his homoerotic passion establishes a clear dichotomy between the two forms of desire as debilitated or empowered states of being. Apollo begins by invoking his love for Hyacinth: "Your anger charms me," he wryly comments to the temptress, "and yet," he continues, "all the time I think of chaste, slight hands." The contemplation of Hyacinth's hands provokes a rush of associated images for the delicate sensuality of the boy's hands, "veined snow; / snow craters filled / with first wild-flowerlets; / glow of ice-gentian," – suggesting the ice flower image of *Sea Garden*'s salt-encrusted flowers and H.D.'s image for homoerotic desire. Further, as William Ulmer elegantly describes the sexual/textual open-endedness of Shelleyan quest romance, the stream of Apollo's images "subjects desire to an open-ended process that gives value no place to rest. . . . [the] metaphors . . . seek to incarnate unrealized desires. . . . engendering a metonymic series of figures mutually associated as surrogates of [the beloved]."[40] I would add that Apollo's metonymic stream of images for the boy's hands include homoerotic and female "unrealized desires."

Apollo's monologue then shifts abruptly to the contrastingly static and self-defeating desire offered by the temptress and her garden. Superficially enticing, like the Romantic Venusbergs of *Sea Garden*, the temptress's paradise conceals a subtext of death and decay in its imagery of confinement, stagnation, and finally extinction. The bereaved Apollo rejects the lurking sexual threat posed by the lower paradise and incites the temptress – a classic Venus figure with "red lips" and "russet hair" – to keep her garden and its corrupt pleasures to herself:

Take the red spoil
of grape and pomegranate
the red camellia,
the most, most red rose;
take all the garden spills,
inveterate,
prodigal spender. . . . (CP 202)

The garden associated with the temptress's charms shares the highly charged color, sensuous glut, and abjection of late summer paradises such as "Garden" in H.D.'s Imagist volume. Like the Decadent Romantic Venusberg, the paradise approaches putrefaction: Overripeness to the point of rottenness is latent in images such as "red spoil" with its double meaning as both the trophy of sexual conquest and its assured decay, and "garden spills," which are at once overluxuriant plants and discarded slops. In the remaining lines of Apollo's description, the dense catalogue of heavy petaled and strongly perfumed flowers, which overaccumulate to the point of suffocation, recalls both metaphorically and semiotically the redundancy and claustrophobia of the "Sheltered Garden":

prodigal spender
just as summer goes,
the red scales of the deep in-folded spice
the Indian, Persian and the Syrian pink,
their scent undaunted
even in that faint,
unmistakable fragrance
of the late tuberose,
(heavy its petals,
eye lids of dark eyes
that open languorous
and more languorous close – the east, . . .)
take these. (CP 202)

The Venusberg's traditionally narcotic influence is suggested in the image of closed eyes that concludes the passage. Further, the Decadent garden's characteristic imagery of confinement accumulates in the "deep in-folded spice," the later "whorls" of "clustered peonies," and other references to the garden's dense vegetation. Apollo's allusion to the love bower as "swales" or swamplands in his angry injunction, "Keep all your riot in the swales below," defines the garden as a realm of erotic stagnation. Apollo's parting threat to the temptress, "You have your tense, short space / of blazing sun," alludes to her inevitable self-destruction in the caustic "sun" of a predatory passion; similarly, H.D.'s poem, "Hymen," described by Susan Gubar as a "somber meditation on the predatory nature of heterosexuality," dramatizes a suggestively violent form of sexuality in its "hot sheltered glen." The metaphorical rape that climaxes the poem's marriage ceremony projects the bride's initiation into eros in a colorfully charged love bower where the plunderer bee "slips between the purple flower-lips" as "the sun lies hot across his back" (*CP* 108, 109).[41]

"Hyacinth's" alternative landscape of mountain and sea ledge, to which Apollo imaginatively retreats, forms an exhilarating contrast to the stasis of the deadly swales of predatory passion. Apollo's visionary landscape associates the upper regions, both high and expansive, with the inviolate homoerotic attachment to Hyacinth; and his reverie generates images of transformation, creative/erotic intensity, and renewal. While Apollo complains that Hyacinth's death has left him feeling "worthless / weary, world-bedraggled," "nevertheless," he asserts to

> mountains
> still the rain
> falls on the tangle
> of dead under-brush
> freshens the loam,
> the earth and broken leaves
> for that hoar-frost
> of later star or flower,
> the fragile host
> of Greek anemones. (*CP* 204–5)

The lower paradise is merely seasonal, but the mountain haunt perpetually renews itself: Apparently cast out, "dead underbrush," Hyacinth will be reborn, as loam gives way to "later star or flower." Again H.D. uses the Victorian Hellenists' code for homoeroticism in the white light evoked by the star/frost/flower image cluster. (And we are reminded, in the distinction between H.D.'s enflamed scarlet temptress and the Hyacinth, associated with white light, of Pater's "that white light, purged from the angry bloodlike stains of . . . passion.") Like the imagined landscape of poems such as "Pursuit," the territory of Apollo's homoerotic desire remains indeterminate. Apollo's preferred mountain refuge exists in the gaps of "ridge," "hollow," and "wind-indented snow":

> All, all I gladly give
> who long but for the ridge,
> the crest and hollow,
> the lift and fall,
> the reach and distant ledge
> of the sun-smitten,
> wind-indented snow. (*CP* 206)

The impression of an infinitely deferred desire created by the continually ebbing landscape demonstrates the Swinburnian poetic of absence that H.D. initiated in *Sea Garden's* chase poems.

Apollo reasserts the triumph of his homoerotic passion over "the swales below" in his reference to the memory of Hyacinth as "one last flower" "upon the mountain slope" which "cleaves" to "the wet marge of ice" (Apollo of course preserved the memory of Hyacinth in the hyacinth flower that he created from the boy's blood.) Defying the temptress's solicitations, Apollo responds:

> For you and autumn yet
> can not prevail
> against that flame, that flower,
> (ice, spark or jewel,)
> the cyclamen
> parting its white cyclamen leaves. (*CP* 204)

The white, blatantly sexual image of the iced cyclamen recalls H.D.'s "Sea-Violet" and forms a further example of H.D.'s systematic white imagery for same-sex love. The triumphant cyclamen indicates the flowering and opening of homoerotic desire, as Apollo celebrates his enduring attachment to Hyacinth over the blighting desire of the lower paradise. "Hyacinth" therefore uses the Romantic antithesis as a narrative strategy to displace the temptress image founded on a predatory heterosexuality with a metaphoric projection of same-sex love.

The dramatic monologue allows H.D. to don a male mask, giving her access to a homoerotic configuration of desire. I suggest, however, that the poem may encode the Aldington-Yorke-H.D. love triangle, which H.D. depicted elsewhere as rupturing the spiritual communion she had shared with Richard Aldington. Intertextually, "Hyacinth" inscribes the refrain from Swinburne's lament on loss, "Hymn to Proserpine," which H.D. appears to have associated with her own psychic paralysis following Aldington's abandonment (P&B I, 76). The "Hymn's" refrain – "wilt thou yet take all Galilean / but these thou shalt not take," – is echoed by Apollo's anguished refrain in "Hyacinth" – "take all for you have taken everything . . . but do not let me see you taking this" – rebuking the temptress for having come between his love for Hyacinth. H.D. also quoted the lines from Swinburne's "Hymn to Proserpine" in *Asphodel* as Hermione curses an apparently malevolent deity who has "taken" the Aldington figure. H.D.'s recasting of her attachment to Aldington as a homoerotic bond in works such as *Hipparchia*, to be discussed shortly, frequently contrasts their sympathetic union with the polarizing dynamic of Aldington's attraction to the sexually active yet superficial Dorothy Yorke. As a revisionary strategy, the male mask provides H.D. with a device for projecting a heterosexual union based on "sameness" rather than the strict sexual difference inscribed in traditional representations of heterosexual love. Indeed the pivotal mask of the boy androgyne that hovers over *HER*'s love scene between the two women appears as frequently in H.D.'s narratives of a wished for heterosexual intimacy contained in works such as *Hipparchia*.[42]

In that novella, H.D.'s autobiographical heroine, Hipparchia, assumes the mask of the boy Hyacinthus slain by Apollo during her lovemaking with the virile Marius (based on Richard Aldington). The fluid, transformative nature of their sexual intimacy is imaginatively rendered through the homoerotic myth as Hipparchia recreates herself, beneath Marius, in the image of the boy Hyacinthus: "With the mouth caught inward by firm line of white teeth, it was a boy, stricken in adolescence. . . . Hipparchius slain by Helios" (*Hipparchia* 29, 30). Later, in the company of the scarlet courtesan, Olivia (based on Dorothy Yorke), who has seduced Marius away from Hipparchia, Marius recalls the subtle and protean power of Hipparchia's "homoerotic" sexuality in the "vision" of the slain boy, "underlip caught inward by a firm line of white teeth," that "for a moment challenged the vulgarity of the new shade of scarlet" (31). H.D. consistently depicted Yorke as a classic "harlot," "doomed to self-extinction," as Julia remarked of Arabella in *Bid Me to Live;* and throughout *Hipparchia,* she emphasizes her heroine's resemblance to the hyacinth, "honey flower."

As a tale of revenge, "Hyacinth" recreates H.D.'s fantasy that Aldington rejects Yorke for the higher love he experienced with H.D. The similarly drawn opposition between the shallow eros of the enflamed seductress and the homoerotic intensity of the bond between Hyacinth and Apollo in both "Hyacinth" and *Hipparchia* suggests that H.D. encodes in the poem her conviction that Aldington's sexual betrayal had violated their sacred, sympathetic bond for a more conventional and self-destructive passion. The poem therefore illustrates H.D.'s manipulation of the male homoerotic masks of the Decadent Victorian dramatic monologue to uncover the sexual politics of her heterosexual as well as homoerotic experience.

Until the early 1930s, H.D. frequently appears to have preferred to imagine her relationships with both men and women in terms of a male homoerotic connection. Personally, H.D.'s assumption of the boy Aesthete mask in relation to her male mentors enabled her to overcome her fear of psychic and erotic appropriation while maintaining the required worshipful, desiring, and passive stance without endangering her art. As a masking praxis, H.D.'s adherence to the Decadent boy mask deliberately countered the masking practices of her male contemporaries' poetic theories, which vehemently rejected the Aesthete persona for successive masks of "impersonality" (Eliot) or "virility" (Pound). As I have begun to suggest, however, H.D.'s female impersonations of the male Aesthete androgyne involved more than the insertion of a boy subject position. Throughout the 1920s, H.D.'s female poetic wore the complex systems of codes, tropes, and linguistic practices that had written the forbidden sexuality/textuality of the boy androgyne in fin-de-siècle Victorian Hellenism. In the next chapter, I investigate the influence of Pater and Wilde, in particular, on H.D.'s inscriptions of the male androgynous body during the 1920s.

The Aesthete Androgyne

Chapter Three

Writing the Decadent Boy Androgyne
Whiteness, Diaphaneitè, Poikilia, and Male Statuary

Reflecting on her recent writings in notes she entitled, "H.D. by Delia Alton," H.D. tellingly described "the theme and center" of her *Hippolytus Temporizes* and *Hedylus* to be "the portrait or projection of the intellectualized, crystalline youth, whose prototype is again found, or first found in the actual Greek drama" (221). Even as her reference to the crystalline youth indirectly suggests Pater's crystal man – frequently his homoerotic ideal of spiritual and physical beauty – H.D. unconsciously echoes Pater's early exclamation over the timelessness of the beloved fair youth in his essay, "*Diaphaneitè*": "Over and over again the world has been surprised by the heroism, the insight, the passion of this clear crystal nature."[1] Indeed, H.D. would seem to be considering the genealogy of her crystalline youth backward, from Aestheticism to the Classicism where she herself "again found" the androgynous type she had earlier discovered in Swinburne's "Hermaphroditus" and other poems.

Following *Sea Garden*, H.D. appears to have found both a radical individualism and a compatible philosophy of erotic/spiritual twinship in the persona of the Decadent boy androgyne whose "higher" love for his male mentor reconciles both intellect and eros. H.D.'s primary mask for female desire in works such as the verse-play *Hippolytus Temporizes* (1927), the novel *Hedylus* (1928), and poems from the volumes *Hymen* (1921), *Heliodora* (1924), and *Red Roses for Bronze* (1931) is largely perceived through the desiring, masculine "gaze" at youthful male beauty familiar in the works of Pater, Wilde, Swinburne, and other Aesthete poets.

Victorian critics such as Richard Dellamora and Linda Dowling are currently exploring the "alternative masculinities" and forms of desire created by Victorian Hellenists who skillfully maneuvered the Greek system of mentoring associated with Plato and the Dorians to encode male same-sex love.[2] Victorian "Dorianism," which, according to Richard Dellamora, derived from "the practice at Sparta of friendship and love between an adult male citizen soldier and a younger one preparing to achieve the same status," conjured male homoerotic love coupled with a Spartan discipline, cleanliness, and athleticism often associated with Greek marble statuary of nude male bodies (*Apocalyptic* 44). Recent critical inquiries into the influence of nineteenth-century philologist C. O. Muller's *History and Antiquities of the Doric Race* on Pater, Wilde, Ruskin, and others suggest that Muller's book inspired Pater's account of the Dorian man–boy twinship: "a clean, youthful friendship, 'passing even the love of woman' " in which "the beloved and the lover, side by side, . . . above all at the battlefield become, respectively . . . the hearer and . . . the inspirer, . . . the elder inspiring the younger with his own strength and noble taste of things."[3] It is believed that Dorian Gray, Wilde's model for supreme male beauty, was named after Muller's homoerotic Dorians. And Pater employs the Apollo/Hyacinth myth in his modern, homoerotic tale, "Apollo in Picardy," evoking, among other things, the Dorians' titular deity, Apollo. Decadent Hellenists also summoned the better known philosophic and academic Platonic man–boy continuum: Indeed, after his guilty verdict was announced, Oscar Wilde began his impassioned defense of male–male desire with a reference to the "pure," "perfect," and "intellectual" bond between men, "such as Plato made the very basis of his philosophy."[4]

Critics have explored extensively H.D.'s poetics of spiritual and erotic "twinning" encompassing maternal eroticism and the bond between androgynous lovers. In the next two chapters I will suggest that during the early phases of her career, H.D. transposed the Decadent Platonic/Dorian philosophy of male–male love onto her boy Aesthetes and their Artemisian or Apollonian twins in order to configure female desire. As we have seen in "Hyacinth" and other works such as *Hipparchia*, H.D., like Pater, was enamored of the Hyacinth/Apollo myth. And, referring to the Dorians (who took possession of Lacedaemon) in *HER*, Hermione's opening fantasy of a twin "sister" who would "run, would leap, would be concealed under the autumn sumac or lie shaken with hail and wind, lost on some Lacedaemonian foothill" explicitly draws upon the Victorian's athletic, homoerotic conception of Dorianism. Indeed, the spare landscapes and wild, vanishing spirits of *Sea Garden* may describe for H.D. a Dorian ("Spartan") ideal of Imagism. Further, classical statues caught in marble "frieze," prismatic likenesses of Pater's crystal man or Swinburne's transparently veined Fragoletta, haunt the poetic white bodies of H.D.'s early poetry and prose.

In this chapter, I focus particularly on H.D.'s encodings of female desire through the Victorian Hellenists' principal icon for Platonic and Dorian male–male love – the nude male bodies of Greek statuary that poets such as Swinburne, Pater, and Wilde summoned frequently as objects of the male homoerotic "gaze." H.D.'s adaptation of "statue love" and the variety of trace images it spawned for the loved male body such as whiteness, crystal, marble statuary, the burning "hard gemlike flame," or the transparently veined white body, enabled her to write the elusive body of mother–daughter eroticism, love between equal men and women, and homoerotic love.

I begin this chapter by discussing H.D.'s debt to what I will refer to as the "scene" of Platonic/Dorian transgressive desire – the eroticized masculine "gaze" at Greek statuary that H.D. may have first encountered in Swinburne's poetic fantasy of the *Hermaphrodite*, "Hermaphroditus." I proceed with a quite lengthy discussion of how such metonymic associations with the Decadents' originary figure of Greek statuary as whiteness, *diaphaneitè*, and *poikilia* ("dappledness" or "intricacy") not only serve as codes for the male–male continuum but create a disruptive body tropology. By rendering him as a glimmering linguistic and bodily trace, these metaphoric disfigurations undo the boy beloved's object status, distinguishing him from the traditional concrete female icon in an ensuing more fluid interaction between male artist and male beloved (text). I conclude by demonstrating that H.D. uses the Decadents' vanishing body of male–male desire in narratives of female desire similarly to disfigure the female Image/text of male modernism.

I "Statue Love"

No one would argue that in Wilde's *The Picture of Dorian Gray,* the male gaze at Dorian's ageless, beautiful male body and hence the configuration of man–boy aesthetic/erotic attachment becomes the site of the novel's Decadent Aestheticism. In Wilde's deliberately perverse narration of Aestheticism, the inverted sexed/gendered body of Dorian Gray is the central objet d'art celebrating the artifice of Victorian fin de siècle. Meditating admiringly on the artist Basil Hallward's fair young model Dorian, Lord Henry exclaims in the opening chapter, "A new Hedonism – that is what our century wants. You might be its visible symbol."[5] "His merely visible presence," Lord Henry later rhapsodizes, "suggests the new manner in art, the fresh mode of looking at life. . . . Grace was his, and the white purity of boyhood, and beauty such as old Greek marbles kept for us. . . ." (41). Admittedly these appreciations of Aestheticism issue from Wilde's villainous Lord Henry Wotton, a parody of nineties' decadence, in a novel that will record the lapse of Aestheticism into vice. Nevertheless, the staging of these three central characters – Lord Henry, Basil Hallward, and Dorian Gray – in Chapter One may be regarded as a striking reproduction of the "scene" of late-Victorian transgressive desire/Aestheticism. The spectacle of the boy model's displayed androgynous beauty like "old Greek marbles" before the adoring, aesthetically discriminating and sensuous gaze of the older male artist(s) (in Dorian's case, Basil and Lord Henry) appears repeatedly in various Aesthetic documents, ranging from Pater's essay on Winckelmann to Swinburne's "Hermaphroditus." In this scene, recurring alike in both consciously serious and perverse renderings of nineties' Aestheticism, the Greek, sculpted, androgynous male body writes the Aesthete's new program for poetry as a version of male–male desire. Hence the only "real" love for Dorian in the novel and thus the "purest" Aesthetic passion – that of his loyal painter Basil – is represented as a version of the Greek homoerotic ideal and exemplified through allusions to famous male artists and their boy models: "For it was really love – had nothing in it that was not noble and intellectual. . . . It was such love as Michael Angelo [sic] had known . . . and Winckelmann, and Shakespeare himself" (97). Similarly, critics often cite as evidence of the homoerotic passion that fuels Victorian Aestheticism Pater's allusions to art historian Winckelmann's romantic friendships with young men and specifically to his caressing of nude male statuary: "He fingers those pagan marbles with unsinged hands, with no sense of shame or loss."[6] Inspired by Pater's essay on Winckelmann, Wilde employed the code of statue love in his poem, *Charmides,* based on Boccaccio's legend of a young boy whose obsession with the statue of Venus compels him to make love to the marble goddess (Wilde 753–69). In Wilde's poem, which Richard Ellmann terms "polymorphously perverse," the scene of transgressive desire catches Charmides in the act of caressing the woman statue, a female stand-in for the erotic relation between the male artist and his poem.[7] Ellmann concludes that the poem, which Wilde considered his "best," gives Wilde "full scope to describe male beauty."[8] Finally, such classic Decadent fantasies of androgyny and man–boy homoeroticism as Swinburne's "Hermaphroditus" credit the homoerotic/aesthetic scene of statue love as the poem's occasion: Swinburne acknowledged that his ode to male androgyny was modeled after the famous statue, *Hermaphrodite,* which Dellamora observes includes him in "a line of poetry by male writers, including Theophile Gautier's 'Contralto,' " inspired by the androgynous statue in the Louvre (*Masculine Desire* 82). In these Aesthetic discourses of Wilde, Pater, and Swinburne, therefore, the white, sculpted, erotic body's staging of desire and the creative process emerges from the implied erotic/aesthetic interaction between the older male artist and his boy text.

Far from expediting the escape into art, therefore, the deliberate artifice of the statue in association with the loved male body creates a transgressive sexual politics. Artifice enacts the necessary denaturalization of the normative erotic body, traditionally defined as female and natural. (I discuss the homosocial aspect of the Greek ideal and its implications for the woman writer in Chapter Four.) Pater implicitly associated female beauty with the lesser beauty of nature, and male beauty, exemplified by Greek statuary, with the superior beauty of art in a quote from Winckelmann: "To [those who are observant of beauty only in women] the beauty of Greek art will ever seem wanting, because its supreme beauty is rather male than female . . . the beauty of art demands a higher sensibility than the beauty of nature . . ." ("Winckelmann" 192).[9]

H.D. appears to have recognized and manipulated the Decadent Aesthetic code of statue love throughout her poetic and prose narratives of desire. As I mentioned earlier, she referred to her Imagism metaphorically as the play of "light and shadows" on the "marbles" of the Louvre; and critics such as Untermeyer expressed the general impression of H.D.'s work as "sculpted." Poems such as "Toward the Piraeus," which reimagine H.D.'s relationships with her mentors on a male–male Greek continuum, often articulate eros as the transgressive male gaze at sculpted male beauty. An apology to Pound for her early chastity, "Toward the Piraeus" (*CP* 175–9) argues that if its female speaker had "been a boy" (178) she might have "worshipped" him, but as a woman she feared sexual/creative obliteration – "you would have broken my wings" (176). Purposefully assuming the boy–man eroticism of the Dorian ideal, H.D. reimagines the Pound figure as a mature lover/warrior and herself as his enraptured boy follower. Both male bodies become luminous spectacles/statuary in alternating scenes of Aesthetic transgressive art/desire. Watching male beauty is desire as the boy-H.D. "rent with an ecstasy" describes how he would have "stood, / and watched and watched / and burned," "glad . . . / to watch you turn / your great head, set on the throat, / . . . / burned and wrought like the olive stalk, / and the noble chin / and the throat" (178). And by the same token, Pound as loving mentor, the speaker elaborates, would have "found my hands, / beyond all the hands in the world, / cold, cold, cold, / intolerably cold and sweet" (179). The boy's cool hands recall the eroticism of the "chill" statue while drawing on the white encodings and the popular metonymy of white hands for the Decadent body (to be discussed shortly).

In H.D.'s "Pygmalion," "Red Roses for Bronze," the titular poem of H.D.'s volume *Red Roses for Bronze*, and "Charioteer," the explicitly or implicitly male speakers are sculptors who dwell lovingly on the bodies of their male subjects. "Charioteer"'s speaker, a brother, "taut with love, / more than any bright lover," mourns the loss of his charioteer brother and vows to "fashion a statue / of him" "to embody this image; / an image to startle, / to capture men's hearts" (*CP* 191, 192). And the obsessively jealous, possessive lover/sculptor of "Red Roses for Bronze" hopes to "sate" his "wretched fingers in ecstatic work" by fashioning, hammering, "strok[ing]" in stone an image of his unrequited love (*CP* 211).[10] While neither of the male lovers evoked in H.D.'s "Myrtle Bough" – Harmodious and Aristigiton – is a sculptor, the legendary lovers and warriors fought side-by-side in battle according to the custom of Dorian love, and one lover is moved to invoke his beloved as marble statuary: "O sleeping ivory . . . rouse your marble self" (*CP* 249, 250).

H.D.'s most overt debt to the Aesthete's scene of transgressive desire occurs in a reference to H.D.'s lesbian narrator in *Paint It Today* as a "sister" of Wilde's Charmides, the youth who fell in love with a statue (59). Chapter Six of the novel, entitled "Sister of Charmides," puts a feminist spin on the Aesthete's code of statue love while acknowledging H.D.'s sister–brother bond with her Wildean precursor by designating Midget as a twin sister to Wilde's fair youth. H.D. is well aware of the homoerotic implications of this exchange: Earlier, Midget had imaginatively become a "sister of Charmides" (or of Pater's Winckelmann) as she gazed at the *Venus de Milo* with eyes that longed to trace like fingers "the curve of the white belly and short space before the breasts brought the curve to a sudden shadow." But she "dared not" betray "the whitest passion" while in the company of the uncomprehending Basil (a type of Aldington) (60). And we recall that Hermione's physical attraction to Fayne is conveyed through the "luminous" mask of "marble" boy statuary during the women's kiss in *HER*. Further, H.D. joins the tradition of Aesthete poets who used the statue of the *Hermaphrodite* to fabricate fantasies of bisexuality and androgyny in *Paint It Today*. Even as lines from "Fragoletta" and "Hermaphroditus" run through her mind, H.D.'s heroine Midget – like Swinburne and Gautier before her – is transfixed by the *Hermaphrodite,* whose "gentle breathing image modeled in strange, soft, honey-colored stone" provokes painful memories of her forsaken bisexuality (65). (As I mentioned, H.D. frequently visited a reproduction of the statue when in Rome (Guest 51).) Elsewhere, in a typically heterosexual projection of the male–male Greek continuum (*Bid Me to Live*), H.D. evokes Winckelmann's sensuous "fingering" of "pagan marbles" in Pater's essay: Attempting to bring Rafe (Aldington) back to the reciprocating and fluid sensuality of their intimacy before the war, Julia recalls how they once mutually caressed Michelangelo's statue of a (probably male) nude. During this moment of cross-gender sensuality, " 'Our hands had run over that marble torso as they said Michelangelo's did after he had gone blind'. . . . The very touch of the fingers of Michelangelo had been transferred to theirs. . . . Other cities had been buried. Other people had been shot to death. . . . [but] there was something left between them" (72).

II · The Decadent Vanishing Body as Subversive Body Trope

Those properties Pater, Wilde, and Swinburne loosely associated with Greek male statuary – whiteness, crystal, light – also write a vanishing body, a darting shape that mimics the elusive play of language and desire. The differently sexed/gendered male body, like the body of female desire, must evade the object status of conventional inscriptions. The traditional I–you subject/object position therefore unravels in the transition to the homo-erotic. Pater's, Wilde's, and Swinburne's phantasms of the loved male body exist most often in Aesthetic texts not as unitary, objectified, figurines of simulated marble, but as disfigurations in which imagined qualities of the sculpted male body such as whiteness, transparency, or burning light leave crystalline traces of the originary figure. These metonymic images are often explicitly or implicitly linked to the Aesthetes' scene or fantasy of male romantic friendships in which the animate statue, a marble phantasmagoria of cool white boy statuary, burns with the energies of the male–male continuum of creativity, life, eros, spirit, or intellect. In works such as Pater's essay "*Diaphaneitè*," as Dellamora argues convincingly, the diaphanous quality Pater ascribes to his male hero functions as an early analogue to the sculpted loved male body he later presents in the more overtly homoerotic essay on Winckelmann (*Masculine Desire* 112). Thus the Aesthetes' frequent allusions to the white androgynous statue, burning gem, and suffusion of white or refracting colored light may be read as simultaneously configuring and disfiguring the feminized boy body in transgressive gender narratives of Aestheticism.

The Romantic/Victorian diaphanous body as visual trope is usually whitely transparent or crystalline, and often flecked or dappled with contrasting or dazzling effects of light, color, and tracery. Pater's diaphanous man is variously, "a thread of pure white light," "that fine edge of light," "transpar[ent]," and "clear crystal" (213, 209, 211, 212). Derived from the Greek "to show through," Romantic/Victorian *diaphaneitè* eludes socially constituted scriptings of the sexual/textual body by crossing its outer boundaries and/or recreating them in the temporary play of visual effect. Evinced by "evanescent shades" for which "the world has no sense fine enough," Pater's diaphanous type, like Derrida's vanishing sign, does not constitute an object so much as the fading trace of erotic and linguistic play ("*Diaphaneitè*" 209). Earlier, Shelley's female transparency "the shape all light" in *The Triumph of Life* confounds the hierarchical relation between male "I" and female "you" by figuring desire as a nonreferential "shape" made visible by *diaphaneitè* (Shelley 453–70).[11] (Sir Walter Raleigh comments in his *History of the World* that "Aristotle calleth light a quality inherent or cleaving to a Diaphanous body.")[12] Paul de Man's famous discussion of Shelleyan disfiguration by way of the "shape all light" observes that Shelley's "shape" "is referentially meaningless since light, the necessary condition for shape, is itself . . . without shape." De Man's further claim that Shelley's "shape" splits light into "the illusion of a doubleness which is not that of self and other" also suggests the power of such tropes to destabilize the subject/object gender dyad of I–you poetic discourse.[13] In *The Picture of Dorian Gray,* Basil avows that Dorian "is never more present in my work than when no image of him is there. He is a suggestion . . . of a new manner. I find him in the curves of certain lines, in the loveliness and subtleties of certain colors. That is all" (Wilde 24). And even Pater's famous figure for the fineness and multiplicity of the heightened Aesthetic consciousness, the transparently burning "hard gem-like flame" that concludes *The Renaissance,* may be said to write the vanishing body of the boy androgyne, extending Pater's discourse suggestively to sex/gender multiplicity.[14] Another example of homoerotic disfiguration, the burning gem, cuts the smooth surface of the conventional, seamless body into glittering facets, figuring among other things, Victorian "split" masking in an erotic spectrum of (male) sex/gender selves. (Similarly Shelley's famous image for multiplicity, "Life, like a dome of many-colored glass, / Stains the white radiance of Eternity," may also extend to more fluid definitions of male desire, particularly in the context of Shelley's homoerotic *Adonais* where it appears.) Indeed, *diaphaneitè* replicates the process of masking and coding – the diaphanous object acts both as veil and transparency to reveal and conceal Aestheticism's forbidden discourse.

By contrast, Pater in particular construes the traditionally female icon he rejects in the opaque and decaying matter of the femme fatale. Dellamora observes that in "*Diaphaneitè*" Pater conjures the masculine, dagger-wielding "half-daemonic" figure of Charlotte Corday as the "antitype" of the diaphanous man (*Masculine Desire* 98). Unlike the possessor of *diapha-*

neitè who introduces a fresh impulse, Pater's most famous femme fatale, La Gioconda, is world-weary; she contains all the base "maladies" of the "soul," and of history – "the animalism of Greece, the lust of Rome . . . the sins of the Borgias" (*Renaissance* 98). Indeed, Pater's *Renaissance* like Yeats's *Autobiographies* makes the femme fatale the scapegoat in a very different sexual and historical agenda: After he writes of[f] the antique bodily "deposits" of the Mona Lisa ("It is a beauty wrought out from within upon the flesh, the deposit, little cell by little cell, of strange thoughts, and fantastic reveries and exquisite passions") – whose stricken beauty would "trouble" the "white" Greek goddesses of Classicism – Pater ushers in the new poetic of male transgressive desire in the form of the male erotic body, the specular "gem-like flame" of his "Conclusion." Significantly, in the essay on Morris, "Aesthetic Poetry," from which he mined much of his "Conclusion," Pater's vision of poetic experience writes the androgynous diaphanous body more deliberately: ". . . exotic flowers of sentiment expand, among people of a remote and unaccustomed beauty, . . . frail, androgynous, the light almost shining through them. . . . the coloring is intricate and delirious. . . ."[15]

The descriptive language that figures and disfigures the Aesthetes' boy androgyne may therefore be included among those "excessive" and "superfluous" decadent details that also illustrate what Naomi Schor describes as the power of the feminine-gendered detail to disturb the smooth surface of masculine unity and centricity.[16] *Diaphaneitè* in the preceding examples passes through the body registering as trace. In other writings of the male androgyne, however, *diaphaneitè* defies the bounds of the canonical body by opening it up and illuminating its hidden contents within. The more consciously erotic narrations of Aestheticism in Wilde, Swinburne, Rossetti, and others inscribe the male androgyne as a transparent human body whose delicately veined tracery and blood response – red, violet, and pulsing – can be seen beneath the white translucence of the skin. In the case of the boy Aesthete (rather than the femme fatale) the veined white body often suggests the erotically charged (scarlet, pulsing) white statuary, although it frequently gives place to far-flung metaphors such as Swinburne's reference to forms of eros as "berries under snow" or "amber in cold sea," and other grotesque combinations of red and white, heat and chill (*P&B* I, 135). Such decompositions of the body emblematize an open textuality as well as sexuality in which closed fictions of linguistic unity between "word" and "thing" are split into autonomous, progressively decomposing parts. In *The Cult of the Detail*, historian of eighteenth century, Frances Wey, is particularly threatened by this aspect of "decadent style," "where the unity of the book decomposes to give way to the independence of the page, where the page decomposes to give way to the independence of the word."[17] We recall that Eliot and Pound objected particularly to the autonomy of Swinburne's language, which "uprooted" "adapt[s] itself to an independent life of atmospheric nourishment."

Further, Linda Dowling argues that the Greek term *"poikilos,"* which often describes the play of light or texture and translates variously as "dappled," "pied," "intricate," or "flashing," belonged specifically to the homoerotic vocabulary or code of late-Victorian Aestheticism.[18] Dowling notes that in his Oxford lectures Pater himself associates *poikilia* (the noun form) with "an effeminate or feminine tendency," and uses the term specifically to refer to "minute and curious loveliness" and "daintiness of execution."[19] A term used by Plato in the *Symposium* to indicate homosexual love (and known to Oxford and Cambridge undergraduates), *poikilia's* range of meanings certainly apply to Aesthetic inscriptions of the fair youth as the whitely prismatic body, illuminated by the play of light and shadow.

Before turning to a discussion of H.D. and the vanishing body, I conclude this discussion with a reading of Swinburne's "Fragoletta" (*P&B I*, 92–4), a famous and representative example of the transgressive (male) body as a specter of the Greek curly haired, androgynous boy sculpture (although it is not formally drawn from statuary like "Hermaphroditus"), which was among H.D.'s favorites of Swinburne's poems. Swinburne's well-known ode to the loved hermaphroditic body sings its disfiguration through *diaphaneitè*, intricacy, and the grotesque – clearly demonstrating theories of horrific detail and disruptive body tropes formulated by Mikhail Bakhtin ("The Grotesque Image of the Body" in *Rabelais and His World*). As Mary Russo comments in her pioneering essay on Bakhtin and the female grotesque ("Female Grotesques: Carnival and Theory"), Bakhtin's "carnivalesque" is often the inspiration behind feminist theory's translocation of "issues of . . . abjection and marginality . . . to the field of the socially constituted as a symbolic system."[20] While Russo is interested primarily in the female abject, I would add that Bakhtin's theory applies as well to "queer" theory and to other figures of abjection such as the feminized male. Significantly, Bakhtin notes in passing that the theme of the androgyne, "popular in Rabelais' time" (23), demonstrates his disassociated "dual" body.

"FRAGOLETTA"

Fragoletta, Swinburne's androgynous boy/girl, in the poem that bears his/her name rhetorically answers the narrator's wondering question, "How should [Love] greet thee? what new name / ... could move/ Thee?" (93). Although it may refer affectionately to a diminutive of the Italian, *fragola,* "strawberry," the name also points to intense fragility unto transparency (*diaphaneitè*) as the sign of the ambiguous boy/girl's difference. The narrator is fearful of crushing this painfully delicate body, which hovers in a liminal state between body whole and body broken at the peak of its strange eroticism. He "dare[s] not kiss" it" "lest my lip/Press harder than an indrawn breath, / And all the sweet life slip / Forth, and the sweet leaves drip, / Bloodlike, in death" (12). Kristeva's theory of abjection focuses specifically on the double body's abject details, which include the ruptured body and its wastes (blood, excrement, etc.). The Decadent body's (Fragoletta's) proximity to what Kristeva would term the abject spilling of its blood (only a breath away) intensifies the impression of liminal or imminently collapsing sexual/textual boundaries. "It is as if," Kristeva comments of the abject body, "the skin, a fragile container, no longer guaranteed the integrity of one's 'own and clean self' but, scraped or transparent, invisible or taut, gave way before the dejection of its contents" (*Powers of Horror* 53).

Although the beautiful youth remains intact, Fragoletta's white body bears what would have formerly been regarded as the Decadent mark or crimson brand of illicit passion – "And where my kiss hath fed / Thy flower-like blood leaps red / To the kissed place" (94). However, the red "fleck" (*poikilia*) of abjection also shows easy visual access beyond the constituted bounds of the body's white sheath. Beyond its metaphoric significance as a corrupt stain in discourses on impurity, the incriminating flush or bruise is also a subversive body trope that disturbs the placid surface of the normative sexual/textual body. Similarly, in Swinburne's "Laus Veneris" (P&B I, 13–30), Venus's transgressive sexuality is immediately apparent from Tannhauser's opening meditation on the telling "fleck," or "speck" that bruises the white neck – "Kissed over close" – of the sleeping Venus. He gazes admiringly at the white skin that "wears yet a purple speck / Wherein the pained blood falters and goes out; / Soft, and stung softly – fairer for a fleck" (13). Piercing the body's envelope, the offending speck opens onto "other" vistas within the hidden recesses of Venus's body. Later in "Fragoletta," the narrator muses, "I dreamed of strange lips yesterday / And cheeks wherein the ambiguous blood / Was like a rose's. . . ." The illicitly "flecked" or transparent body reproduces Bakhtin's grotesque image whose "artistic logic . . . ignores the closed, smooth, and impenetrable surface of the body and retains only that . . . which leads beyond the body's limited space or into the body's depths" (Bakhtin 317, 318). As a metaphor for narrative, Fragoletta's "ambiguous blood" like Venus's telltale mark, supplies the clue to a submerged story of desire.

The narrator of "Fragoletta" calls the boy/girl a "double rose of Love's" (an endearment H.D. echoes while regarding the *Hermaphrodite* in *Paint It Today*), more fascinating for his cross-gendered charms, thus exemplifying what Bakhtin terms the grotesque image of the "double" or "dual" body. By contrast, the narrator's unfavorable description of the redundantly female "maiden" replicates Bakhtin's self-referential "body of the new canon" as merely "one body," "self sufficient," "a closed sphere" (321). Her hair is arranged in impeccable "Fold over simple fold / Binding her head." She is made up of achromatic tones, without accidents or modulations of color, light, and translucence: "Her breast-blossoms are simply red, / Her hair mere brown or gold." The maiden's body articulates erotic indifference rather than difference – "her mouth is cold." Fragoletta, however, is a "mysterious" flower, "strange," and "ambiguous"; and Swinburne further distinguishes his/her difference by altering the traditional red rose-cheek analogy of the love lyric. His flushed cheeks have the nearly imperceptible, "ambiguous" (suggestive of unhealthy) tint of the unopened flower, "like a rose's – yea, / A rose's when it lay / Within the bud" (92). The faint luminescence of the bud also suggests the embryonic potentiality of the Decadent double body. Moreover, while the maiden's hair "binds her head," Fragoletta has "a serpent in [his] hair, / In all the curls that close and cling," bearing a hint of the double and unruly Medusan body (94).

His curls "that close and cling," bespeak the affective, generative sexuality of the body that in Bakhtin's words, "shoots and branches . . . outgrow[ing] its own self . . . conceiv[ing] a new, second body" (Bakhtin 316, 317).

III   H.D.'s Crystalline Poetic

Pater's "fine edge of light" refined "to the burning point" of male–male sexual dissidence is surely discernible from the early ungendered *Sea Garden* in H.D.'s "sculpted," "fluted," and glittering Imagism – "Violet . . . you catch the light – / frost, a star edges with its fire" – (*CP* 26). And later, male–male desire announces itself in the crystal ice flower that articulates Apollo's unfolding desire for the erotic son ("Hyacinth") – "that flame, that flower, / (ice, spark, or jewel,) / the cyclamen, / parting its white cyclamen leaves" (*CP* 204). Similarly, throughout H.D.'s poetry, her many prayers to the shrine of the white goddess, such as the invocation of H.D.'s volume, *Heliodora*, evoke the fragility (*poikilia*) and transparency (*diaphaneitè*) of the faintly glowing Decadent body, "like a rose's – yea," "when it lay / within the bud":

> *drift of rare flowers,*
> *clear, with delicate shell –*
> *like leaf enclosing*
> *frozen lily-leaf,*
> *camellia texture,*
> *colder than a rose;* (*CP* 147; emphasis H.D.'s)

H.D.'s later efforts to clear her "crystalline" poetic of charges of Romanticism affirm her responsiveness to the elusive ice/fire encodings and transgressive energy of the Decadent body. Like Pater in his "Conclusion," H.D.'s protestations emphasized the "concentrated" "energy" rather than static frigidity of "crystal": "For what is crystal or any gem but the concentrated essence of the rough matrix, of the energy, either of overintense heat or overintense cold that projects it?" ("Delia Alton" 184). Elsewhere in "H.D. by Delia Alton," H.D. would seem to be tracing a crystalline path from the early Imagism through the crystalline youth of works such as *Hippolytus Temporizes* and *Hedylus* to the feminist transmutation of the

Decadent "jewel" body that allows access to the mother's body in the later *Trilogy*. H.D. suggested that her fair youths had formed an early "projection" of the mother/"matrix" in her later poems – "the projection of the jewel or the crystallization of the jewel or jewels in the matrix" (221).

The white body of H.D.'s poetry is subject to what one critic has called "erotic liminality," which, I will argue, derives from white Decadent/ Romantic disfigurations of the normative.[21] H.D. is particularly drawn to the popular Decadent synecdoche of languid, white hands – often delicately veined – that for Swinburne, Wilde, and others destabilize the conventional male body through descriptive codes for male effeminacy such as fragility, *diaphaneitè*, and whiteness. Further, Decadent disfigurements of the *hands,* those socially constituted agents of writing, work, and love, are also powerful indicators of alternatively dissenting discourse, practice, and erotics. Lord Henry's "cool, white, flower-like hands" that seem to "have a language of their own" (*Dorian Gray* 31) gesture toward the linguistic and erotic transgressions of the finely tuned, "gentle, sensitive mind" the modernists often eschewed (Yeats's "Ego Dominus Tuus," *VP* 368). H.D.'s association of the self-identifying sister love between Fayne and Hermione (*HER*) with Swinburne's portrait of female narcissism, "Before the Mirror," is triggered not only by the ghostly "white sister" in the mirror but by her languid white hands. Hermione quotes the passage in which Swinburne's self-enamored heroine remarks, "*my hand, a fallen rose, . . . lies snow-white on white snows, . . . and takes no care*" – lines that may signify both the forbidden eros of masturbation and the passive attitude of the girl's voyeurism (*HER* 126, 127, emphasis H.D.'s). We recall that in H.D.'s "Toward the Piraeus," H.D. imagines the soothing male–male intimacy between herself-as-boy and Pound in his taking of her/his hands, "you would have summoned me . . . and found my hands, beyond all the hands in the world, / cold, cold, cold, / intolerably cold and sweet" (*CP* 179).

"Hyacinth" in particular presents the metonymy of diaphanous white hands as the vanishing body of homoerotic desire. Apollo's ode to the diaphanous body, like Swinburne's "Fragoletta," declares his unconventional love by singing the body's linguistic and metaphoric disintegration. Decadent *diaphaneitè* enters the poem almost immediately in Apollo's long meditation on the red-veined glowing intricacies of Hyacinth's white hands – an onrush of red and white images that recall the abject veining beneath

Fragoletta's translucent body (and familiar ice/fire erotic metaphors such as Swinburne's "berries under snow" or "amber in cold sea"):

> . . . all the time
> I think of chaste, slight hands,
> veined snow,
> snow craters
> filled with first wild-flowerlets;
> glow of ice-gentian,
> whitest violet;
> snow craters
> and the ice ridge
> spilling light;
> dawn and the lover
> chaste dawn leaves bereft –
> I think of these
> and snow-cooled Phrygian wine. (*CP* 201)

Neither the boy body of Apollo's desire nor the body of the text is neatly bounded off. Rather, the rapt cascade of differential images subjects both hands and text to rapid shifts and decenterings, and, as I mentioned in Chapter Two, resembles William Ulmer's description of Shelley's similar technique of spewing metaphoric surrogates for the beloved, giving "value no place to rest."[22] At the same time, multiple projections of *diaphaneitè* permeate transparency after transparency without end. Even the successive acts of permeation themselves are progressively deferred as the tightly contained binaries of "ice-gentian" or "whitest violet" spill over in the loosely joined "ice ridge/spilling light"; or when *diaphaneitè* becomes absence in the penultimate "dawn and the lover / chaste dawn leaves bereft –."

H.D. creates a similarly "open" space for androgyny in *Hedylus* from the loosely formed *diaphaneitè* or visual "play" occurring between twin mother–son erotic bodies. There the Oedipal son, Hedylus, is a specular white reflection of his mother, Hedyle: "uncanny in their likeness," Hedylus's face is "a live blue star reflected in a chill pool, a flaming red-lotus that sees its face pale and removed in a marble-oblong of fresh water." Together, mother and son present a shimmering spectacle of "purple" veined transparencies, exotic and "pale," "flaming" and "chill." Entranced,

Hedyle murmurs to her son, "I don't believe any man begot you. There's no man in you" (*Hedylus* 31).

I conclude here with a brief discussion of how the gendered duality of *diapheneitè* and opacity encompass the female/body text in H.D.'s early revisionist mythmaking.

IV Diaphaneitè and Women's Writing

Not all early-twentieth-century women writers accessed the bodily codes of Victorian Aestheticism through the male mask. Exclusively lesbian writers such as Renée Vivien, who also modeled much of her poetic after Swinburne, identified themselves as female Aesthetes, claiming Swinburne's Sappho in "Anactoria" as their model of androgyny rather than Fragoletta or Hermaphroditus.[23] (All appropriations of the Decadent body, however, male or female, may be considered forms of male masking, because, arguably, even Swinburne's Sappho is a "mask" for male homoeroticism.) Vivien and Natalie Barney displaced the male–male Greek ideal of high Aestheticism with imagined Sapphic communities of women and reversed the misogyny of Pater's crystal man, equating whiteness and *diaphaneitè* with the "Female Principle" and attributing the "bestiality" and "cruelty" Pater had condemned in women's love to the "Male Principle."[24] In Vivien's novel about her tumultuous affair with Barney (*A Woman Appeared to Me*), her autobiographical heroine attributes "the unjust" and "the base" to "the Male Principle" while "everything unbearably lovely and desirable emanates from the Female Principle" (*A Woman Appeared to Me* 7). During a philosophical debate about the virtues of female–female desire, another character ("the Androgyne") shouts angrily at her male opponent, "I accuse you . . . of being unable to conceive of a love at once ardent and pure, like a white flame. That was the sort Psappha vowed to her melodious adorers" (8).

The sexual masking practices of H.D.'s poetry and prose are more complicated, in part because of the complexities and contradictions of her bisexuality. In her poetry, the Artemisian heroine who shares the diaphanous properties of the male Aesthete is often secondary to the Oedipal son who becomes H.D.'s primary mask in *Hippolytus Temporizes* and other works.

However, H.D. overtly assumed the mask of the female Aesthete in her more private writings. As Susan Friedman elaborates in *Penelope's Web,* H.D. was more apt to explore the exclusively female narratives of procreation, motherhood, and lesbian desire in her prose novels and in philosophical expositions such as *Notes on Thought and Vision.* H.D. may, perhaps, have been cautioned by an article on Renée Vivien, "A Pagan Poet," appearing in the *Egoist* while she was assistant editor (1916) that made an issue of Vivien's sexual personae. The author open-mindedly praised the lesbian poet's "courage" in adhering "to her feminine identity when the simple expedient of a masculine poetic disguise would have saved her from bourgeois reproof." Her gender bias emerges, however, in her reservations about the implicitly feminine confessionalism of Vivien's prose, where "her inspiration falls short": "In prose she was, generally, the woman, the somewhat effaced human woman she seems to have been in life."[25] "The Pagan Poet," which appeared in the year of *Sea Garden's* publication and of H.D.'s search for new directions in her writing, may have alerted her to the problematic of masking and the woman poet. Within the next few years H.D. wrote her defensive letters to Cournos concerning her need to work through the "emotional tangle" besetting her "personal self" in the novel form before reassuming the impersonal "clairvoyant poet." And in those successive experiments with narrative, H.D. would frequently shed the "expedient of a masculine disguise," applying, like Vivien and Barney, Decadent Aesthetic codes of whiteness or *diaphaneitè* toward explicitly female visions of creativity, eros, and the materiality of the body.

H.D.'s transformations of Decadent Romantic *diaphaneitè* in the revisionist myth making of her prose, in particular, frequently associate the white body directly with women's writing, lesbian love, and the womb, or the "double body" of pregnancy. In *HER,* we recall, Fayne is the "white sister" of Swinburne's "Before the Mirror," and her image grafted onto Hermione's own appears in the familiar star cluster of renewed desire following Her's bout with madness: "Her saw Her as a star shining white against winter daylight" (225). Elsewhere tropes of darkness and luminosity represent the insensitive husband's sexual/psychic invasion of the clear female space. As Rafe enters Julia without regard for the doctor's order that she refrain from sex so soon after the birth of her stillborn child (*Bid Me to Live*), Julia feels herself fall into a "gap in her consciousness, a sort of black hollow, a cave, a pit of blackness; black nebula was not yet concentrated into clear thought" (12, 13). The "black" hole of female excision displaces her womb and extends to its frigid surface – the "wound" of hostile male penetration literally threatening bodily as well as psychic obstruction: "If the wound had been nearer the surface, she could have grappled with it. It was annihilation itself that gaped at her" (13). By contrast, diaphanous articulations of the pregnant female body or of the unborn child form gender-specific metaphors for female creativity in the expositions of "the *gloire*" and "the overmind," H.D. derived from her famous jellyfish experiences in the Scillies. Although Julia's open letter to Rico (based on D. H. Lawrence) urges an androgynous aesthetic of "the *gloire*," a suffusion of light that is "both" sexes and "neither" (*Bid Me* 176, 177) – "the child is the *gloire* before it is born" – as Susan Friedman observes, the *gloire* itself is "imaged in a uterine globe" (*PW* 165). H.D.'s mystical jellyfish experience, in which she felt herself enclosed by an amorphous, transparent dome, is specifically associated with her pregnancy in 1919, and would become, in *Notes on Thought and Vision,* the uterine center from which female eros and creativity proceed: a "cap, like water, transparent, fluid, yet with definite body, contained in a definite space. It is like a closed sea-plant, jelly fish or anemone."[26] Similarly, in *Asphodel* Hermione's pregnancy forms a dual body, "Herself had woven herself an aura, a net, a soft and luminous cocoon" (179). H.D.'s distinguishing metaphor for female self-realization and rebirth – the butterfly and the cocoon – frequently takes the form of a crystal enclosure in works such as *Bid Me to Live* and in "Leuke," the white island section of *Helen in Egypt.*

In those texts where the eclipse of *diaphaneitè* signifies the excision of women's writing, H.D. represents the print/sign of male desire as a blot on the white semiotic space of women's language. In *Bid Me to Live,* Rafe carelessly crosses out lines from Julia's poem while commenting, "a bit dramatic. . . . It's Victorian" (54). Significantly, Julia's poem appears to be a version of H.D.'s "Eurydice" (*CP* 51–5), written during the period that *Bid Me to Live* describes. In "Eurydice" tropes for *diaphaneitè* and occultation determine the articulation of women's writing and being in a feminist revision of the Orpheus–Eurydice myth. Here, Orpheus's disobedience of the injunction not to look back at Eurydice (thereby banishing her once more to the underworld) is interpreted as a devastating incidence of the male gaze, which metaphorically blocks the *diaphaneitè* of women's writing – "you who passed across the light" (53). Eurydice is relegated to a hell of black excisions: "Everything is lost, / everything is crossed with black, / black upon black" (*CP* 52). The poem's momentary imaging of an alternative female potentiality in language calls up the ghost of Eurydice's "face" as Orpheus must have seen it, reflecting the earth's light at the mouth of the dark cavern where she stood, a dazzling effacement, defined only by "reflex" of "white" light that bounds off earth at the "raw fissure" and courses through the "veins" of the transparent "wind-flower."[27] In response to the rhetorical question, "What had my face to offer?" Eurydice's description of her face at the moment Orpheus fixes his gaze on her enacts the process of *diaphaneitè*, literally a "showing through":

> What had my face to offer
> but reflex of the earth,
> hyacinth color
> caught from the raw fissure in the rock
> where the light struck
> and the color of azure crocuses
> and the bright surface of gold crocuses
> and of the wind-flower,
> swift in its veins as lightning
> and as white. (52)

Elsewhere, in "Fragment 40," an extended translation of a line from Sappho, H.D. conveys the liminality of female eros and language through the trope of the diaphanous body. In this instance she assumes the female homoerotic, Sapphic mask (although the poem probably refers to her bereavement over Aldington) in her elaboration of Sappho's lyric, "love . . . bitter-sweet":

> I had thought myself frail;
> a petal,
> with light equal
> on leaf and under-leaf.
> I had thought myself frail;

a lamp,
shell, ivory or crust of pearl,
about to fall shattered,
with flame spent.

. . .

then the day broke. (174, 175)

In the moment between dusk and dawn, the Sapphic body of love is at the height of its luminescence; like Fragoletta's fragile, tenuous body, it barely keeps the set boundaries of inner and outer. The poem concludes with the image of the ruptured body as necessary to the articulation of "love": "Yet to sing love / love must first shatter us."

Chapter Four

Across Gender, across Sexuality

H.D.'s Male Masking and the Sexual Narrative: Hippolytus Temporizes; "Heliodora"

This chapter continues to inquire into the literary, political, linguistic, representational adventures issuing from female modernist uses of the Decadent boy androgyne. H.D.'s maternal-erotic quest romance, *Hippolytus Temporizes,* perhaps best illustrates H.D.'s deployment of the male mask, the open sexual narrative, the white body of androgyny, and Romantic twinning she derived from Victorian Hellenism. Before discussing the play, however, it will be useful to survey and elaborate upon the Decadent conventions related to the male Aesthete that most attracted H.D. and her contemporaries. Why might a modernist woman writer deploy a culturally stigmatized and (frequently) literally outlawed form of sexuality to explore female desire? How might Decadent male–male homoerotic literary conventions and codes offer better models for the unity of eros, intellect, and legitimate political power than those available in modernist (heterosexual or lesbian) imagings? What might the strategy of adapting the Decadent boy mask afford a lesbian or bisexual writer?

I   The Male Aesthete as Fair Youth or Wildean Prototype and Modernist Woman Writers

"Art is Individualism and Individualism is a *disturbing and disintegrating force,*" Oscar Wilde wrote in *The Soul of Man under Socialism.* Jonathan Dollimore demonstrates that Wilde's definition does not concern human essences but "is inseparable from a transgressive desire and a transgressive aesthetic."[1] Thus, if male modernists rejected the male Aesthete in the name of impersonality, many women writers found reason to embrace the Wildean persona of the sexually transgressive artist/narrator. Famous Wildeanisms including Wilde's Aesthete pose, his suggestive aphorisms, and the phrase, "the love that dare not speak its name," associated with Wilde (although Lord Alfred Douglas originated it), became the identifying features of the sexually heretic authorial mask. Indeed, modern women writers such as Willa Cather sometimes unconsciously implied their intimate connection with the Aesthete artist. The argument of Sharon O'Brien's persuasive essay on Willa Cather's homoeroticism, "The Thing Not Named," as its title indicates, rests on the assumption that (although Cather hated Wilde personally) she encodes the female intimacies that fuel her writing by unconsciously echoing the famous phrase "the love that dare not speak its name" in a key passage on creativity and the artist: "Whatever is felt upon the page without being specifically named there," Cather writes, "that, one might say, is created. It is the explicable presence of the thing not named."[2] O'Brien's essay operates reasonably on the premise that Cather knew the half-confession associated with Wilde so well that its unconscious echo in her discussion of creative energy signals a return of the woman author's repressed homoeroticism. I suggested earlier that both Katherine Mansfield's and H.D.'s conception of Oscar Wilde and the Decadents as a transgressive community of artists enabled them to posit a dissident authorial presence. And, I argued in Chapter One, volumes such as Swinburne's *Poems and Ballads* offered the example of an open sexual narrative and, simultaneously, a rebel "author" who presides over the moods or passions of the poem: The moments represented by the poems therefore comprise points on a continuum of the fictional author's imagined sexuality.

Oscar Wilde openly claimed his deployment of what I will call "split" masking in the composition of his *The Picture of Dorian Gray,* where, he professed, each character bears the traces of an authorial "self" or "selves." Wilde wrote to Ralph Payne Wilde:

> I am so glad you like that strange many colored book of mine: it contains much of me in it. Basil Hallward is what I think I am; Lord Henry, what the world thinks me; Dorian what I would like to be.

Barbara C. Gelpi comments that each of Wilde's selves "watch[es] the other selves and offer[s] comments upon or even engag[es] in dialogues with the self at stage-center."[3] Similarly, Wilde's *Poems,* described by Richard Ellmann as "polymorphously perverse," deliberately inserted a sexually heretic author at "stage-center" overseeing the volume's Greek, eroticized masks of Narcissus, Charmides, Antinous, and others. In "Helas!," the proem to the collection, the narrator announces his intention "To drift with every passion till my soul / Is a stringed lute on which all winds can play," thus inserting himself as the willing mediator of endless sex/gender variety.[4] Without its heretic authorial mask, Swinburne's or Wilde's songs of forbidden love automatically engage a normative "I" and thus run the risk of being read in toto as a moralizing discourse on perversity. Swinburne's shrewdest defenders, including himself, argued coyly against his detractors that this was the true intent of the *Poems and Ballads.*

H.D.'s volumes such as *Hymen* or *Heliodora* create the phantasm of a shaping power, "H.D.," who explores a range of female emotions and desires. Lacking this "H.D.," the poems would lose much of their transformative and revisionary power. As I will demonstrate in *Hippolytus Temporizes,* for example, the mother–son couplings of the boy Aesthete and his statuesque Artemisian beloved enable her to inhabit both masks and to create an androgynous space between, just as Wilde's technique of split masking allows him to play all parts in *The Picture of Dorian Gray.* Such uses of split masking in modernist women's writing thus reinstate the both/and vision of a "double self" feminist critics have associated with a female aesthetic.[5]

In the preceding chapter, I began to discuss H.D.'s white erotic bodies in relation to the Victorian codes of Dorianism and Platonism. Women writers eagerly assumed the Aesthetes' Greek, Platonic philosophy of love, thus restoring romantic/sexual "sameness" to women's texts from its exclusion in anti-Romantic modernism. Indeed, contemporary feminist theories about the links between female modes of relating and a women's aesthetic occasionally, if reluctantly, prompt comparisons with Romantic Aestheticism. Marilyn Farwell acknowledges that Adrienne Rich's "lesbian continuum" of women-centered relationships and creative reciprocity resembles, "admittedly," a "Romantic/Aesthetic relationship."[6] Sharon O'Brien notes that among Cather's first models for the role of the artist was the male Romantic Aesthete, and she cites Cather's debt to "Romantic theory" in her writings' emphasis on "feminine" traits such as "sympathy."[7] Clearly the neo-Platonic sexual politics of Romantic Victorian Aestheticism provided both women modernists and their critics with an authoritative mask for feminine modes of desire.

Critical inquiries into the influence of Trinity College Professor Reverend J.P. Mahaffy and his discourses on Greek homosexuality agree that his Platonic ideal of romantic male friendships formed the basis of Wilde's and others' Hellenic poetic.[8] (Linda Dowling points out at least one instance in which Swinburne used the term "Platonist" to describe the homosexual proclivities of a friend in the late-Victorian literary circle.[9])

Using this model, Wilde elaborated a "continuum" of male-centered relationships: Wilde wrote in his Commonplace Book approvingly, "The refinement of Greek culture comes through the romantic medium of impassioned friendship."[10] As I have suggested, the young, fair, and untaught Dorian Gray and the older, world-weary Lord Henry in *The Picture of Dorian Gray* are perhaps the most well-known (although not the most admirable) examples of the Greek, Dorian, erotic continuum. And insofar as the Dorian and Platonic codes can be separated, the more philosophic and academic Platonic ideal better explains Basil's creative, spiritual, and erotic adoration for Dorian ("for it was really love . . ."). Swinburne's eloquent array of classical lyric masks for (male) androgyny and same-sex love forms something of a paradigm for Decadent male masking forged from the Greek continuum. His paradigm may have emboldened contemporaries such as Pater and Wilde to create similar anthologies in Pater's *Imaginary Portraits* or Wilde's *Poems*.[11] The Greek boy–man relation is assumed both within the narrative of Swinburne's "Fragoletta" or Wilde's *Charmides* (*Poems*) and without, between the older male "author" who masterminds the collection and the fair youth (Hyacinth, Narcissus, Antinous, etc.) that is the erotic object of his song.

Feminist transpositions of Romantic Victorian neo-Platonism pervade late nineteenth- and twentieth-century women's literature. Paradoxically, despite the Greek system's classification of women's love as inferior and bounded, the Aesthetes' adaptation of the Greek continuum forms an earlier male example of Adrienne Rich's famous "lesbian continuum."[12] Like Rich's continuum of sexual and nonsexual women's relationships, the

Greek system is based on nurturing romantic friendships that do not necessarily include sexual intimacy but rather define eros, in Rich's words, as
a diffuse and omnipresent energy not limited "to any single part of the
body or solely to the body itself."[13]

According to Janet Kaplan, Katherine Mansfield's early fascination with
Wilde was linked to his "elevation of the Greek ideal of male friendships."
Kaplan speculates that Mansfield used this model to articulate "her sexual
attraction" to women such as her friend Maata and "in her early attempts
to write about sexuality" toward men. An early journal entry (1906) describes her erotic feelings for "a Dorian-like young man."[14] As I have
suggested, H.D. also frequently positioned herself imaginatively on a male
continuum with her male mentors or instigators in poems such as "Hyacinth," "Toward the Piraeus," "The Charioteer," or "Red Roses for
Bronze" where the male–male relation surpasses a limited and predatory
heterosexuality. Ethel Arnold suggested a neo-Platonic female continuum
in her little known New Woman novel, *Platonics,* which came under attack
because its plot deemphasized the marriage of one of its protagonists in
favor of the (only posthumously acknowledged) homoerotic female friendship the marriage had displaced.[15] H.D.'s most lesbian novel, *Paint It Today,*
relies heavily on neo-Platonic codes of Aestheticism to configure the lesbian coupling that concludes Midget's quest to join physical with spiritual
love.[16] Most notably, the novel is framed by discourses on Plato and Shelley, or suggestive conflations of the two – as in *Paint It Today*'s early allusion
to Midget's search for a twin love via Shelley's translation of Plato in the
epigraph to *Adonais:*

> Thou wert the morning star among the living
> Ere thy fair light was shed,
> Now having died thou art as Hesperus giving
> New splendor to the dead. (12)

And although H.D. might not have known that Swinburne singled out
Cathy's ardent "I am Heathcliff" (*Wuthering Heights*) as his favorite expression of Romantic twinning, Hermione's litany over Fayne's sleeping
body recalls Cathy's pronouncement: "I am Her. Her is Fayne. Fayne is
Her."[17]

Finally, as I have demonstrated in H.D., female assumptions of the

Aesthete mask also involved impersonating the homoerotic male andro-gyne's body. Indeed, modernist women writers' myths of sexual and aes-thetic origins often take the form of conversion stories centering on the revelation of their own sex/gender "otherness" mirrored back by the an-drogynous youths of Victorian Hellenism. I referred earlier to Mansfield's recognition of herself as "child, woman, and more than half man" in Wilde's androgynous pose. Further, Mansfield appears to have consciously encoded her bisexuality through the Aesthete mask in her first writings: Claire Tomalin's biography of Mansfield describes as "undisguisedly les-bian" an early unpublished story, "Leves Amores," in which an ungen-dered but clearly Aesthete "I" discovers her/his creative and erotic powers during a visit to a prostitute in a tawdry London setting.[18] H.D. and Frances Gregg appear to have identified themselves with the male hermaphroditic or androgynous bodies of Swinburne's *Poems and Ballads*. And at the age of fourteen, Willa Cather literally adopted a male identity as "Dr. William Cather" and impersonated a boy in a series of carefully posed photographic portraits. O'Brien observes that in Cather's college writings the same im-pulse prompted Cather to identify herself with the "man-womanly" model of androgyny she derived from "Romantic Aesthetics" (O'Brien 96–116, 159).

In these instances and in H.D.'s poems such as "Hyacinth" or "Toward the Piraeus," the modernist woman writer responds not only to fin de siècle Greek codes for male homosexuality but also to what "queer" Vic-torian theorist Thaïs Morgan describes as the Decadent practice of "inter-sexuality" – cross-gender inventions of homosexuality that made it possible, for example, for *male* writers such as Swinburne and Baudelaire to open up "a discursive space in which . . . male lesbianism might be thought."[19] Conjuring male homoeroticism by analogy, these Decadent (French and English) poets transpose their own male–male desire onto the lesbian bodies of their Sapphic poetry. H.D.'s "Hyacinth" and "Toward the Piraeus" demonstrate such queer literary crossings undertaken by the *female* bisexual or lesbian author who identifies as the boy androgyne in a mythical male–male coupling (only to reposition herself further as the heterosexual "twin" of H.D.'s male lovers and mentors, Richard Aldington and Ezra Pound). Hence, H.D. creates space for what critics have termed the "boy lesbian."[20]

However, although the movement across gender and sexuality afforded

H.D. and other women writers' many sexual and textual opportunities,[21] transsexual masking also traded in important sex/gender differences – most obviously that of the female body – for the universal indifference[22] of an assumed male body. Such figurative cross-dressing might therefore give body to a feminist poetic while paradoxically subsuming the subversive potential of the women writer's own female body. Women writers who appealed to the Greek continuum of boy–man eroticism in Victorian Hellenism often unwittingly acquired the misogyny of its "homosocial" and hierarchical configuration. I begin with a discussion of H.D.'s male masking in *Hippolytus Temporizes* before concluding my consideration of the Aesthete androgyne by examining the ways in which H.D.'s Decadent cross-dressing began to afflict her writing during the late 1920s.

II Mother–Son Twinnings: Hippolytus Temporizes

Male modernist theories of masking often rejected the slippery, unrequited maternal-erotic narrative of the male androgyne. However, H.D.'s Argument to her verse drama, *Hippolytus Temporizes*, indicates immediately that her attraction to Euripides' play lies in its fatal mother–son erotic pairings. H.D. asserts that the plots of *Hippolytus* – Phaedra's ill-conceived obsession for her beautiful stepson and Hippolytus's distant Oedipal worship for the goddess Artemis – have gained the play legendary status as "the prototype of unrequited love for many centuries."[23] "Hippolytus is his mother again," H.D. continues in the Argument, "frozen lover of the forest which maintains personal form for him in the ever-present vision, yea even the bodily presence of the goddess Artemis" (7). In H.D.'s version of "the familiar story," therefore, Phaedra's famous sexual deception of Hippolytus in the guise of Artemis is secondary to Hippolytus's roving passion for the goddess shade of his mother. Indeed, unintentionally recalling Eliot's chief example of Romantic excess, John Walsh's Afterword to *Hippolytus Temporizes* describes H.D.'s Hippolytus as a "reverse" version of Hamlet (it is his *father* who remarries), pronouncing the play's ruling emotion to be "the madness of mother-obsession."[24] However, unlike Eliot's interpretation of *Hamlet* or his own "Prufrock," H.D.'s modernist quest romance perceives unrequited love as a symptom not of emasculation or psychic collapse, but of the necessarily unrequited maternal eroticism that animates her tale of female desire. Each character in the various mother–son twinnings of *Hippolytus Temporizes* searches for a mysterious "she" whose only identifiable trait is a maternal presence: Hippolytus longs for the elusive warrior goddess Artemis who hunted beside his dead mother Hippolyta and who has become "the mother," "the nearest," "a spirit . . . as she" (29); Artemis reluctantly desires this beautiful boy shade of her beloved warrior twin, Hippolyta; and even Phaedra, who would appear to be lusting only after a boy lover, actually perceives in Hippolytus the ghost of a lost female "sister" as her ardent prayer for his love to Aphrodite – a deliberate echo of the call to the "sister" swallow in Swinburne's "Itylus" – suggests: "O swallow fair / O fair sea-swallow . . ." (53).

Unlike the masking narratives of Eliot and Yeats, H.D.'s transformation of Euripides' play into a maternal-erotic quest romance seeks rather than repels symbiosis with the mother/twin. The sexual embrace that lies at the center of the play's plot – Phaedra's elaborately contrived ruse to trick Hippolytus into sexual intimacy by posing as Artemis – becomes, by contrast, a striking emblem for the maternal eroticism that necessarily "exceeds" its "object," the love requited or otherwise that is always already a ruse, a substitution, a replacement for the lost maternal presence. Far from a languishing narrative of frustrated desire, however, H.D.'s tale of the crystalline youth is a vital tracing of erotic stratagems. Both sides of the mother–son pairings are alternately agent and object of this sexual history in the making and the creators of an erotic presence (their own and the beloved's) spun from a mutual, ongoing quest to capture, affix, read each other. An elaboration of H.D.'s early "Pursuit," H.D.'s *Hippolytus Temporizes* is also a more interactive and female version of Shelley's Alastor-poet's search for the wood spirit who flees him through the forest (*Alastor*). Compelled separately by his or her love for the elusive "she," each character in *Hippolytus Temporizes* finds "her" and a former self momentarily in the other – a temporary stay against the belated desire that drives and forms them. Their union, sexual or otherwise, resembles Rich's definition of sexuality as a diffuse energy, encompassing and extending beyond the body, which H.D. evokes poetically as an effusion of the "white" phosphorescent "body" that is the height of an androgynous and pervasive eros in Romantic Victorian poetics.

H.D.'s play finds a compelling source in Pater's *Hippolytus Veiled*. Like H.D.'s, Pater's Romantic mythology bears little resemblance to Euripides's tale of a hearty Hippolytus and his merry band of worshippers, but uses the Greek play to explore the intensity of the "crystalline" Hippolytus's fixation on Artemis's "all-embracing maternity." Although Pater's Hippolytus possesses a serviceable mother, he dedicates himself to the worshipful study of the goddess who is his "new mother," "his great mother," an eroticized presence "gliding softly through [his dreams] with abundance of salutary touches."[25] H.D. was probably directly influenced by Pater's androgynous depiction of the delicate youth and austere, statuesque Artemis. In H.D.'s play, Artemis notes Hippolytus's "fragile and imperious length, / your pale set features / and your woman's grace" (27). Hippolytus exults at his first sight of Artemis, "O fair, / like some rare / young warrior / with his glittering arms and spear" (13). Pater's Artemis and Hippolytus provide models for H.D.'s diaphanous pairing of crystalline erotic bodies. In *Hippolytus Veiled*, Hippolytus is a "crystal" youth, a "star flashing" and Artemis, the familiar crimson/white, hot/cold eros he gathers each dawn with the flowers "of purple and white frost" he places "against [her] white marbles [shrines]" (*Hippolytus Veiled* 252).

The mother–son configuration of H.D.'s *Hippolytus Temporizes*, however, further transforms Pater's masks for "forbidden" desire into a code both for equal relationships between men and women and for the mother–daughter bond. Like Wilde's *Charmides*, Pater's *Hippolytus Veiled* arguably encodes the Greek ideal of boy–man mentorship in which the older man nurtures and educates the younger. While Pater's Phaedra is the type of the femme fatale, associated not only with "sickly perfumes" and gaudy attire, but also pejoratively linked with the heterosexual institutions of marriage and procreation, Artemis is the fatherless boy's appointed mentor – an austere and masculine figure whose sylvan ways he literally studies (he is a scholar of Artemisian lore) and strives to emulate. As Eileen Gregory observes, however, H.D.'s Hippolytus "Mirrors and bespeaks the female body."[26]

Sharon O'Brien suggests that possible interpretive strategies for determining when a male character comprises a female mask rather than an opposite-sex character include "textual clues" that contradict the protagonist's assigned gender, such as the "over-identification" between mother and son (O'Brien 217). The Oedipal dyads of H.D.'s early work – Hedyle-Hedylus, Hippolyta-Hippolytus – are frequently spiritual and erotic twins, each projecting an androgynous mirror of the other so that one might well ask, with the narrator in H.D.'s passionate poem on androgyny, "Myrtle Bough," "are these two maids / or pages with bright shoon?" (*CP* 248). Chodorow's model of the prolonged pre-Oedipal attachment between mother and daughter is discernible in Hedylus's struggle to separate from the all-powerful mother who "still encloses me as if I never were born" (*Hedylus*).[27] Similarly, Hippolytus believes that his mother, Hippolyta, "is my strength"; "her white soul lives in me" (27). In actual instances of Victorian cross-dressing on the stage, Martha Vicinus demonstrates, women frequently take the part of "the liminal son." A flexible and powerful mask for female agency, the "son's" maleness guarantees a measure of power and subjectivity while remaining provocatively poised in between a still active identification with the mother and an imminent initiation into a privileged male identity. The liminal son's bond with his mother destabilizes traditional male–female power relations; both are at once desiring and desired, alternately powerful and needy. Further, H.D. enhances the erotic liminality of her mother–son pairings by assuming both roles in an instance of Decadent split masking, creating a continuous and fluid identification between man-woman and woman-man.

I begin with a close examination of H.D.'s "Proem" to the play (4–5), Hippolytus's prefatory prayer, which Gregory lucidly locates as the moment when Hippolytus "temporizes," "in the aftermath of [Hippolytus's] lovemaking with one he assumes to be Artemis" in which "he prays to her and imagines he holds her, seeing [her] luminous bones beneath the flesh."[28] Here, as Gregory observes, "love of the absent mother is inextricably associated with the 'white' erotic body," which, I add, finds a source in Decadent Romanticism. In this highlighted scene of postcoital eroticism, Hippolytus's dream of the maternal white body does not differ from his earlier virginal quest, but serves as an appropriate preface to a tale of deferred desire in which sexuality is a diffuse energy that is not entirely "of the body."

Even after he has, presumably, possessed his beloved, Hippolytus summons the white body of displacement, doubling, and dissolving grounds that always eludes him. H.D.'s "Proem" is worth quoting in full:

I worship the greatest first —
(it were sweet the couch,
the brighter ripple of cloth
over the dipped fleece;
The thought: her bones
under the flesh are white
as sand which along a beach
covers but keeps the print
of the crescent shapes beneath:
I thought:
between cloth and fleece,
so her body lies.)

I worship first the great —
(ah sweet, your eyes —
what God, invoked in Crete,
gave them the gift to part
as the Sidonian myrtle-flower
suddenly, wide and swart,
then swiftly,
the eye-lids having provoked our hearts —
as suddenly beat and close.)

I worship the feet, flawless,
that haunt the hills —
(ah, sweet, dare I think,
beneath fetter of golden clasp,
of the rhythm, the fall and rise
of yours, carven, slight
beneath straps of gold that keep
their slender beauty caught,
like wings and bodies
of trapped birds.)

I worship the greatest first —
(suddenly into my brain —
the flash of sun on the snow,
the fringe of light and the drift,
the crest and the hill-shadow —
ah, surely now I forget,

ah, splendor, my goddess turns;
or was it the sudden heat,
beneath quivering of molten flesh,
of veins, purple as violets?) (4–5)

Isolated as the proem to *Hippolytus Temporizes,* this open-ended quest poem
haltingly remembers the sexual embrace through a process of displacement
and forgetting, articulating the height of desire, like Swinburne's "Fragoletta," as an elusive visual trek through the transparencies of the eroticized
body. The form of the proem itself, a series of abortive invocations – "I
worship" – from which Hippolytus digresses involuntarily into an ardent
song to various parts of the Artemisian body, stylistically recreates the double sexual/textual body: Hippolytus's ardent asides hover and vanish beneath the formal prayer of love like a textual "unconscious." The process
of forgetting, remembering, and displacement thus shapes Hippolytus's
poem, which fades in and out from formal utterance to the associative
dream of a vanishing body and back again. The infinite regress of phosphorescent prints and erasures both writes his ecstasy of sexual requital
while replicating the chaste but desiring Hippolytus's opening search for a
Hippolyta/Artemis through clues in the wooded landscape where the in-
appropriate (and often phosphorescent) detail marks her path. The virginal
Hippolytus had "ask[ed] of every stone upturned, / . . . and the earth /
sprinkled with unaccustomed silver drift / of sand / and delicate seed pearls
/ from the east, / Artemis, / Artemis, / Artemis, / has she passed?" (14, 15).
    In the proem, Hippolytus's gaze at the imagined "white" body sets the
diaphaneitè of a forbidden and infinitely deferred maternal eros in motion
as he looks through and thereby illuminates its coverings only to experience
further coverings. Traveling easily through cloth, fleece, white flesh, and
the "print" of white bones under the coverlet, which like sand along a
beach "covers" yet "keeps the print of the crescent shapes beneath," Hippolytus engages in an ongoing search for the trace "of one long since
forgotten," a conflation of mother and Artemis. Since desire for the mother
is always already on the run, unrequited love (chastity) and sexual consum-
mation are not in opposition, nor do they form a linear, progressive narrative, but rather give on to a sexual/textual chase of signifiers. Lisa M.
Steinman refers to Shelley's similar technique of textual regress, which I

have linked in H.D. with the activity of maternal eros, as a "visionary inversion" in which tropes enact "a regress of consciousness": "For any image of a given mental activity there is always a further image to represent consciousness of that activity, suggesting an endless succession."[29]

In the proem's concluding stanza, the poem's already erratic glimmers of the white body are interrupted by a further loss of orientation and a heightened eros: "suddenly into my brain – / the flash of sun on the snow –." This seizure or abrupt epistemological shift in which Hippolytus's dream of Artemis becomes shockingly vivid begins with the light distractions of *diaphaneitè*. Sun reflects and deflects wildly off snow, the "dips," gaps, and opacities of "crest" and "hillshadow," signaling a more profound obliteration than the associative shifts of before. The brain's sudden erasure – "Ah, surely now I forget" –, is abruptly displaced by Hippolytus's almost painfully acute awareness of Artemis's physical presence – "my goddess turns" – which as suddenly becomes in Hippolytus's imagination the hallucination of the passionate and transparently veined decadent body: "Or was it the sudden heat, / beneath quivering of molten flesh, / of veins, purple as violets?" Posited as a final distraction in a series of forgettings, the culminating vision of the erotic body as molten, purple flesh is not a phallic image of male sexual climax, as we have often been taught by male modernist narratives to expect, but a spectacularly vivid enactment of the Decadent, diaphanous body whereby the transgressive gaze permeates the canonized body/text to reveal its hidden abjection.

Later, Phaedra's and Hippolytus's retellings of their night of passion do not differ significantly from the dream of the white body in the play's proem. DuPlessis notes in a study of Mina Loy's sexual narratives that in female texts the sex act is often represented differently than in conventional sexual narratives: "more playful perhaps, with a variety of tones" or "just like any other action in the poem."[30] Although Phaedra has formerly been designated as the Paterian crimson femme fatale, she recounts her night of love by way of the phosphorescent trace emitting from the white body, seen, heard, and embraced: "(O night, luminous with phosphorescence / and more bright / than day-star / climbing heaven's stair at noon)" (81). Hippolytus replies, "Lady, / I know your dream, / I feel your thought, / ... / last night, I too, / lay bathed in phosphorescence/ like white dew /

... / O her hands were cool" (81, 93). H.D.'s reference to "cool hands" recalls the body of homoerotic love in "Hyacinth," and both representations of coitus issue from the Decadent Romantic code of fragility: "That thing that held me," Hippolytus recalls, "was a broken bird, . . . and O, the white was luminous / . . . / O goddess, child-like / and so pitiful . . ." (96, 97). Phaedra and Hippolytus are both awash in phosphorescence, and their double accounts also suggest the uterine body that is H.D.'s "overmind," the womb consciousness of female creativity and desire. Further, Hippolytus's vision, in which the beloved is both mother and child, evokes the mother–daughter bond behind the mother–son masking.

That Phaedra is in fact a fraud makes little difference. When the battered and nearly dead Hippolytus of the final act at last encounters an embodiment of the "real" Artemis, he fails to recognize her. Her memory displaced by the Artemis-Phaedra-Hippolytus that gave him rest, Hippolytus longs for the decadent detail that marked the eros of that night – the border of pink roses on the hem of Phaedra's white dress, which is absent from Artemis's more spare and severe attire. Phaedra, perhaps, speaks most poignantly for H.D.'s female sexual narrative of an infinitely deterred maternal eroticism: Wistfully correcting Hippolytus in the midst of rhapsodically lamenting the departure of the woman he believes to have been Artemis, she protests, "Say rather that in some other arms, / you'll feel her shape, / that in some other form / count her heart-beat" (79).

III "White Song": Decadent Auditory Masking in Hippolytus Temporizes

"I was realizing a self . . . that was an octave above my ordinary self – and fighting to realize it," H.D. later wrote of *Hippolytus Temporizes* (qtd. in "A Note to the Text" p. 152). From the opening lines of the play, in which Artemis picks up the strains of Hippolytus's distant prayer for her presence and responds, "I heard the intolerable rhythm / and sound of prayer," transgressive *sound* works to dispel the "set measure and stated time" of the conventional romance narrative much as *diaphaneitè* metaphorically violates the symmetry of the female image. Constant thematic references to rhythm, echo, hearing, and so on, as well as stylistic manipulations of repetition, dissonance, and alliteration thus compose a maternal-erotic narrative as musical score in which voices appear to trace one another without regard for the stable positions of "I" and "you." The endlessly reverberating "white song" (H.D.'s phrase, p. 115) which engages Artemis and Hippolytus calls across the divide of language to a maternal voice whose loss continues to compel it. Written to be heard, H.D.'s verse drama uses auditory troping and aspects of prosody she inherited from Swinburne and others to realize a female self an "octave above" the socially sanctioned sexed/gendered selves of male modernism.

Auditory masking in *Hippolytus Temporizes* therefore becomes a means of speaking transgressive desire/language that vocally disturbs the subject–object resonances of conventional desire. The Decadent white body's metonymic streams of visual imagery and refracting, diffracting effects find auditory analogues in the echoes, dissonances, and outpouring of associative "sounds" that break down barriers between the lovers. Voices cross and recross, interrupt, improvise, and exchange themes in a dialogue that enhances the activity of the visual trace while distracting from the two remote, grounded figures at stage center. Such auditory play replicates the movement of desire and language to create for female desire a "rhythmic space" that does not admit the conventionally opposed utterances of "he" and "she." Indeed, it is hard to say who is calling whom in *Hippolytus Temporizes* and whether sexual power resides with the caller or with the listener. Artemis's attention to Hippolytus's "mad wood-speech" and ardent prayers literally catalyze her into audible, bodily, and erotic presence – she exists as "aether" "breathed" by the forest until she "hears" her followers' prayers – thus redefining the aggressive operations of desire as a function of listening as well as of speaking. As we shall see, Hippolytus's quest is also driven by his attentiveness to "the very pulse and passion of [her] feet" (14) echoing in the wild sounds of the forest. The voices of the lovers therefore become auditory masks, forming and reforming the subject positions of the pursued and pursuer in the boy lover and the various manifestations of his mother Hippolyta.

H.D.'s experimental "white sound," which leads or displaces the "concrete" meaning in *Hippolytus Temporizes*, finds an earlier model in Romantic Victorian sexual histories and is among the feminine traits that modernists such as Pound, Eliot, and others condemned in their program for modern poetry. The ruinous siren song of Romanticism thus included the seductive potential of word sounds as well as effeminate imagery in male modernist theories of poetry. Andrew Ross amply demonstrates that poetic modernism privileges "the eye" and severely mistrusts the "ear" (Ross 31). "Speech varies, . . . all our eyes are the same," Eliot instructs (*SE* 243). Eliot and Pound objected particularly to Swinburne's famous alliterative technique, in which a differential sequence of associative sounds appears to determine word choice with apparent disregard for linear thought or clear delineation of characters. In "The Hounds of Spring" from *Atalanta in Calydon,* which H.D. admired, for example, complicated patterns of consonant sounds give the impression of an alliterative chase that leads the meaning:

> When the hounds of spring are on winter's traces,
> The mother or months in meadow or plain
> Fills the shadows and windy places
> With lisp of leaves and ripple of rain. (*Atalanta,* lines 65–8)

Swinburne's alliterative patterns often produce provocative combinations – "lisp of leaves and ripple of rain" – or unsettling instances of synesthesia as in "The heavens that murmur, the sounds that shine, / The stars that sing and the loves that thunder" in "The Triumph of Time" (a favorite of the young Pound's). Indeed, Eliot singled out specifically Swinburne's allusion to "Time with a gift of tears; Grief with a glass that ran . . ." in *Atalanta in Calydon* to illustrate the point that Swinburne's fascination with alliteration destroys the visual metaphors that would result from a simple reversal in which "time" would be more reasonably paired with "the glass that ran" and "grief" with "a gift of tears" (*SE* 284).

Eliot uses the rhetoric of pathology when describing the evasive signification effected by sound in those writers (almost always Romantics) who do not have their "eye on a particular place" (*SE* 209). Such implicitly sexual/textual perversion produces "a foreign idiom" prone to "acts of lawlessness" in which the auditory is "abnormally sharpened." The resulting "hypertrophy," Eliot continues, overwhelms "the visual and the tactile so that the inner meaning is separated from the surface. . . ."[31] Swinburne's attention to sound over meaning is cited by both Eliot and Pound as detrimental to the concrete objectives of modernism and by extension to modernism's masculinist agenda. In Swinburne, "the meaning and the sound are one thing," Eliot objects; Swinburne "works" the word without concern for the implicitly masculine use of logic and sharp imagery (*SE* 283). Similarly, Pound, using the scientific rhetoric cultivated by the Imagists, disparages Swinburne's excess of "the rhythm-building faculty" at the expense of "the word-selecting, word-castigating faculty" (*LE* 293). The result of this deficiency, Pound suggests, contributes to Swinburne's abnormal fixation on "unusual and gorgeous words" (293, 294): He valued words not "as words," but as "sound" (*LE* 295).

As several critics have pointed out, Swinburne himself claimed to value "song" and spoken word over written language.[32] And Swinburne's writings of transgressive desire relied strongly on the manipulation of transgressive sound both thematically and stylistically. Swinburne's *Poems and Ballads* is a collection of ballads and dramatic monologues singing various sexualities through an array of auditory masks for the voice of the poet. The Romantic Victorian technique of split masking, therefore, may be accomplished both visually and vocally, the songs of the fictive "author" representing multiple sexual selves even as they realize their desire through odes to the Decadent body. Further, transgressive sound is frequently incorporated thematically in *The Poems and Ballads'* forbidden songs of love. Thaïs Morgan demonstrates that Swinburne's lesbian "Anactoria" deliberately parodies the biblical "The Song of Songs."[33] Further, Sappho, the speaker of the poem, does not pray to the heterosexual Venus for Anactoria's love – "Are there not other gods for other loves?" – preferring a goddess of greater diversity, possessing "A mind of many colors, *and a mouth / Of many tunes and kisses*" (*P&B* I, 66; emphasis mine). In the extensive sound troping of the poem's sexual narrative, lesbian love creates "music" and the loved body a "song" – "thy body is the song, / thy mouth the music" (66) – and Anactoria imaginatively becomes a "lyre" that Sappho plays and that by turns "plays" her. Dellamora notes that in Sappho's often violent embrace, "the sounds of the tortured lover become Sappho's music" (*Masculine Desire* 77, 78), but the beloved's "sighs" also rupture her own body: "Thy sharp sighs / Divide my flesh and spirits with soft sound" (64). Sappho concludes her monologue to Anactoria with the triumphant assertion that her "songs" recording the "music" of Sapphic love will one day, "Cleave to men's lives, and waste the days thereof / With gladness and much sadness and long love" (73).

Kristeva's conceptualization of "the chora" in *Revolution and Poetic Language* provides a sound metaphor for the visceral matter of abjection (the subject of her *Powers of Horror*) – both of which belong to Kristeva's pre-Oedipal, "semiotic" modalities of language.[34] Like bodily effluvia, "the *chora*" issues from "cracks" in the "symbolic surface" of language, thereby allowing the "vocal," "kinetic" "rhythm" as well as the "shadow" of the mother to appear.[35] Unlike Eliot, Kristeva speaks favorably of the *chora*'s ability to break even the specular image. However, in most cases, my discussion of "white sound" will not consider the dissonances and echoes of *Hippolytus Temporizes* as necessarily prior to the visual trace, but as a means to a rhythmic rather than graphic space created by the deconstructive activity of sound-troping and poetic song.

Elsewhere, H.D. frequently uses "white sound" in conjunction with the white erotic body to configure female sexuality. Hermione's moment of reconciliation with her lesbian desires (*HER*) finds her alone in an icy forest of sight and sound images that perfectly illustrate the eruption of Kristeva's *chora*. Emerging from her breakdown into the winter forest, Her[mione] rediscovers her love for the betraying sister, Fayne, not only in the "phosphorescent values" (her phrase) evinced by the familiar image cluster of white hands, phosphorescence, and star-frost, but also in the white sound emitting "like a violin string," "a white string," a "silver string," from the "cracks" of the icy ground:

> The ice cracked as she made tentative slipping movement. The sound it gave out suggested something beneath hammering the under surface. . . . The crack widened, actually snapped suddenly. . . . Reverberation cut like a white string, cut like a silver string. . . . Then her thought widened and the tension snapped as swiftly. It's like a violin string. It's like Fayne exactly.

> When she said Fayne a white hand took Her. (*HER* 225)

Earlier in the novel, Hermione's growing awareness of her bisexuality is also signaled by a sound eruption of the *chora*. Shortly after their first meeting, Her begins to sense the significance of Fayne's appearance in her life initially as a premonitory distant beat, "like a dynamo vibrating with electricity from some far distance," which eventually finds voice in Swinburne's poem "Itylus" (*HER* 123). Hermione searches hurriedly through her volume of Swinburne's *Poems and Ballads* to find the passage that "beat from somewhere outside" and discovers it, appropriately, in the stanza describing the slain boy Itylus's cry for his mother Procne:

> *The sound of a child's voice crying yet.*
> *Who has remembered me, who has forgotten,*
> *Thou hast forgotten, O summer swallow*
> *But the world will end* . . . the world will end . . .
> the world will end . . . *when I forget.* (124, 125; emphasis and ellipses
>   H.D.'s)

The passage coalesces Philomel's call to the "sister" swallow with the boy child's cry for maternal love, reaching backward and forward toward the lost mother, Fayne, through the song of H.D.'s Romantic "foremother," Swinburne.

Finally, H.D. used a combination of vocal and visual references to describe her own experience of psychic/erotic events that exceed concrete description: Her vision of Niké and Helios in the "pictures on the wall" at Corfu, she wrote (in response to Freud's labeling of the event as a "dangerous symptom") was "really a high powered *idea*, simply overstressed, *over-thought*, you might say, an echo of an idea, a reflection of a reflection, a 'freak' thought that had got out of hand. . . ."[36]

HIPPOLYTUS TEMPORIZES

In H.D.'s *Ion,* another play focusing on the Oedipal son's search for his mother, H.D. defines her extremely loose method of translation as a deliberate departure from "the sustained narrative of the original."[37] "The broken, exclamatory or evocative *vers-libre* which I have chosen . . . is the exact antithesis of the original." Ion and Creusa's quick exchange of fragmented, rebounding retorts is intended to convey "a tense feeling of ecstasy and an undercurrent of hysteria, as if the pent emotions of a childless woman and a motherless boy might, at any moment, break through the surface of hard-won reticence" (*Ion* 40). Although the pace is slowed in *Hippolytus Temporizes* and the jarring volley of words between Creusa and

Ion is displaced by the trailing echoes of voices that always seem to just miss each other, *Hippolytus* also pointedly rebels against the rhythms of "sustained narrative" to evoke the poignancy of maternal longings. Artemis's opening line, "I heard the intolerable rhythm / and sound of prayer," which also concludes the play, thematizes the *chora*, the ruptured, "intolerable" rhythms that fracture the surface of language/desire in the play. Later, Hippolytus declares that his "song" of Artemis's "bright name" (11) has "inflamed and torn the dispassionate air / with sound of flute / and note of songs / and meter –" (12). When he hears the conventional dance music of ritualized romance, Hippolytus bids the musicians, "O tear the strings, / have done with mockery / of set and stated time / of word and meter; . . . what word / can tell the sudden rhythm / of her white feet?" (39, 40). (In "Fragoletta" the narrator invokes illicit love through sound imagery, "O broken singing of the dove" (*P&B* I, 94).) Both conventional music and conventional iconography are inadequate simulations of the *chora*. Hippolytus protests to Artemis that the white statues he places at her shrine cannot compel white eroticism, "but song may yet entrap you, / fire and rhythm / may yet contain the ecstasy / and the heat / cold like white lightning –" (14). Transgressive song is also "wild" song, and Hippolytus therefore imitates the animal calls of the forest, donning the vocal masks of the linnet or the serpent in order to persuade Artemis through the untamed "madness of wood-speech" (10): He strives to learn the "bird notes" of the linnet, "and so follow / like a wild linnet, Artemis, Artemis –" "I have intrigued for many days," he reveals, "to meet / some kindly serpent / who might name your name, / so I might lay in wait / to lure, to hiss / like a wood-creature, Artemis, / Artemis –" (10).

Listening is also desire in *Hippolytus Temporizes,* as I have mentioned, and the maternal auditor shares in the forbidden discourse. Lacan includes the listener in the erotic, psychoanalytic narrative: "Provided that it has an auditor . . . every Word calls for a reply" and there "is no Word without a reply."[38] Although Artemis (shivering) protests emptily at the conclusion of the play, "No song of his / lured me / with poignant note; / no shrill song-note / of mine / responded to his piercing flute; / no, / I was mute," Artemis's first reply to Hippolytus's prayer is her ontological change from aether into auditory, erotic presence (119). Earlier, Hippolytus indicates the active presence of his actual mother, the dead Hippolyta, behind his love for Artemis in his ardent belief that "she [Hippolyta] listens now / in every bright and evanescent leaf, / she hears" (28).

Complicity between Hippolytus and Artemis is also characterized by auditory/erotic belatedness. The deferral of maternal eroticism is represented most overtly by the play's "chorus" of Artemis's maidens, whose echoing song appears to issue from the dead Hippolyta:

> *O love, peace,*
> *never in any porch*
> *or portico*
> *can love come,*
> *never to us,*
> *eternal, tenuous,*
> *who died young,*
> *long ago,*
>   *long ago.* (73; emphasis H.D.'s)

Further, Artemis's reply/summons to Hippolytus reaches him belatedly in the midst of her flight, as she assumes a "voice" only to elude him – "I heard the intolerable rhythm / and sound of prayer, / so I have hidden" (8). Having answered Hippolytus by assuming erotic being, she calls to him by leaving elaborate visual and auditory tracks for him to follow through the echoing heights and "impassible stairs / of rock / and forest shale" (8). Even when Hippolytus encounters the voice of Artemis in the forest, their replies often evade the question: Both respond simply with the echo, "wild, wild, wild, wild . . ." as if distracted by the "wildness" of their longings (12).

Stylistically, much of the dialogue is governed by sound rather than visual image in intricate patterns of alliteration, internal rhyme, and repetition. Although H.D.'s briefer and more incantatory method of dwelling on one- or two-word lines does not share the often breathless pace and density of words of Swinburne's style, H.D.'s lines possess Swinburne's alliterative urgency and sense of inevitability as sound rather than image propels them forward. Hippolytus's admonishing speech to Artemis on her failure to save his mother, for example, becomes a seductive recitation of subtly differential alliterative patterns:

. . . you, you, you,
goddess . . .
let her so perish,
who protect
the gull,
the swallow,
the wild owl,
the tern. (29)

The list of birds is determined not by logic or visual metaphor, but by
open vowels and alliterative "l" sounds, which become increasingly more
complicated as "gull" gives way to "swall-ow," which leads to the striking
intricate echo, "wild owl," and the addition of alliterating "w's." Passages
such as these give the impression of a love trance in which sense is deliberately skewed by the lover's fascination with words. The love call to the
sister swallow in Swinburne's "Itylus" is similarly incantatory and preoc-
cupied with an almost maddening ("intolerable") play of alliteration: The
refrain changes from "O sister swallow" to "O fair swift swallow" to "O
fleet sweet swallow," to "O sister swallow" to "O fair swift swallow" to
"O soft light swallow," and so on (P&B I, 61–3). And, as I have mentioned,
Swinburne's "Itylus" is clearly echoed in Phaedra's song to Aphrodite, "O
grace of wild, wild things, / O swallow fair / O fair sea-swallow . . . O
swallow, swallow, / listening everywhere –" (53). Finally, the following
excerpt from the dialogue between Hippolytus and Artemis demonstrates
H.D.'s use of alliterative play to create the impression of voices that trace
each other, even as Artemis accuses the youth of "trapping" her:

Artemis: . . .
ah, you, you most,
you trap, you trick, you take –
I traced this runnel
from the farthest hills
to this sea-shelter,
this remote sea-cove,
lonely, immanent, where peril
I thought had made all safe,
but you,

you like a bird,
Hippolytus,
must follow –

Hippolytus: O fair –

Artemis: Have I no peace,
no quiet anywhere?
you trick,
you trap, Hippolytus,
a goddess in your snare.

Hippolytus: Say rather
you have trapped,
have stricken me – (18)

The most complicit sounds in the passage linger delightedly on the tripping notes of Artemis's "you . . . ," "trick," "track," "take," which she repeats as "trick," "trap," and which Hippolytus further varies in his reply, "you have . . ." "trapped," "stricken" (me). The echoing of slightly divergent sound plays evokes the mutual enthrallment of the lovers and underscores the trick, ruse, stratagem that must define the quest for the erotic mother. (Notably, Artemis's accusation, "You like a bird must follow," harkens back as well to Philomel's call to the sister "swallow" and particularly the lines of "Itylus" that Hermione and Fayne treasured, "The wild birds, . . . follow and find the sun.")

Ignoring the boundaries of the closed sexual narrative, the play's "white song" projects beyond the conclusion of *Hippolytus Temporizes*. Destroyed by the jealous Theseus's curse, Hippolytus now "has his home forever, / in white song" (115), while Artemis leaves the scene of her beloved's death to pursue yet another chase, ending as she began:

I heard the intolerable rhythm
and sound of prayer,
I must be hidden
where no mortals are,
no sycophant of priest
to mar my ease;
climbing impassible stairs

of rock
and forest shale
and barriers of trees. (136–7)

IV Male Masking and the Homosocial Narrative

Whereas H.D.'s mother–son dyads mask a range of relationships to both women and men, H.D.'s Greek man–boy homoerotic pairings occurred most frequently as a code for the imagined brotherhood the early H.D. vainly desired between herself and her male modernist contemporaries. H.D.'s strategy for avoiding what Rachel DuPlessis has termed "romantic thralldom" to her male mentors involved repositioning herself poetically on a Greek continuum of man–boy mentorship derived from her Decadent precursors. As Eve Sedgwick observes, although the boy protégé of the Greek homoerotic ideal is the "object" of his mentor's desires, "The love relationship . . . had a strong educational function." "Along with its erotic component," she stresses, "was a bond of mentorship; the boys were apprentices in the ways and virtues of Athenian citizenship." Unlike the relationship between male poet and woman muse, "For the Greeks, the continuum between 'men loving men' and 'men promoting the interests of men' appears to have been quite seamless" (*Between Men* 4). Further, the guise of the boy androgyne, H.D. suggested in several poems, including the apology to Pound for her early chastity, "Toward the Piraeus" (*CP* 175–9), enabled her to avoid the constant threat of expulsion from the (male) poetic community accompanying the inevitable arrival of rival muses. H.D.'s boy mask guaranteed a place in the poetic brotherhood unaffected by the comings and goings of women such as Dorothy Shakespear, Brigit Patmore, Dorothy Yorke, and others, who had interfered with H.D.'s poetic twinships to Pound, Aldington, and Lawrence.

This particular deployment of the male–male continuum thus inherited the misogynist configuration of "homosocial desire" frequently attending literary appropriations of the Greek system whereby the scapegoating of women either as "foul" body or "gift" effects cultural and erotic bonds between men. Sedgwick includes among her many examples of the configuration she derives from René Girard's literary theory of "mimetic

desire" and the love triangle and Gayle Rubins's anthropological exploration of the cultural "traffic in women,"[39] Shakespeare's antithesis between
the Dark Lady and Fair Youth of his *Sonnets,* which poise the inferior,
"foul," and animalistic female beloved between the two men. Most recently, Earl Jackson, Jr.'s *Strategies of Deviance: Studies in Gay Male Repre-*
sentation points out that the sanctioned "homoeroticism" between men in
classical Greece and in Victorian Hellenism was both patriarchal and hierarchical, particularly in its Platonic distinction between a "heavenly (masculine) and earthly (female-directed) eros." "Women," Jackson asserts,
were envisioned "as irreducibly corporeal beings whose passions were ex-
hausted in physical gratification, and bound to the animality of reproduction."[40] H.D. appears to have drawn upon this Decadent homosocial
dichotomy, demonstrated by Pater's crystal man and the femme fatale, to
diffuse the threat of the Bellas and Brigits while imaginatively sealing a
compact of work, community, and love between herself as boy and her
modernist contemporaries.

Inscriptions of the female as foul body or mere woman in relation to a
superior male–male love are rampant in H.D.'s early work. Thus "Hyacinth" casts out the russet femme fatale (Yorke) in favor of a more spiritual, erotic love between the crystalline Hyacinth (herself) and Apollo
(Aldington) – a wistful reversal of the actual affair that ended her marriage.
"Towards the Piraeus" clearly establishes the boy's (H.D.'s) distance from
the beloved male poet's (Pound's) sexual life with women, evoked here as
a violent and passing "kingly storm" that leaves the older poet free to en-
joy a more spiritual eros with the "boy": Having spent his "heat," the
Pound figure of H.D.'s transsexual fantasy returns to white love, finding
the boy's hands "cold, cold, cold, / intolerably cold and sweet" (*CP* 179).
The mere love of women is suggested in "Charioteer," where a male
sculptor describes himself as "taut with love, / more than any bright
lover" (191) for his dead charioteer brother. Evincing the Decadent legacy
of male–male love and the code of male statuary, the poem's sculptor
vows to erect a statue to his love that will surpass all beauty, including implicitly that of a woman – "an image to startle, / to capture men's hearts,
/ to make all other bronze, / all art to come after, / a mock . . ." (*CP*
192). "Red Roses for Bronze" takes this sentiment further as its
apparently male speaker, crazed with "anger," "hatred," and "jealousy"

toward his arrogantly cynical, womanizing, beloved determines to demonstrate his more compelling love in sculpture. The sculptor's fury mounting as he watches his cynical and worldly beloved flirting casually with two women "chattering, / chattering / by the fountain-rim," he resolves to begin his sculpture,

> making of mouth and eyes
> a thing of mystery
> and invidious lure
> so that all, seeing it, would stare,
> so that all men (seeing it)
> would forsake all women
> (chattering). (214)

In the closing stanza of the poem, the sculptor bitterly asserts his claim to the superior love between men:

> such is my jealousy
> (that I discreetly veil
> with just my smile)
>
> that I would clear so fiery a space
> that no *mere woman's love* could long endure. (215; emphasis mine)

H.D.'s poetic dismissals of "mere woman's love" involved her in a feminist's "double cross": While the white (or bronze) body of the Decadent male androgyne protects the woman writer from male excisions, it also crosses out or despoils her own woman's body.

The erasure of the female is poignantly illustrated in H.D.'s "Heliodora," a poem of homosocial desire in which the woman poet, serving as "gift" or object of transaction rather than foul body, mediates the desire between two "brother" poets. Ostensibly based on a tradition among Greek poets such as Meleager who presented poems to one another as gifts, the act of naming the absent muse, Heliodora, becomes the challenge of H.D.'s poem as two poets vie to fix the female beloved in the most potent poetic phrase. Dale Davis, Caroline Zilboorg, and Rachel DuPlessis have suggested that the two apparently male poets are types of Aldington and H.D., and Zilboorg argues that "Heliodora" specifically replicates the early intimacy of their collaborative sessions on Greek poetry.[41]

H.D. casts herself in the role of the older poet (she was Aldington's senior by five years), the Apollo to Aldington's Hyacinth. During the course of their poetic dueling, the poets' passions rise suggestively toward one another, allowing for an easy reciprocity of passionate and intellectual exchange. The erotic and creative camaraderie is, however, created at the expense of female subjectivity. Striving to "name" the object of their desire, the legendary poet Heliodora, the brother poets form a homosocial love pact based on their shared drive to objectify (capture) the female muse in the "perfect" poetic phrase. H.D., the muse of the London literary circle, thereby runs the risk of writing herself out of the poem.

The passion of "Heliodora" (*CP* 151–4) is clearly homoerotic. Although the poets compete for the absent female beloved, their actual poetic challenge resides, I suggest, in their dangerous approximations to "the love that dare not speak its name." The poem's opening phrase, "He and I sought together," places the charged interaction of "Heliodora" between the two men:

> He and I sought together,
> over the spattered table,
> rhymes and flowers,
> gifts for a name. (151)

The spattered table of a casual, long, and drunken meal sets the scene for the ensuing night-long competition to "name" their desire: "We strove for a name, / while the light of the lamps burnt thin / and the outer dawn came in." As the poets "quibble" "over a girl's name," their first attempt at situating their desire – "He said, . . . 'the narcissus that loves the rain.' " "I said, 'the narcissus, drunk, / drunk with the rain' " – both draws upon a familiar Decadent Romantic mask for male love and indicates that the speaker is willing to go further than his companion toward articulating the moment's drunken passion. The other poet, however, wins the contest immediately thereafter with the phrase, " 'The rose, the lover's gift, / is loved of love.' " The narrator's exclamation, "He said it / 'loved of love,' " may evoke his admiration for the winning phrase, but also signals the poem's movement toward articulating the "unspoken" homosocial desire between the two men that is assured by the female conduit – "he said it [!]" In the following lines, the poets become increasingly intimate, sparking each other's desire, as the winning poet (Aldington) leans suggestively forward and offers yet another more daring "name":

> I waited, even as he spoke,
> to see the room filled with light
>
> . . .
>
> Then he caught,
> seeing the fire in my eyes,
> my fire, my fever, perhaps,
> for he leaned
> with the purple wine
> stained on his sleeve,
> and said this:
> 'did you ever think
> a girl's mouth
> caught in a kiss,
> is a lily that laughs?' (151, 152)

The passage would seem to encode the homoerotic "kiss" between the brother poets: The girl's "mouth" is suggestively reinscribed by the passionate "purple wine stain" on the leaning poet; and just as the girl's mouth is "caught in a kiss," so also the brother poet has "caught" the "fire" in his partner's eyes, evoking the men's mutual desire to possess the other's desire through the mediation of the symbolic female. Their passion continues to escalate, and the older poet enjoys a heady self-identification with his aroused and newly initiated brother: "So I saw the fire in his eyes, / it was almost my fire, / (he was younger), / I saw the face so white, / my heart beat, / it was almost my phrase." Conceding to his friend's skill, the older poet confirms his companion in the "brotherhood" afforded by the homosocial bond: "I saw it now / as men must see it forever afterwards; . . . / it was his pour in the vat / from which all poets dip and quaff, / for poets are brothers in this" (152). The brotherhood sealed, the narrator allows himself a titillating moment of homoerotic desire:

> I watched him to the door,
> catching his robe
> as the wine-bowl crashed to the floor,
> spilling a few wet lees,

(ah, his purple hyacinth!)
I saw him out of the door . . . (154)

The disruption of the spilled wine – both a careless drunken gesture and an outburst of purple eros – prompts a reciprocal thrill in the speaker – "ah his purple hyacinth!" – which also tellingly conjures the homoerotic tale of passion between Apollo and Hyacinth that H.D. had elsewhere summoned toward her relationship with Aldington.

While H.D.'s figurative cross-dressing in "Heliodora" makes possible an erotic and artistic community with her male contemporaries, the poem simultaneously names H.D. the female poet as the absent Heliodora, the "gift" of exchange that was subsequently discarded by "Aldington-Pound-Lawrence." As Dale Davis observes, "like Lesbia, Delia, Cynthia and Zenophile," Heliodora was remembered solely for the poems she inspired.[42] The victim of a feminist double bind, H.D. therefore assumes a mask that preserves both the silence of the excluded, feminine "other" and the silence of the masculine transsexual pose that has ceased to struggle with difference. Commenting on the hazards of literary male impersonation, Ann Herrmann observes that the cross-dressing female scriptor risks assuming the sexual "indifference" of the "masculine," thus subsuming her potential for subversion: "A return to one's original sex [the feminine] means . . . preserving the possibility of a different relationship to language, meaning, and power."[43] By the late 1920s H.D. appears to have fallen victim to the double bind of sexual "indifference."

The Femme Fatale

Chapter Five

Toward a Revised Myth of Origins
From the Diaphanous Androgyne to the Abject Femme Fatale

By the early 1930s, H.D. was suffering from the writing block that would baffle her for nearly a decade. Susan Friedman theorizes that H.D.'s aesthetic of androgyny, twinship, and bisexual desire reached a figurative dead end in *Nights* (1931), where H.D. expressed her "death wish" through the chilling suicide of her heroine – the female half of the novel's androgynous pairing (*PW* 218). Hiding behind the male mask and unable to fully reconcile her "two loves separate," H.D. came to associate bisexuality, as Friedman notes, with "being cast out of a 'home' category," and androgyny with "living in limbo – neither man nor woman" (*PW* 310). Perhaps not incidentally, H.D.'s chief Romantic mask of boy androgyny through the 1920s – Swinburne's Hermaphroditus – now formed an ironic commentary on the gender impasse of H.D.'s male masking. Unlike its celebratory brother poem ("Fragoletta"), "Hermaphroditus" is a distressed ode on androgyny as sexual "indifference":

Love stands upon thy left hand and thy right,
Yet by no sunset and by no moonrise
Shall make thee man and ease a woman's sighs,
Or make thee woman for a man's delight. (*P&B* I, 90)

H.D. could no longer find a fluid, androgynous space between boy Aesthete and mother muse, but remained caught in the "limbo" of their mutual negation. Clearly, by the early 1930s, the play had gone out of H.D.'s Decadent Romantic revisionism. Several critics have focused on the ways in which H.D.'s analysis with Freud (1933, 1934) began the process of self-creation that would allow for the more woman-centered mythos of the later poetry. "Freud-as-mother," Friedman observes, "brought back . . . the primal mother of the daughter's pre-Oedipal desire," thus reconciling H.D. with her bisexuality (*PW* 313). In turn, H.D.'s recognition of the erotic mother she sought in both men and women opened up a matrilineage of mother muses in her later poetry, inspiring and authorizing "the daughter/poet who no longer imagines her writing self as masculine" (*PW* 327). I would add that H.D.'s insights into her "mother-fixation" necessitated a shift from the Swinburnian boy masks of androgyny that had mediated her representation of both mother–daughter eroticism – through the Oedipal boy–mother relation – and heterosexual love – in the "Greek" boy–man continuum.

I will argue in these concluding chapters that H.D.'s rediscovery of the maternal femme fatale, provoked by her psychoanalysis with Freud, her involvement with Kenneth MacPherson and avant-garde cinema, her Pre-Raphaelite revival, and H.D.'s long experience as a woman poet among the modernists, generated a second myth of Romantic origins. This revised sexual history displaced *HER*'s poetic of Swinburnian boy androgyny with a cultural script of Romantic origins based on the nineteenth-century cult of the femme fatale. The fatal woman figures largely in H.D.'s Pre-Raphaelite revival, which began in the late 1920s and early 1930s during several intimate collaborative discussions with Pre-Raphaelite descendant and New Woman Violet Hunt over Hunt's biography-in-process of Elizabeth Siddal – Rossetti's abused model/wife and the prototype of the Pre-Raphaelite woman (*The Wife of Rossetti,* published 1932).[1] H.D. subsequently began rereading William Morris and the Pre-Raphaelites in 1934 (between sessions with Freud),[2] and by the midforties was engaged in a massive research project[3] into the work and lives of Siddal and the Pre-Raphaelites that culminated in several prose works centering on Pre-Raphaelitism, including H.D.'s own unpublished, fictionalized, autobiographical novel of Siddal, "White Rose and the Red" (1947–8) – in which she recast herself as Elizabeth Siddal and her Imagist contemporaries as the Pre-Raphaelite Brotherhood –; a second Pre-Raphaelite autobiography, "The Sword Went Out to Sea" (1946–7); and a volume of detailed, careful notes on the Pre-Raphaelites (1947) that would inform almost everything she wrote thereafter.

H.D.'s Pre-Raphaelite revival has not received any scholarly attention largely because, as Susan Friedman rightly observes, the novels are often incomprehensible and do not quite "work" either as "fiction, biography or history." However, H.D.'s reimagining of her World War I story among her Imagist mentors – Aldington, Pound, and Lawrence – from within the character of Siddal and the Brotherhood does work effectively as an historicized agenda for her later poetry and a later rescripting of the earlier myth of Romantic origins, *HER*. I am suggesting that H.D.'s proposed return to Pre-Raphaelitism, enacted by the time travel of herself and the Imagists back to the Victorian cult of womanhood in "White Rose" and related texts, functions as an alternative sexual/textual program for a "female" modernism to *HER,* the no longer viable myth of boy androgyny and personal awakening that served H.D. for a little over a decade after the Imagist movement.

H.D. herself repeatedly suggested that she regarded her Pre-Raphaelite writings as a grand strategy or master plan (script) for her later poetics. She described the Pre-Raphaelite novels as the culminating compilation of her "story," "legend," and as the "prose phase" that necessarily preceded "the poetry" (*Compassionate Friendship* 94). She continually stressed the momentousness of her return to the Pre-Raphaelites who had "renewed [her] faith at the end of the war-years" ("Delia Alton" 195). "In 1945" – the year she seriously undertook her Pre-Raphaelite research – "my life began," H.D. wrote in "The Sword Went Out to Sea" (222). "I had actually adjusted my opera-glasses the wrong way round, to the Greek scene," she commented, referring to her earlier work; but (she) found "new direction" in the Pre-Raphaelite legend ("The Sword" 176). H.D. variously termed her renewed link to the past as a "re-birth" (7), "the foundation stone of my life" (222), a "reincarnation," and as "the only thing that matters" (181, 182)[4]; and persistently referred to her revival of the Pre-Raphaelite quest for the female "Rose" as a mission: "[The Pre-Raphaelites'] dreams shall not be in vain, nor they forgot while I am alive to remember them" ("The Sword" 277).

I suggest that H.D.'s Pre-Raphaelite rescriptings of *HER* form the literary, historical, and cultural blueprint for H.D.'s later poetic. Like the earlier script, *HER,* H.D.'s new cultural case history continues to draw on the Romantic past as a feminine myth of origins. However, her Decadent revisionism – now formed from feminist transformations of Freudian and Pre-Raphaelite family romance – has shifted to suit the changing purpose, scope, and orientation toward the feminine of H.D.'s later poetic. As critics have pointed out, the later feminist mythos represented in H.D.'s *Trilogy* and *Helen in Egypt* is distinguished both by its movement away from the male mask and attendant myth of androgyny toward a more immediate female–female connection[5] with the mother muse, and by the cultural, rather than personal quests of these female, "epic" poems whose schemes for a Woman's Age contrast with the masculinist mythos of male epics such as Eliot's *Waste Land* and *The Four Quartets* or Pound's *Cantos.* Critics have further noted H.D.'s deployment of equal brother–sister bonds rather than same-sex androgyny as the relational model for love between men and women in her more inclusive notion of a female era when "no man will be potent, / important, / yet all men will feel / what it is to be a woman" (*CP* 460).[6] DuPlessis observes, for example, that in *Helen in Egypt,* "The lover and woman [Achilles and Helen] are imagined as brother-sister quest-ers, so that . . . spiritual, sexual, forces define the relationship. The quests of Helen and Achilles are finally not journeys toward love for each other, but a single quest to identify the source: the mother" ("Romantic Thrall-dom" 419). The Pre-Raphaelite quest for the "Rose," then, offered H.D. a poetic model for the searching, psychoanalytic narrative of maternal long-ing she had recreated in Freud's presence and for a cultural myth of wom-anhood from which to fashion a female modernity. In "White Rose and the Red" and other Pre-Raphaelite writings, H.D.'s representatives of male modernism/modernity do not stray from their early Romanticism, but as-semble reverently around the icon of the Pre-Raphaelite woman in mutual fascination with the erotic mother/sister twin.

Over the course of her career, H.D.'s gender narratives may be said to move from rejection to reconciliation with the two primary objects of her poetic/sexual anxiety defined by *HER* – namely, male modernity (Lowndes/Pound) and the forbidden mother ("Faustine") behind the sister love. In the earlier case history of H.D.'s poetic development, she ap-proaches the mother obliquely through masks of boy androgyny and resists the male modernist discourse by rejecting entirely the male offender Lowndes/Pound. "White Rose and the Red," however, reconstructs H.D.'s poetic around the femme fatale foremother and transports male modernity back to the maternal feminine. H.D.'s imaginative transposition of the Imagist circle into the Pre-Raphaelite brotherhood masterfully heals the breach of the early myth by returning H.D.'s male mentors to their Romantic selves before their defection took them to destructive, even fascistic extremes. Pound-as-Swinburne, Lawrence-as-Morris, and to a certain extent, Aldington-as-Rossetti are once again the sensitive, nurturing, and sympathetic artist allies H.D. had lost to the "modern cult of brutality" in the patriarchal forces of war and its accompanying "man-is-man, woman-is-woman" aesthetic. Simultaneously, H.D.'s conception of the maternal foremother herself shifted radically from boy androgyne to abject femme fatale. As I demonstrate in the next three chapters, H.D. would cast off the vanishing body of male "indifference" – Hermaphroditus – for exploded and explosive female bodies that matter.[7]

In the remainder of this book, I propose to examine H.D.'s later Decadent revisionism not simply as another transformation of the feminine past, but as a larger feminist revisionary circle traced by both early and later scripts. As such, H.D.'s changing figuration of the erotic mother, from white androgyne to the more visceral femme fatale, and of her male contemporaries, from the misogynist anti-Romantics of the earlier scripts to the Romantic twin she termed the *"héros fatale"* (*Compassionate Friendship* 30) in her later Pre-Raphaelite agenda, maps a woman poet's changing patterns of anxiety over the course of a career. The lifelong trajectory of authorship anxiety plotted by these narratives thus offers a uniquely female version of Harold Bloom's career-long cartography of a single (male) poet's "anxiety of influence" and its corrective strategies over the long term.

Although Bloom's father–son model of male anxiety does not adequately describe the experience of female writers, nor, as I have argued, the mother–son and erotic, male–male configurations of modernist anti-Romanticism, his "phases" do acknowledge the changing faces of anxiety inherent in the poet's frequently lifelong process of sexual/textual identity formation. Bloom's argument that the male poet, having spent his career forging his "own" (male) poetic identity, can at last fearlessly "open" his "poem" to his former agon(s) in the final phase of development (termed

"*Apophrades*"), adheres roughly and perhaps more poignantly to the brave course of H.D.'s female anxieties – toward both the mother and her male mentors – which established its "I" repeatedly and against even greater odds. This chapter therefore traces H.D.'s narratives of anxiety, first toward anti-Romantic male modernism and second toward the maternal body, arguing that these dual repressions contributed to her writing block in the 1930s. The career-long mapping of sexual/aesthetic development formed by *HER* and the later Pre-Raphaelite works thus proceeds from early feminist initiation narrative to an abject tale of survival more suited to the battle-scarred woman poet of a later phase, as I will show. Like Gilbert and Gubar's savvy Victorian women writers, H.D. would learn to "use" her agon – here the femme fatale and figurations of her male contemporaries – to combat twentieth-century male myths of poetic modernism. After tracing H.D.'s narratives of anxiety toward the father/patriarch in the form of her male mentors, I proceed to examine the turning point in H.D.'s attitude toward the maternal femme fatale that began to occur in the late 1920s, early 1930s with her exposure to Violet Hunt's biography of Elizabeth Siddal, *Wife of Rossetti,* and her new enchantment with the screen femme fatale (Greta Garbo) during H.D.'s experiments with avant-garde cinema. In the next chapter I focus on H.D.'s refiguring of the father as the Romantic twin in her later myths of Pre-Raphaelite origins. I conclude in the final chapter by discussing H.D.'s poetic presentation of the abject femme fatale as the cultural leader of H.D.'s female modernist epic, *Trilogy*.

I   H.D. and Her Modernist Contemporaries: Early Scriptings

Long after the dissolution of the London circle, H.D.'s anxiety of authorship was kept painfully alive by the misogynist institution of anti-Romanticism that launched persistent critical attacks on her "escapism." I therefore begin this section by tracing the anxious role of H.D.'s Pound- and Aldington-figures in early scripts such as *HER,* where the poet heroine achieves a lone poetic identity through separation from the male agon. I proceed by examining H.D.'s mounting defensiveness toward anti-Romantic male modernism in those narratives of anxiety issuing from reviews, notes, and interviews of the 1930s, composed after the early scripts had ceased to suffice.

As I suggested in Chapter One, H.D.'s villainization of Lowndes-Pound in the early script of her poetic development, *HER,* strives for complete dissociation from the oppressive erotic and linguistic implications of male modernism. At this crucial postwar, post-Imagist juncture in her career (1926–7), H.D.'s acute anxiety of authorship compels her toward what Bloom would call a necessary "misprision" of the agon, Pound. *HER* distorts her early companion's considerable role in introducing and cultivating the Romantic myth of twinship they both shared, expanding instead upon Frances Gregg's equally profound but different contribution. In the earlier *Paint It Today* (1921), the Pound figure first appears as the vessel for H.D.'s anxiety. Often dryly referred to simply as "the youth" or "the erstwhile fiancé," "Raymond" enters and exits briefly in the interstices of H.D.'s female homoerotic plot. Midget's elaboration of Raymond's abuse might describe any of the slick, insensitive male modernists that frequent these early histories:

> When she was nineteen, she had parted with the youth, having gained nothing from him but a feeling that someone had tampered with an oracle, had banged on a temple door, had dragged out small, curious, sacred ornaments, had not understood their inner meaning, yet with a slight sense of their outer value . . . had not stolen them, but left them, perhaps worse, exposed by the roadside, reft from the shelter and their holy setting. (7)

Accordingly, both scripts offer sanctuary for their heroines in the Romantic myth of the boyish sister love.

Significantly, H.D.'s early dramatizations of male modernist insensitivity to the feminine sex/text most frequently seize upon fictionalized scenes of her contemporaries' anti-Romanticism. The defamatory Pound- or Aldington-personae of H.D.'s early prose myths of Romantic origins therefore function simultaneously as vehicles for H.D.'s personal bitterness and as composite figures of a more urgent agon – the critic agents of male modernity who persistently attacked her poetry in the name of an "escapist" Romanticism. *HER, Asphodel, Murex,* and other works limit the Pound and Aldington figures to brief cameo appearances where they are shown at their most arrogant, exclusionary, and self-absorbed in the act of deriding the implicit effeminacy of the Romantics – a scene that H.D. must have witnessed ad nauseam, judging from the regularity of its appearance in the early fictional histories. Pound first introduced H.D. to the Victorian Romantics and was already gaining a reputation as a man of letters during the years fictionalized by *HER*. However, the only poetry that "belongs" to H.D.'s Lowndes-Pound is his mocking, drawling rendition of the American Romantic poet, Longfellow, whom Pound grouped with the "vague," "cosmic," British Romantics he abhorred. Hermione's musings, during one of several walks with him in Farrand forest, on why she cannot love George are cut short by his parody of Longfellow, which on the instant seems reason enough not to love him:

> *This is the forest primeval, the murmuring pines and the hemlocks,* (George intoned dramatically; she knew why she didn't love him) *"bearded with moss and with garments green, indistinct in the twilight."* She knew why she couldn't love George properly. . . . George being funny, nasal intonation, being funny, *this is the forest primeval* . . . George . . . was a hideous harlequin being funny on a woodpath. "Noaaw this is the fawrest *pri*-meval. (65, 66; emphasis H.D.'s)

The recurring scene of George being funny on a woodpath at Longfellow's expense comes to stand for more than youthful irreverence. His smugly hostile parodies of Longfellow issue from the same male silencing system that in *HER* prompts George to rebuke Hermione – "Don't talk such rot" or "yore pomes are rotten" – and that, outside *HER*, was already determining the critical reception to H.D.'s post-Imagist poetry. *HER* argues for the value of a female, Romantic poetic against a snide, self-important, anti-Romanticism as George's "Noaaw this is the fawrest *pri*-meval" rebounds against Hermione's reverent chantings of "Itylus" and her hunger for the Romantic poetic – Swinburne's – that will rejoin her to her "female" erotic and writerly selves. Hermione feels linguistically marooned by male modernism's emphatic disinheritance of their mutual Romantic past: If "words were her plague and words were her redemption," "George with his parody of their New England Poet was cutting her again from moorings" (67).

An almost startlingly parallel scene occurs in H.D.'s *Murex*, where H.D.'s sexual/writerly anxiety again prompts her to depict the betraying male modernist (here, Aldington) at his worst, badmouthing effeminate Romanticism. Male anxiety meets female anxiety in these fictional histories where the male modernist defensively parodies Romanticism and the female modernist winces at his implicit slanders of women's writing. "Murex" ostensibly details the deadening effect on H.D.'s work and life effected by Aldington's adultery; however, "Freddie," who appears seldom and in flashback, is also the mouthpiece for the critical anti-Romantic jibes that contributed to H.D.'s psychic paralysis after World War I. As in *HER,* the offending male modernist is reduced to brief anti-Romantic sallies into the story's predominantly homoerotic dialogue – this time between the female narrator and various specters of the "other woman." Among Raymonde's most resonant memories of Freddie is his insolent recitation from William Morris's "Helen," followed by a brash dismissal of the Pre-Raphaelites' implicitly feminine aesthetic of intricacy and detail: " 'O glory of eyes, O glory of hair, O glory of glorious face most fair.' Raymonde heard the mocking, the throaty sous-entendre that nothing was worth taking seriously, that there was no reason for anything and certainly none for William Morris. . . . 'O glory of face – that excruciating blighter [he said], he writes poetry like wallpaper patterns' " (133, 134).

During the 1930s, "anxious" excerpts from H.D.'s reviews and notes on poetry indicate that she was feeling increasingly more vulnerable to the worsening critical attacks on her Romanticism. Michael King observes in his overview of H.D.'s critical reception that "throughout the thirties" H.D. was viewed as "a relic," "a technical invention," and an "escapist."[8] In 1931, the *Manchester Guardian* tersely dismissed H.D.'s self-indulgent tendency to "expand and romanticize" her Greek material, which "neither reflects the Greek nor gives the effect of it on the modern mind."[9] Douglas Bush's sweeping book-length repudiation of Romanticism from its roots in the eighteenth century to its influence on the twentieth (*Mythology and the Romantic Tradition* 1937) summarized the generally hostile tone of H.D.'s modernist reviewers. Bush scathingly denounced H.D.'s "turbid romantic emotionalism" and "fundamentally romantic and precious conception both of Greece and of poetry" as being more escapist even than the Romantics themselves (503, 505, 506).

H.D.'s hurt and outrage pervades her public pronouncements of the period. In a "note" on the "aims" of her poetry written in the same year that Bush's book appeared (1937) for the *Oxford Anthology of American Literature,* H.D. feels the need to begin by defending her work against the anti-Romantic "final indictment" of her "sort of poetry" – "We don't live. We don't see life. And so on."[10] Defensively, and almost apologetically, H.D. thereupon opens her discussion with the qualification, "In order to speak adequately of my poetry and its aims, I must, you see, drag in a whole deracinated epoch [Romanticism]." H.D. proceeds to justify her Romanticism by demonstrating the insensitivity of male anti-Romanticism, once more summoning an anecdote detailing a male modernist's (probably Aldington's) cynical observations on Romantic poetry's inability to address the harsh realities of "life": Upon wading through the rubble of a bombed-out neighboring house during World War I, H.D. recalls, her bemused companion gave a "decisive foot-ball kick with his army boot" to a fallen volume of Browning, demanding dramatically, " 'What is the use of all this – now?' " H.D. responds emphatically that for her, "*Fortu* and the *yellow-melon flower* . . . were . . . never so clear as at that very moment." Later in the informal note, H.D. implies, perhaps not without justification, that the anti-Romantic attacks against her work are turning her creative powers to gall. She declares among the purposes of her poetry the desire "to tear, if it be even the barest fragment of vibrant, electric parchment from hands not always worthy to touch, to fingers whose sterile 'intellectuality' is so often a sort of inverted curse of Midas" (1287, 1288).

H.D.'s anxiety was particularly obvious in book reviews where the author's anti-Romantic stance gave her a chance to strike back. Reviewing the *Poems of Sappho,* by Edwin Marion Cox, in an unpublished essay she entitled "Winter Roses" (published in a different form in *The Saturday Review,* 24, 1925), H.D. begins by dryly conceding that Cox is "our superior in scholarship," but she proceeds to condemn his "too gentlemanly, too scholarly too bloodless" book particularly for its "very modern" omission of Swinburne's translations, one of which she regards as "forever and ever wedded to that particular fragment [of Sappho's]."[11] Finally, H.D.'s most confrontational narrative of anxiety toward organized, critical anti-Romanticism is contained, appropriately, in her *Criterion* (July 1933) review of the distinguished anti-Romantic Irving Babbitt's *On Being Creative.* H.D. associated Babbitt with another French philosopher known for his anti-

Romanticism, Julien Benda, whom Richard Aldington had recently translated (1927) in yet another modernist tribute to anti-Romanticism. H.D.
is contemptuous beneath her studiously "scholarly" attack on Babbitt's
treatment of Keats's "Ode to a Nightingale":

> The rigidity of his anti-romantic standards is leading Professor Babbitt into
> an extremely specious type of criticism, of a kind that gives away with one
> hand and takes back with the other. It is not really illuminating to make
> remarks like 'Keats' *Ode to a Nightingale* is an exquisite poem of escape.' It
> is an exquisite poem, the intentionally derogative qualification 'of escape'
> becomes superrogatory. . . . (*Criterion* 17)

H.D.'s tone grows icier as she accuses Babbitt of the same facile "lack of
sensibility" she evoked in her fictionalized Pounds and Aldingtons, "One
begins to suspect that Professor Babbitt, like his French colleague, Julien
Benda, achieves the integrity and tidiness of his views on art and literature
by virtue of a certain lack of sensibility. It is easy to deny the emotional
basis of art if you do not feel it."

II   The Femme Fatale: Rewriting the Erotic Mother

The "crystalline" quality (*diaphaneitè*) of H.D.'s poetic body formed the
primary target of modernist attacks on her "escapist" Romanticism. If
H.D.'s detractors could not blame her for piling on sensuous detail with
"escapist" abandon, they perceived the same suspicious avoidance of life
in the feminine fragility, tentativeness, and transparency of her imagery.
"What is one to say," wrote Douglas Bush, "of a kind of beauty which
vanishes the moment one's eye leaves the page?" (Bush 501). Stung as she
was by modernist attacks on her "escapism," H.D.'s decision in the 1930s
to move away from the fire and ice of her early poetry did not, however,
direct her toward the passive, flawless, female objects Yeats and others
equated with modernist "concreteness" and the "movement downward
upon life." Rather, H.D.'s new compulsion toward "bodies that mat(t)er"[12]
took her back to that other dreaded image of Romantic (feminine) excess,
the aggressive, Medusan, Romantic foremother whose threatening materiality had induced a male modernist purge on the decadent decaying mat-

ter, characterizing for example, the powerful sexuality of Pater's Mona Lisa: "It is a beauty wrought out from within upon the flesh, the deposit, little cell by cell, of strange thoughts and fantastic reveries and exquisite passions" ("Leonardo Da Vinci" 125). Thus New Critic and modernist sympathizer Frank Kermode asserts extravagantly in his *Romantic Image*, that Yeats's inclusion of Pater's passage on Mona Lisa as the first poem in his *Oxford Book of Modern Verse* "at once" lifts her "out of the stale ecstasies of 'decadent' appreciation," recreating her as "an emblem of both the *paysage interieur* and the concreteness of modern poetry" (Kermode 58). H.D.'s return to the femme fatale positioned her against male modernist attempts to trim feminine superfluity.

As I have attempted to demonstrate, for both modernist woman writers and Decadent Aesthetes alike, the vanishing body of the male androgyne cleared a space for difference and erotic/linguistic play. Further, the blood traces beneath the lucent white skin frequently divulged the boy androgyne's hidden abjection, albeit within the "pure" white body that outwardly appeared evacuated of its sexual content. However, as Earl Jackson, Jr., points out, although the Aesthetes celebrated the male body of masculine desire through references to Greek love, their "Neo-Platonic disavowal[s] of 'literal' homosexual desire" simultaneously desexualized male eros (Jackson 4). We might surmise that the hygienic male youth with his participation in discourses of purity, whiteness, and spiritual love also exhibited the cultural somatophobia (misogynist or heterosexist) that denies sexually transgressive men and women writers a gendered, sexualized, affective, and interactive body. Thus, Thaïs Morgan's argument that Decadents such as Swinburne projected male–male desire on the Sapphic bodies of their lesbian fatal women ("Anactoria," "Faustine," etc.) suggests that the often violent, visceral songs of lesbian eros restored a passionate body to male–male sexuality.[13] Similarly, from the 1930s onward, H.D. cast off her primary mask of male indifference – Hermaphroditus – increasingly summoning the power of the perversely profuse, the horrific, and the maternal, body in the mask of the Romantic femme fatale.

If, according to Kristeva, "identity, system, order" are defined by what is purged or excluded, then the return of the abject – the body's outgrowths and wastes – might bombard and disperse neatly pared-down, modern aggregates of patriarchal centricity (*Powers of Horror* 4). H.D.'s *Trilogy* encourages the outcast dejects of World War II to learn the wisdom of the abject: "Be indigestible, hard, ungiving," the narrator instructs the "straggling" company of artists, "and the shark-jaws / of outer circumstance / / will spit you forth" (*CP* 4; 514). Poetry and language must also be unassimilable, projectile, monstrous: "Depth of the sub-conscious spews forth / . . . many incongruent monsters / / and fixed indigestible matter" (*CP* 32; 534). But foremost, *Trilogy*'s dejected bodies accumulate in the feminine somatic overflow of the poem's pivotal dark Venuses. H.D.'s femmes fatales thus deploy a female tropology powerful enough to force the feminine into representation and political power. Unlike the vanishing body of the male androgyne, which eluded male masks of modernism but often left the ensuing gap bodiless and sexless, the swarm and litter of abjection adhering to *Trilogy*'s Venus, Mary Magdalene, and others, returns upon that linguistic and bodily space, filling and overfilling it with rebounding female signification.

Indeed, the Decadent femme fatale has always been a remarkably fluid and resistant linguistic/sexual body, whether in her guise as the pornographic object of the male "gaze," or as the agent of the sexually transgressive text. Nina Auerbach notes that Pre-Raphaelite paintings such as Rossetti's *Beata Beatrix,* in which "a woman's trance is the single medium of radical, and magical, change," surpass the limitations of Rossetti's male "frame." Helena Michie expounds, similarly, "the Pre-Raphaelite painting, is itself the icon of Victorian female sexuality. . . . Larger than life, emblazoned on the wall, the women in Pre-Raphaelite paintings are glowing emblems of female power and sensuality. Every hair takes on a life and a power of its own."[14] As I mentioned in Chapter 4, Thaïs Morgan and Richard Dellamora demonstrate the lesbian fatal woman's importance in Victorian encodings of male–male desire. And Morgan's study of contemporary dominatrix pornography as a vehicle for feminine subjectivity traces the figure of the dominatrix back to the "fin-de-siècle femme fatale," focusing specifically on figurations of the Medusa.[15] The Decadent femme fatale is, of course, a prototype for Gilbert and Gubar's "madwoman" writer, as they suggest in *Sexchanges.*[16] Further, although she is not directly alluded to in Kristeva's study of abjection (*Powers of Horror*) or Bakhtin's theory of the grotesque body (*Rabelais and His World*), the femme fatale is the unspoken emblem both of Bakhtin's Medusan, devouring, sprouting, and writing "dual bod[ies]"; and of the "abject mother" Kristeva locates behind her analysis of Celine's abjection – a "descent into the hell of naming" which, Kristeva herself professes, "might just as well" have "been motivated" by "Baudelaire" (134).

The Baudelairean or Swinburnian femme fatale is surely behind Monique Wittig's sexual/linguistic agenda in *The Lesbian Body* "to bring the real [lesbian] body violently to life in the words of the book" (10). *The Lesbian Body*'s passionate dismantling of loved, female bod[ies] toward Wittig's program for the violent rend[er]ing of language/sexuality clearly derives from fin de siècle love poetry. Wittig borrows the Decadents' intricately veined, garish, and often dismembered loved female bodies, as well as the deliberate perversions of biblical language[17] that constitute their love poems to abjection: "*I* await an apotheosis a glorious end in this place where the primary colors are not lacking," Wittig's lesbian narrator intones to her "incomparable Sappho," "*I* tremble before the bright red efflux from your arteries . . . *I* see the dark blood emerge from the blue of your veins, in places it is congealed violet, *I* am illuminated by the gold and black of your eyes . . ." (21). And when Wittig's narrator croons to the beloved, "*I* invoke your help m/y incomparable Sappho, give m/e by thousands the fingers that allay the wounds, give m/e the lips the tongue the saliva which draw one into the sweet slow poisoned country from which one cannot return" (Wittig 16), we are reminded of Swinburne's "Anactoria," in which Sappho seeks to feed on the milk, honey (and poison) of her beloved's body unto its total consumption:

> Ah that my mouth for Muse's milk were fed
> On the sweet blood thy sweet small wounds had bled!
> That with my tongue I felt them, and could taste
> The faint flakes from thy bosom to the waist!
> That I could drink thy veins as wine, and eat
> Thy breasts like honey! That from face to feet
> Thy body were abolished and consumed,
> And in my flesh thy very flesh entombed! (*P&B* I, 68)

Wittig's strategic linguistic/bodily invasion of the Decadent, Sapphic body, her exhaustive list of dismembered body parts, does not perform the same disfiguration enacted by Paul de Man's tricks of light and specularity in "Shelley Disfigured." Her narrator's journey into the teeming vistas of a traditionally closed sexual (lesbian) body rather strives to enact the "lived, rending experience that is m/y writing" in the hope of forcing the female "I" (which she also bisects as j/e) into representation (Wittig 10).

Moreover, as I suggested during my earlier discussion of Swinburne's "Faustine" and the encoded "kiss" between Fayne and Hermione (HER), in addition to love, the Decadent fatal woman might also embody the mix of fear and elation stimulated by the "perverse" identity forced upon women who love women. Sue-Ellen Case's excellent "Tracking the Vampire" gives personal testimony to the value of the Decadent, vampire femme fatale as a focal point both for the pain and the "reveling in an illegitimate homosexual state of desire": Her adolescent discovery of Rimbaud's vampire femmes fatales offered "a way of deconstructing my own milieu to ease the pain of exclusion as well as to confront what we have long, on the street, called 'the recreational use of the lesbian.' " But at the same time, Rimbaud's (female) vampires inscribed the disempowering "identification with the insult, the taking on of the transgressive, and the consequent flight into invisibility."[18] Finally, as Susan Edmunds argues, the aggression, sexual anger, and sadomasochism of the mother–daughter dyad in H.D.'s later works has often been slighted in favor of more "peaceloving" feminist interpretations.[19] As I will discuss shortly, for the early H.D. and others, the Decadent femme fatale with her history of violence, sadomasochism and emotional torment could express uniquely female–female experiences of sexuality, erotic enthrallment, competition, and the negotiation between self-identification and difference in relation to an "other woman," be she mother, sister, lover, friend, or rival.

Here, and in my final chapter on H.D.'s Trilogy and the abject femme fatale, I shall show H.D. consciously or unconsciously deploying most of the typologies of the femme fatale suggested. However, I begin with a discussion of H.D.'s pronounced ambivalence toward the maternal-erotic agon implied by the Romantic femme fatale in her early work, before considering H.D.'s gradual turning toward the fatal woman in the narratives generated by her fascination with the screen femme fatale and her readings in Violet Hunt's Wife of Rossetti.

III   The Femme Fatale: Early Scriptings

As I argued in Chapter Two, H.D.'s resentment toward the femme fatale manifested early and vehemently with *Sea Garden*'s sharp contrast between liberating white, vanishing, landscape/bodies of androgyny and stifling, overflowered Venusbergs of conventionally feminine sexuality. However, while the early H.D. used the Romantic foremother reviled by her contemporaries to pronounce against the evils of sexually divisive, manipulative, male–female relations, she also inadvertently revealed her own female anxieties and yearnings toward an "other" female body. The abjection of *Sea Garden*'s overripe, oversweet, decaying Venusbergs bespeaks an uncontained, rampant (female) sexual energy that both attracts and terrifies its author. "The Gift" (*CP* 15–19) – the only poem of the volume in which an apparently female narrator addresses her dark Venus – hymns to the delights and tortures of the beloved's burgeoning landscape/body. She mocks the pain of unrequited love and the histrionic language of the abject lover – "Do not dream that I speak / as one defrauded of delight, . . . / . . . who gasps: / these ripe pears / are bitter to the taste, / this spiced wine, poison, corrupt" (16). Nonetheless, it is precisely the streaking, spreading, overripe Venusian body that makes inroads in her resistance: "Your garden sloped to the beach, / myrtle overran the paths, . . . / / The myrrh-hyacinth spread across low slopes, / violets streaked black ridges / through the grass / / The house, too, was like this, / over painted, over lovely –."

I argued that in "Hyacinth" (*CP* 201–6) Apollo's rebuke toward the flaming femme fatale in favor of Hyacinth's "white hands inviolate" suggests a jealous outcry against the combative sexuality of Aldington's "other" women, the Brigits and the Bellas that interfered between their spiritual twinship. However, Apollo might also function as an unconscious mask for a female author experiencing a strong countercurrent of homoerotic desire and sexual anger toward the temptations of an "other" woman. The speaker's address to the russet fatal woman is fueled by erotic longing, sexual rage, and envy for the physical power and abundance of this "inveterate, / prodigal spender" who takes "all" and whose demonic "fervor" the narrator cannot match: "What can I offer?" "she" asks rhetorically, "lush and heady mallow? / the fire-grass / or the serpent-spotted / fire flower? / O take them, / . . . / and more swiftly go" (202, 205). Although ostensibly condemning the fatal woman's corrupt and consuming appetites through images of decay – "take the red spoil / of grape and pomegranate" and of devouring – "your flaring will / should sweep and scorch, / should lap and seethe and fill / with last red flame / the tender ditch and runnel" – H.D.'s narrator would also seem to stand helplessly in awe of the spoiling, lapping, seething, somatic/semiotic body that compels her/him toward the safety of "white hands inviolate."

The proliferation of fatal women in H.D.'s early poetry, typified by the Venus of "The Gift," the mistress of "Hyacinth," or Phaedra in *Hippolytus Temporizes* thus form dark sister/mother doubles to H.D.'s Greek boys and boyishly androgynous sister loves. Throughout the early work, the fatal woman may be seen as the antithesis of the boy mask, venting either H.D.'s mixed fear and attraction toward female sexuality, the erotic mother, and homoerotic thralldom; or in the more heterosexual narratives, what Helena Michie calls, "sororophobia" – encompassing "both the desire for, and the recoil from identification with other women."[20] In the following discussion, I examine the femme fatale as a vehicle for these conflicts in H.D.'s early prose gender narratives. I focus first on a deliberately lesbian version of the femme fatale – H.D.'s figurations of her betraying first woman lover, Frances Gregg – and second, on an example of the mistress as femme fatale – H.D.'s depiction in "Murex" of the friend who was among the first of Aldington's infidelities, Brigit Patmore.

HOMOEROTIC THRALLDOM

FRANCES GREGG. Critics have uncovered the problematics of H.D.'s relationships with men; most notably, Rachel Blau DuPlessis's article, "Romantic Thralldom in H.D.," demonstrates the passively "feminine," "all-encompassing, totally defining love between unequals" that characterized H.D.'s divisive, gender-coded attachments to her male mentors and threatened to efface her as poet ("Romantic Thralldom" 406). H.D.'s early depictions of Frances Gregg as the femme fatale seem to evoke the problematics of female–female "sameness" and "difference" and particularly H.D.'s ambivalences toward the sexual power and proximity of an "other" woman's body. The repeated lapses of H.D.'s Gregg-figures into demonic personae – Faustine, Hecate (dark aspect of Artemis), witches, etc. – in *HER, Paint It Today,* and *Asphodel* suggest an aspect of H.D.'s lesbian sexuality that leaped the comfortable bounds of the supportive woman-identified "sister love" into less acceptable realms of lust, sexual wrath, competition, and sadomasochism. Although I shall offer a psychoanalytic grounds specifically for H.D.'s recoil from "sameness," in this examination of H.D. I also discuss H.D.'s female–female eroticism as distinct from the issues of either gender oppression or gender identity[21] in the hope of yielding a more complex and sexual H.D.

Psychotherapist Joyce P. Lindenbaum observes that in certain lesbian couples one woman may feel that she has become "lost in her partner": "Along with the blissful experience of mother–infant oneness comes the terror of possible identity loss, object-loss, and complete dependence."[22] Lindenbaum cites Nancy Chodorow's theory that this form of symbiosis is more apt to emerge in woman-to-woman intimacies because they most closely resemble the mother–daughter bond. "How can the women fulfill their original desire to merge, and simultaneously subdue the terror it arouses?" Lindenbaum continues (87). In terms of Kristeva's more psychoanalytic (and less formulated) theory of lesbian sexuality, the phenomenon resembles the pathology that must result from a woman's arrest in the pre-Oedipal stage of mother–child exclusivity (*Tales of Love* and elsewhere). According to Catharine Stimpson's feminist overview of the lesbian novel, H.D.'s homoerotic novels portraying Gregg as the self-identifying female eros affiliate H.D. with those lesbian "texts" in which "characters" "search . . . for alter egos, moral and psychological equivalents which the term 'sister' [or 'mother'] signifies." However, H.D.'s choice of the horrific femme fatale to image the "anxious" and bodily dimensions of lesbian love seems more appropriate to Stimpson's visceral description of the psychic violence that preoccupies narratives treating the breakup of "the mother–daughter exchange," wherein the lover's pain "spurts like blood from the cut of terror."[23] In the mask of the femme fatale, H.D.'s Frances Gregg represents a compelling and frighteningly intrusive sexuality of touch, taste (even to devouring), and other intimacies familiar to the female Decadent body but closed to the white androgyne of the ethereal sister love.

From the moment she appears in H.D.'s first homoerotic novel, *Paint It Today,* Josepha (Gregg) is suggestive of the ominous femme fatale. Midget's first impression of Josepha notes the disconcerting, "unwholesome" pallor and texture of her face juxtaposed against the heavenly promise of her eyes:

> The other girl's face was slightly spotted. Her color was bad. . . . It was her eyes [that captivated Midget], set in the unwholesome face . . . it was her eyes, an unholy splendor.
>
> Her eyes were the blue eyes, it is said one sees in heaven. (*Paint It Today* 9)

In *Asphodel*, Lowndes-Pound would comment that Fayne's face reminded him of a Burne-Jones fury; and indeed the contrast of dazzling, hypnotic eyes against deathly pallor is reminiscent of the Pre-Raphaelite femme fatale. Initially, there is no sharp division between the boyishly androgynous, Artemisian figures and the sinister femmes fatales that cumulatively signal the controlling power of H.D.'s Frances Gregg in *HER* and *Paint It Today*. "Josepha's" or "Fayne's" ability to draw out the young heroine's mythopoeic powers arises both from her sisterly "sameness" and from the Gregg figure's brooding, dark sensuality, her fascination with prophecy, witchcraft, and other supernatural forces (in both novels the women call themselves "wee witches"). However, in each novel, the Gregg figure's mounting sexual power over H.D.'s autobiographical heroines is signaled by her increasingly exclusive association with demonic female figures such as Swinburne's "Faustine." The scene of the kiss in H.D.'s *HER* provides a pivotal example.

H.D.'s mingled attraction and anxiety toward the bodily inducements of her homoerotic desire for Frances Gregg is suggested in the ambiguous vampiric disposition of the kiss and its lingering aftermath. Earlier I interpreted *HER*'s juxtaposition of Fayne against Swinburne's evil vampire femme fatale, Faustine, as an infiltration of the heterosexist discourse represented by George Lowndes. However, as Sue-Ellen Case suggests in "Tracking the Vampire," the "kiss" of the female vampire in Decadent literature and film also inflicts a necessary violence on traditional representations of desire. Case points out, among other things, that the blood exchanged by the kiss is perversely "transformed" into "food for the undead"; "[what] the dominant discourse represents as an emptying out, a draining away, in contrast to the impregnating kiss of the heterosexual, becomes an activism in representation" (Case 6, 15). Further, Case argues, a mutually immured, physical representation of transgressive sexuality is encoded by the vampire's traditionally close, palpable setting, the interlocked female–female gaze between the monster and her subject, and the ensuing "revelling in the wounding" of the "kiss" itself. Accordingly, the vampiric kiss between Fayne and Hermione evokes the ambiguities of an "en-trancing" and entrapping "gaze," a quickening and draining "blood revel," that suggests both fear and desire for female–female intimacy. I quote the relevant lines from *HER* fully before further discussion.

> Her bent forward, face bent toward Her. A face bends towards me and a curtain opens. There is swish and swirl as of heavy parting curtains . . . almost across me I feel the fringe of some fantastic wine-colored parting curtains. Curtains part as I look into the eyes of Fayne Rabb. "And I – I'll make you breathe, my breathless statue." "Statue? You – *you* are the statue." Curtains fell, curtains parted, curtains filled the air with heavy swooping purple. Lips long since half kissed away. Curled lips long since half kissed away. In Roman gold. Long ere they coined in Roman gold your face – your face – your face – your face – your face – Faustine.
>
> Seated in cold steel light, drawn back again, away from that blue-white face, face too-white . . . Her Gart saw rings and circles, the rings and circles that were the eyes of Fayne Rabb. Rings and circles made concentric curve toward a ceiling that was, as it were, the bottom of a deep pool. Her and Fayne Rabb were flung into a concentric intimacy. . . . flung, as it were, to the bottom of some strange element . . . as if they had fallen into a deep well, and were looking up. (163, 164)

Set at a traditional site of vampiric seduction, the "decadent" boudoir, the love scene's close, uncanny atmosphere both heightens and participates in the woman's aroused bodily awareness. Karla Jay notes that Renée Vivien's lesbian femme fatale, Aphrodite, is "an indoor goddess" whose temple is "dark and cloistral"; and indeed Vivien's staging of Aphrodite's entrance before her followers in the poem "Venus" recalls Fayne/Faustine's conjuration from between enfolding curtains: "The foliage parts like the folds of curtains/ Before the Venus of the Blind" (Jay 77, 78). Sue-Ellen Case suggests that "the proximity" pervading "vampire lore" may bespeak a tangible, lesbian sexuality in instances of the (female) vampire's kiss. She cites for further support Tzvetan Todorov's work on the power of the supernatural to evoke atmospheric "proximity": "The central diegetic force [in tales of the supernatural] . . . is their atmosphere . . . of proximity. Settings in fog and gloom connect the disparate elements of the structure through a palpable atmospheric 'touching' " (Case 13). In the preceding passage, the curtains' constant movement further emphasizes the tactile by reenacting the bodily contact of the "kiss," as the brushings of wine-colored curtains, parting, closing, opening "almost across me," mimic by atmospheric touching the touching of lips (and more covertly, the spasms of vaginal orgasm). Further, citing Linda Williams's analysis of the "entranced" look between woman and monster in film, Case also argues that the en-tranced "take" preceding the (female) vampire's "kiss" skews the conventional male-subject, female-object relation as the woman's horror and consequent fall into enchantment transforms her from voyeur to participant (Case 10).[24] H.D.'s coded, sexual, narrative closes in on the "face" that seems to draw both women toward the kiss, and afterward, the "eyes" that continue to hold them in "concentric intimacy" until it is unclear who wears the mask of the seducing Faustine. After the kiss, the lingering aura of eye and bodily contact evokes a mutually felt closeness and sexual vertigo – "as if they had fallen into a deep well and were looking up" (164). Finally, like the vampiric embraces depicted in "Anactoria" or Wittig's Lesbian Body, the actual kiss between Fayne and Her is a greedy act of feeding, consuming, and disfiguring. Fayne's mouth "scars" her face and the meeting of lips is accompanied by the recurring incantation from "Faustine," "lips long since half-kissed away." Swooning, Hermione looks up to find that Fayne's face is "blue-white," "too-white," drained by the just passed blood revel of the vampiric kiss. But the initiation is mutual, and the kiss provides "food for the un-dead": In the throes of passion, each woman defiantly issues the challenge that her kiss will breathe life into the passionless "statue" she perceives in the other – "And I – I'll make you breathe, my breathless statue." "Statue? You – you are the statue." Unquoted lines that occur elsewhere in "Faustine" would seem to elaborate on the abject blood revel of the vampire's "kiss" between the women: Faustine's "carved lips" "make my lip a cup / To drink, Faustine; / Wine and rank poison, milk and blood / Being mixed therein" (P&B I, 119, 120).

Catharine Stimpson unintentionally conjured the "blood revel" in her evocative simile for the lesbian jealousies depicted by certain novels – "like blood from the cut of terror." Apart from the scenes of their desire, H.D.'s fictionalizations of Gregg's sexual betrayals frighteningly compound the devouring, blood reality of the (lesbian) body. Gregg's apparent confession of love for H.D.'s then fiancé, Pound (*HER*), and Gregg's surprise marriage to Louis Wilkinson (1912) (*Paint It Today, Asphodel*), appeared in H.D.'s writing to cut closer to the bone than Aldington's desertion. Whereas H.D. mythologized Aldington as having dehumanized her in the role of the passive muse, Gregg's impact was visceral – she "ripped souls from bodies" – intimately nourishing the sexual/creative body only to "blight" it later. The Aldington figures leave H.D.'s heroines in a benumbed state of self-effacement (*Murex, Bid Me to Live,* etc.), but Fayne's betrayal in *HER* ravages Hermione body and soul, sending her into long-term illness and raving dementia in the famous mad scene that some have argued is Hermione's transition into power.[25] *Narthex,* written shortly after *HER* in 1927 or 1928, likens Gregg to a sadistic "Venus" who feeds and starves the psychic "Adonis gardens" of her victims:

> [Katherine] would condemn you to an eternity of abandonment, emotional starvation. . . . Katherine brought tiny roots out, Adonis garden to be swiftly withered. One was all Adon-garden under Katherine's regime, all sudden premature spiritual flowering, to be as prematurely blighted. Katherine ripped souls from bodies. . . . [26]

In a 1930 letter to Bryher, H.D. described Gregg as a "psychic kleptomaniac. She must get and break" (qtd. in "Two Loves" 228). Yet, in *Narthex,* even as the narrator calls Katherine a "psychic vamp," with "a predilection for destruction," her awe and admiration for such monstrous sexual power is unmistakable: Katherine is like "some Asiatic goddess, many-breasted, something monstrous that yet holds authenticity . . ." (262).

Apart from the pain of Gregg's betrayals, H.D.'s mythologies of Frances Gregg as the femme fatale imply the strong (primarily emotional) sado-masochistic element of their lesbian attraction. Rachel DuPlessis's "Romantic Thralldom in H.D." accurately interprets H.D.'s passivity toward her male mentors as cultural construct rather than a phenomenon of traditional "feminine masochism." Susan Edmunds argues that H.D. "had greater difficulty exploring female aggression against men than against

women" in her study of Melanie Klein and H.D.'s psychodrama of daugh-
terly aggression, sadism, and reparation (Edmunds 21–93). Indeed, H.D.'s
recurring reference to Gregg as Swinburne's Faustine suggests that in addition to boy androgyny, Swinburne – infamous for his fantasies of flag-
ellation and author of sadomasochistic poems such as "Anactoria" and
"Dolores" – provided H.D. and Gregg with images for sadomasochistic
forms of lesbian love. Frances Gregg also read Swinburne with her lover,
John Cowper Powys, whose sadomasochistic proclivities are well known
to his critics. And like H.D.'s references to Gregg as Faustine, Powys's
nickname for Gregg, "Sadista," in a long (unpublished) Swinburnian love
poem he wrote to her of the same name, suggests that an aspect of Frances
Gregg's sexuality inspired masochistic endearments.[27] H.D.'s attraction to
Swinburne included his lifelong fascination with sadomasochism, which she
remarks frequently in her "Notes on Pre-Raphaelites." H.D. appears to
have identified her own early poetic of embattled elements with Swinburne's aesthetics of erotic pain. As I noted in Chapter Two, H.D.'s description of Swinburne's childhood surrender to the beauty and cruelty of
the sea captivated H.D.: "Large company of cousins at Capheaton . . .
[Swinburne] buffeted by sea, swimming, bruises, struggle, salt-sting caused
Young S. sensuous pleasure. Cruelty and beauty in S., as in Sea. S. stoic
in face of elements." H.D. was thrilled to discover Swinburne's sadomasochistic fictional autobiography, *Lesbia Brandon,* in the early 1950s and
wrote suggestively to Silvia Dobson about her similar reaction to Swinburne's *Lucretia Borgia,* which she had requested as a Christmas present in
November 1952:

> What a book and what an extravagance! . . . I even found myself lost, lost
> in the fine print, though it tires my eyes – but no, the excitement of this
> is too much to weary one physically or mentally, I do hope you looked it
> over. . . . I can only repeat I hope you had the benefit of all this and enjoyed
> it as much as I am doing, if you know what I mean.[28]

However neither H.D. nor Gregg so readily accepted their own sadomasochistic relationships. Gregg repeatedly displays horror, cynicism, and bitterness toward the roles of sexual/sensual dominatrix she assumed for others
throughout her memoir, *The Mystic Leeway.* She bitterly (and perhaps accurately) portrayed her participation in Powys's sexual fantasies as having

ruined her life and her innocence (*Mystic Leeway* 100–6). Gregg's sense of H.D. as emotionally/erotically cruel, unnatural, and exploitive surfaces in her description of a "lecherous" H.D., who "had no traffic with love," but whose sexuality emanated a "constant . . . drumming, like the communications beyond the bounds of the meager sense of humans, sight, hearing, that insects have as a part of their sexual equipment" (*Mystic Leeway* 65). And at the end of *Paint It Today,* H.D.'s similarly embittered Midget pronounces her "impossible sisterhood" with Josepha as noxious, "as the sulphurous substance they call in London winter, fog" (*Paint It Today* 89). Still, in life, and as we shall see, in art, Gregg's terrible aspect continued to fuel H.D.'s imagination long after the relationship had ended. At nearly fifty, H.D. wrote to Silvia Dobson that she was "still liv[ing] down" her love for "Frances," a love she described as "terrible with banners [that] only emerges or materializes once or twice in a lifetime" (qtd. in Guest 228).

BRIGIT PATMORE. Apart from sour grapes, the rival femmes fatales of H.D.'s heterosexual love triangles in prose works such as *Hipparchia, Asphodel, Murex,* and others, configure the homoerotic anxieties of what Helena Michie has termed "sororophobia" (the simultaneous desire and recoil from female self-identification). Here the stolen man seldom plays more than a minor role as cover or go-between in the female–female struggle to negotiate between sameness and difference. Helena Michie locates sororophobia in "the infinitely capacious figure" of the "other woman" who assumes many conventional literary guises including that of "the mistress," "the lesbian," and "the doppelganger" (*Sororophobia* 10).[29] Among H.D.'s premier models for her fictional femmes fatales, Patmore – potential friend, lover, lookalike, and Aldington's mistress – encompassed all of the above.

Art may have influenced life in the case of Patmore's Romantic imaging. The wife of Coventry Patmore's grandson, her long, curling red-gold hair and soft features contributed to the flamboyant Pre-Raphaelite personae she cultivated in the London literary circle. Less talented than H.D., Patmore was nonetheless adopted as another muse figure to the Imagists; and despite H.D.'s more Attic pose, both women were often mistaken for sisters by outsiders. Patmore seems to have harbored a virulent strain of sororophobia toward H.D., heightened undoubtedly by H.D.'s artistic gift. Her homoerotic, and intensely personal, fictional memoir of Bryher and H.D., *No Tomorrow*, depicts H.D. as an irresistible siren who seduces and torments both men and women, suggesting that Patmore's attitude of envy and resentment and her alleged professions of love for H.D. were well founded. Patmore's mixed emotions toward the more talented and elusive muse of the Imagist circle must have contributed to her flagrant wartime affair with Aldington, which deeply hurt H.D.,[30] into a like articulation of sisterly conflict.

H.D.'s *Murex* inaccurately attributes the end of H.D.'s marriage to Bright Patmore's seduction of Aldington. Raymonde Ransome represses the memory of her husband Freddie's desertion for Mavis Landor, preferring to reside in postwar, postmarriage, psychic paralysis: "this late cocoonblur of not thinking" (96). She is, however, rudely shaken out of her lethargy by the appearance of Ermy (Ermentrude Solomon), whose own husband absconded with Mavis, and who is eager to commiserate. Ermy's insistent proddings force Raymonde to re-member Mavis Landor and eventually release Raymonde from her writing block by returning her to a boyish Spartan, writerly "identity" bearing no trace of resemblance to her sensual double.

Re-membering Mavis Landor (whose fictional name retains Patmore's connection to a Romantic poet) involves reconstructing her as a monstrous femme fatale, a Medusan body whose image rends Raymonde from her cocoon-blur into acute and bloody body consciousness:

> Mavis was a thread that ran on and on and through and through and to jerk that one highly flavored thread out of her life's fabric meant ravelling edges, meant odd searing gash and tear in a fabric of London life that was as her very nerve and vein, fabric of her very body. (101)

Raymonde's Freddie and Ermy's lost husband remain shadowy figures – "It was not any definition of any young man [that Raymonde was seeing in her imagination]. . . . it was the three . . . women" (117). Mavis, however, is depicted with somatic vehemence amid fragmentary references to the "overflowered 1890s," as she evolves from the "supersensual" Flora of Botticelli's *Primavera* to more threatening visions of "a Frankenstein, a creature half-formulated and . . . dangerous," a "hydra-headed" "monster," a "siren to sink ships," a "Circe" weaving the "web of deception" and a Medusan creature who only has to "look" at her victim in order to enthrall him/her (107, 131, 163). In keeping with the contradictions of sororophobia, Raymonde finds herself gripped by a compulsive desire to merge in one body with her dark rival – to "be" her and hers – which erupts in the form of several increasingly urgent questions about the two women's alleged resemblance to one another:

> You think I'm like her? . . . People used to say so. [105] . . . Do you think I'm like Mavis? . . . Do you think, Ermy, that I'm like her? [111] . . . My husband used to say I was somewhat . . . Do you think so? Do or don't you think I'm like Mavis? [112] . . . I seem to have asked you a dozen times and got no answer. Do or don't you think I'm like Mavis? [114]

Even Raymonde cannot understand her obsessive need to identify with Mavis: "Whatever could it matter that she, Raymonde, was or wasn't like this Mavis? . . . Whatever could it matter that she stung, that she prodded Ermy with it?" (114) And when Ermy belatedly responds after a sudden moment of recognition, "Yes, you might have been her sister," Raymonde seems more pained than comforted (125). Further, Raymonde admits to having been entranced herself by Mavis Landor. She too submitted to the vampire's seductive female "gaze." When Ermy recalls, "but she said she loved *me*," Raymonde remembers her own thralldom to the Medusan body: "This [was] also a recurrent hydra . . . Raymonde had heard just that . . . 'you're so young, so alluring. I don't see how anyone can help loving you,' Raymonde heard the low purr of Mavis" (109).

Raymonde's complex relation to Freddie's former mistress cannot be explained solely as a dynamic of conventional, feminine jealousy (whatever that may be); and H.D.'s relation to the "other" woman in *Murex* is more overtly homoerotic than René Girard's narrative theory of "mimetic desire" in the love triangle would allow. Although *Murex* concludes with Raymonde's joyful rediscovery of her rigorous writerly "self" in the form of the helmeted, Greek, boy mask, "Ray Bart," Raymonde's determination to find a writer's refuge in the cool Swiss mountains is reminiscent of Apollo's escape from the russet femme fatale into the memory of Hyacinth "up on the mountain ledge." Raymonde's apparent flight from the dev-

astating aftereffects of her marriage may also be interpreted as a flight from
the violence and passion of the loved female body.

IV   The Siren Revisited: Elizabeth Siddal and
Greta Garbo

During H.D.'s involvement with Kenneth MacPherson and avant-garde
cinema, the rampaging, projectile, bodies of film burst upon H.D.'s consciousness like a ravening Medusan body even as she was reading Hunt's
biography of the Pre-Raphaelite femme fatale, Elizabeth Siddal (before its
1932 publication). H.D.'s poem, "Projector II," marveled at the savage,
writhing, welter of "bodies" thrown against the screen: "shape/upon num-
berless shape / to spring and bear upon us, writhe / and rear . . . / light
that sears and breaks / us / from old doubts / and fears / and lassitudes"
(CP 355, 353). In her prose and film essays, H.D. attributed the disruptive
power of these surging "shapes" to the feminine, and particularly to the
screen siren's self-created tumult of masks that formed a "new" language
of the female face and body. Freud would help to dispel H.D.'s anxieties
toward the Decadent femme fatale, reconciling her both to her bisexuality
and her "mother-fixation." However, film visualizations of the female
body and Hunt's biography of Elizabeth Siddal were already predisposing
H.D. to the erotic, linguistic, and political impact of the Decadent femme
fatale that would find expression in Trilogy (composed 1942–4), Helen in
Egypt (composed 1952–5), and her Pre-Raphaelite novels (1946–8) from
over a decade later. Indeed, when H.D. began to form plans for her fictional autobiography based on Elizabeth ("Lis") Siddal's life, she first "visualize[d]" the work as a "play" or "film" in which she "could imagine
Greta Garbo (and only Garbo) as Lis" (Compassionate Friendship 81).

The broiling images of Violet Hunt's silent, unconventionally beautiful
Siddal may have already entered H.D.'s imagination as she wrote her rev-
erent essay on Greta Garbo's intense, enigmatic "Venusian" beauty in "The
Cinema and the Classics."[31] Nearly ten years after H.D.'s first encounter
with Wife of Rossetti, she proudly acknowledged the profound influence of
Hunt's biography on her "White Rose and the Red." She wrote in a letter

to Pearson, "*Rose* . . . has meant a great deal to me; I felt I had taken right over from Violet Hunt, whom I knew; she knew all of them and I give tribute to Violet in a note, as *I felt myself part and parcel of her own book Wife of Rossetti* – the title of which I gave her" (August 27, 1948; emphasis mine). Despite Hunt's apparent intention in *Wife of Rossetti* to recount Siddal's physical deterioration at the hands of the neglectful, adulterous Rossetti and the Brotherhood, her meticulous inscription of Siddal's proud, grotesque, and disintegrating beauty brings "the real [female] body violently to life in the words of the book" (Wittig 10). Like Gilbert and Gubar and countless writers and critics, Violet Hunt, and subsequently H.D., clearly perceived Siddal's garish self-invention as emblematizing "the unhealthy energies, powerful and dangerous arts" that emit from the "monstrous" woman artist's "very freakishness" (*Madwoman* 29).

Not only did Hunt's life of Siddal reintroduce H.D. to the imposing mythic and legendary masks of Pre-Raphaelite painting – Proserpina, Venus, Morgan La Fay, and others – but Hunt's biography half-records, half-invents, in characteristically Pre-Raphaelite detail, a vivid and formidable portrait of the Decadent female body:

> "Miss Sid," as they came to call her, looked older than she was. More handsome than pretty, tall without being weedy, well-formed, with big white arms and neck almost too columnar. Her eyes were blue, the color of agate, egg-shaped, rather Eastern, pale and unsparkling . . . and prominent, so that she could not have worn a veil without fretting the eyelids. She had no eyebrows to speak of. Her upper lip was short and there was a cleft in the lower one. In repose the face seemed full of character, not all of it good, bearing at times an expression described . . . as sensual and at the same time starved. . . . (Hunt 31)

Like the legendary Garbo, Hunt's Siddal is evasive, solitary, and inscrutable, "she did not go out of the way to make . . . new people like her or feel at ease with her, confounding and puzzling them all by an obstinate withdrawal of personality. [She was] not friendly or chatty . . . turning off the talk the moment it became personal to herself" (45). A prose appreciation of Decadent, female abjection, Hunt's biography traces the "unravelling" (Hunt's word) of Siddal's body, ostensibly from tuberculosis and abuse, particularly as it intensifies the splendor of the Pre-Raphaelite woman's somatic distortions. For example, Hunt's re-creation of an imagined encounter between Siddal and the doctor who will diagnose her tubercular condition, occasions a rapt, spellbinding passage on the particulars of her long, "grotesque" body:

> Fatefully roseate, perniciously lovely, she waited . . . sitting very still, with half-closed eyelids. . . . The contour of the bosom was dissimulated under the plaited folds of her dress, the whole languid torso masked by its sheath of pliable whalebones converging to the low-placed, pointed waist. . . . He noted the long thin feet pushed out from under her skirts. . . . She did not use them much – they were as thin as her hands. He noted those, flabby and blue-veined, and the shape of the arms . . . out of proportion to the rest. . . . Long legs, long fingers, long throat, dullish prominent eyes, luxuriant hair – all characteristic of one type of what we now colloquially call T.B. Distinct curvature of the spine! (63)

Shortly before her death, the ravages of Siddal's disease as seen through Hunt's female gaze only serve to enhance the "cynical, sensual" contours of the Pre-Raphaelite woman's body, as if Dorian-like, the "Blessed Damozel" also undergoes the body's decadency:

> She . . . thinning with shrunk bosom and eyes more prominent than ever . . . in his drawings [Rossetti] registered with Pre-Raphaelite truth, the new outline, in sketches of the once beloved head, mostly pillowed, the bows of hair less opulently outspread, the forehead lined; twists instead of curves in the cynical, sensual mouth of the Blessed Damozel. (279)

By H.D.'s Pre-Raphaelite enterprise in the mid-1940s, she was responding strongly to the somatic jolt issuing from Hunt's Siddal. She made careful notes on several of Hunt's references to Siddal's bizarre beauty. One entry painstakingly recorded various comments made by Siddal's contemporaries: "William Allingham wrote 'her pale face, abundant red hair and long thin limbs were strange and affecting – never beautiful in my eyes' . . . Brown's brief record: 'Saw Miss Siddal, looking thinner and more deathlike and more beautiful and more ragged than ever" ("Notes on Pre-Raphaelites" 38). H.D.'s "White Rose and the Red" (third draft) includes a passage in which Rossetti explains to Siddal that she resembles the women pictured in the horrific "old frescoes from the *campo santo* at Pisa . . . that had started them in their [Pre-Raphaelite] ideas" . . . "And she . . . who [was considered] 'strange and affecting but never beautiful' was like those people on the *campo santo* walls." H.D.'s Siddal recognizes the power of horror in the frescoes that she seems to inhabit. Examining "The Triumph of Death," which dramatizes a hunting party's sudden discovery of three decomposing bodies in a ditch, Siddal muses, "every daisy [was] showing separate[ly] in the grass . . . the look of sudden horror on the faces of the first two [in the party] is intended to make you feel some kind of like horror, seeing a decomposing body . . . the picture . . . might make you feel things" ("White Rose" 76–8).

"Greta Garbo," H.D. wrote in the late 1920s for the film journal *Close Up,* "as I first saw her gave me a clue, a new angle and a new sense of elation. This is beauty and this is a beautiful . . . young woman" ("C. and C." 28). One can easily divine the reasons for H.D.'s association of the Greta Garbo that had given her a "new angle" on beauty with the Pre-Raphaelite prototype of the femme fatale, Elizabeth Siddal. Both women were considered to be sirens, of unconventional, larger-than-life beauty, silent almost to insolence, and in possession of an intensity that radiated beyond the frame (celluloid or picture) of the male gaze. H.D.'s Garbo evinces a rare, enduring "classic" beauty – like "the famous Medician Venus" – in her "mermaid's straight stare, her odd magic quality of almost clairvoyant intensity" (33). H.D. castigated the Hollywood moguls whose attempts to mold Greta Garbo after the conventional "vamp" nearly "eclipsed" her with "pseudo-Lillian Gish affectations," "wigs," and "eyelashes"; but H.D. maintained that "the screen . . . in spite of all the totems must finally respond" to Garbo's "mermaid enchantment" (33).

Other women film critics and literary scholars have written separately on Garbo's and the Pre-Raphaelite woman's similar appeal to an overweening female text. In "Greta Garbo: Sailing Beyond the Frame," Betsy Erkkila notes Garbo's ability to "lose" the "male magus" and "shape the film in her own self-generated image": Becoming "the author as well as the actress of her own myth," "she directs her energies away from the erotic plot toward an other female being beyond the frame."[32] Similarly, Nina Auerbach stresses the power of the Pre-Raphaelite woman's insistent muscular physicality and of her hypnotic "trance," which shakes "off the idiom of victimization along with the cover of the looming male magus"

(Auerbach 39). Among other things, H.D.'s simultaneous fascination with Garbo and Elizabeth Siddal indicated that she now willingly met the "entrancing" gaze of the "other" woman.

Moreover, H.D.'s revelatory experience of Greta Garbo had taken place against a screen backdrop of eerie abjection which, like Pater's Mona Lisa, Garbo soulfully exceeds and contains. H.D. vividly recalled her first sight of Garbo wandering through the urban wreck of postwar Vienna past an amputee in the opening of the little known film, *Joyless Street:* "The performance began with a street (will I ever forget it) and the sombre plodding limp of a one legged old ruffian" ("C and C" 30). Garbo appeared,

> stepping frail yet secure across a wasted city. . . . Before our eyes the city was unfolded, like some blighted flower, like some modernized epic of Troy town is down, like some mournful and pitiful Babylon is fallen, is fallen. . . . [She was] Helen walking scatheless among execrating warriors, the plague, distress and famine is in this child's icy mermaid-like integrity. (28, 31)

H.D.'s Garbo, like Siddal, conjured images of legendary enchantresses – Venus, Helen of Troy, the mermaid/siren. Most striking, H.D.'s lasting impression of Garbo, posed against the "hell" of a wasted city, anticipated *Trilogy's* vision of a female age in which reviled Venusian femmes fatales step "frail yet secure" across the panoramic sweep of war-wracked cities and reeling, abject bodies. H.D. herself played a frozen siren, Astrid, in MacPherson's avant-garde film, *Borderline,* complete with heavy, Garbo-like makeup, dark intensity, and passionate (sometimes bloody) scenes.[33] H.D. hoped that Astrid, like Ibsen's femme fatale, Hedda Gabler, would shine through her character's frenzies and "petty jealousies" – "astral."[34]

In her essay, *Borderline,* H.D. labeled film "the most modern art of portraiture in movement" (19); and H.D.'s new experience with the camera focused her on the incremental details of female figuration that had formed a "language" in Victorian writing and painting. As Hilary Schorr comments in her paper on Victorian fiction and Pre-Raphaelite art, "so often in reading for a plot . . . we come to be reading for a face."[35] Fascinated, H.D. watched Kenneth MacPherson work on "1,000 little sketches for some months [before filming], until there was not one angle of a face, scarcely a movement of a hand or fold of drapery that he had not pre-visualized" (*Borderline* 16). Animated, the female frames of *Borderline* struck H.D. as a jump cut of differential details from Botticelli's *Primavera* in which setting, face, and body all participated in the implicitly feminine drama: "It is odd to associate Botticelli with the cinema but that association is inevitable in some of the interior scenes [of *Borderline*], for instance of Astrid and her shawl. . . . Women . . . are embroidered with delicacy, as that head of [*Primavera's*] Adah against rock-flowers, or they are gouged out with a . . . fury, like the tragic face of Astrid" (18). Her comparison of *Borderline's* Astrid to the enchantresses of Botticelli brought H.D. a step away from the Pre-Raphaelite femme fatale, whose careful rendering and haunted faces moderns such as Yeats often associated with Botticelli. And later, in H.D.'s "Notes on Pre-Raphaelites," she used the film idiom to comment on Pre-Raphaelite portraiture: Noting Rossetti's technique of making "innumerable sketches" of Siddal's face before attempting *Beata Beatrix,* H.D. referred handily to film rhetoric (while remembering, perhaps, Mac-Pherson's sketches): "large face studies = 'close-ups' " ("Notes on Pre-Raphaelites" 13). Further, H.D.'s actual discussion in *Borderline* of film's ability to revive the "stamp" of a "weathered" written language or narrative, uses the powerful register of a legendary demon woman's body by way of example. Demonstrating the ability of film semiotics to render the tired expression "flying upstairs" as "winged," H.D. isolates a dramatic moment in the life of a modern-day Pandora:

> We must see a woman at the foot of a staircase, Lulu, for instance, in Pabst's *Box of Pandora,* and then we must see the entire staircase, perhaps slightly tilted, to give effect of dizzy eminence or of the state of mind of that woman, say in the case of Lulu, waiting to fly up it. . . . The camera . . . shows us that, actually, in vision or retrospection or in anticipation, we "fly" upstairs at a given warning or given signal. (27)

V "The Most Modern Art of Portraiture in Movement": Screen Beauty in Bid Me to Live

The proliferating, zooming shapes of "female" film narrative, H.D.'s "mermaid" Garbo, and the Pre-Raphaelite femme fatale come together in Julia's "first intimation of screen beauty" at the turning point of H.D.'s World War I memoir, *Bid Me to Live* (written intermittently between 1939 and 1950). Clearly drawing on her own discovery of a new Venusian "beauty" in film and Pre-Raphaelite portraiture, H.D. located her war-ravaged heroine's experience of visionary self-realization in her first apprehension of screen beauty at the movie theater Julia attends with Cyril Vane (based on Cecil Gray). The "hell" of ravaged bodies in the theater recalls the war ruin that foregrounds H.D.'s first sight of Garbo in *Joyless Street,* or *Trilogy's* apocalyptic vision of ravened cities and saving Venusian bodies configuring a cultural form of female self-realization. While the curtains are drawn over the screen at intermission, Julia likens the movie house's "smoking" "pit" of wounded soldiers to a Dantean hell:

> The theater lights . . . showed the thousand uncovered heads, all alike, smoothed back, here and there a white arm in a sling. For the most part, the arms in slings wore khaki bandages. That is what she [Julia] saw.
> She was gazing into a charnel-house, into the pit of inferno. . . . Heavy dusty maroon velvet had mercifully slid across the veil of the temple, where just a moment since, a miracle of light and shadow had embroidered in luminous threads the garment of a goddess. (126)

The theater's antique, garish, velvet maroon curtains whose parting reveals "the garment of a goddess," must – perhaps unconsciously – harken back to the Decadent atmospheric touching of parting, velvet "wine-colored" curtains in *HER's* more ambiguous scene of vampiric, female seduction. Screen Beauty herself unreels before Julia in animate, eerily Decadent Pre-Raphaelite frames, from the opening pan of her "tapestried," "flat flowers," "magnified under glass" to such Venusian, Pre-Raphaelite accessories as the dressing table, the diadem, and the looking glass. Among the swamping, protean female masks attributed to Screen Beauty by an enchanted Julia are Botticelli's enchantresses and popular subjects of Pre-Raphaelite art, Venus, the mermaid siren, and the dark myth of Proserpina/Demeter.[36]

> The garden was tapestried in . . . leaves and flat flowers. The flowers were large (magnified under glass) in her hands, Persephone in Enna. She turned and a wind caught the fluttering stuff of the scarf. She twisted it suddenly round her head. Now she was a hooded woman, Demeter, looking out.

She was watching from the rocks (Primavera with her flowers). (*Bid Me* 124, 125)

Julia's homoerotic commune with the movie vamp offers another example of the female viewer "en-tranced" by the dark, seducing face that looks back at her. In the continuation of the passage, Screen Beauty transforms into a drenched, "mermaid" "Venus" "regarding the face the same face" in the mirror, and donning a shimmering, teardrop corona of gems, hence joining the several masks of women "looking," "watching," "regarding," and reflecting Julia's "gaze" in her screen vision:

> She [Screen Beauty] runs back to the house, the screen darkens, she peers through a window: outside, rain twists the branches of palm-trees. . . . She climbs marble steps out of a fairy tale. She is a mermaid. . . . She emerges; drowning, she staggers toward her mirror. Pushing back the wet stuff of the palpably mermaid garment, she regards the face, the same face from a mirror. Venus and the looking glass, Persephone in Enna, Primavera. . . .
>
> Softly, to the tune of out-moded aria, she pushes back the dark hair from the white forehead, and as the screen veers to show her reflected image at still closer range, one sees the flower-scattered rain-drops on her face. The camera swerves, the flower-tears have vanished and she lifts, as if in replica, to replace them, a diadem of brilliants. (125)

Later in the novel, a deliberately parallel "scene" articulates Julia's transformation from postwar, postmarriage, psychic paralysis to erotic self-realization. H.D. takes Julia through a simulation of the screen goddess's passage from a storm-swept Pre-Raphaelite garden, upstairs to a Venusian dressing table and haircomb. Turning female camera "eye"/cinematographer, H.D. incorporates the ornate, glassy detail attending the Pre-Raphaelite Screen Beauty and the swerving, zooming effects of film semiotics to speak the deluging language/bodies of Julia's newly discovered self. Like Screen Beauty, Julia begins her quest in a Pre-Raphaelite landscape (surrounding Cyril Vane's country cottage). There she becomes "see-er," " 'priestess,' " "wise woman with her witch-ball" in a female world of enchantment and sensuality (147):

> There was a strange static quality, the ivy was cut out for a stencil, each leaf was separate and moisture settled symmetrically like rain-drops in a *Pre-Raphaelite painting*. The green showed like green in stained-glass and the

yellow of the occasional early clusters of gorse-blossom was gold glass. Her perception was sharpened, yet she was not thinking. (151, 152; emphasis mine)

As a storm descends and Julia escapes into the house, H.D.'s language deliberately evokes the reeling film semiotics of the earlier passage in which Screen Beauty emerged a dripping "mermaid" Venus, to sit at her dressing table. (Interestingly, H.D.'s reference to Julia's being "blown into [the] door" seems an attempt to conjure the fresh "stamp" of film "language" which revives "weathered" expressions such as "she flies upstairs" through visual details and cues):

> [Julia] lifted the latch. She slid into a darkened space. . . . Her heart was beating, she must have run that last bit. . . . Everything zoomed as if breakers were washing over a ship . . . The stairs had no banisters. . . . She was blown into [the] door, the elements were with her. She would drip away to a pool of water on this hall floor, like some lady from the sea, fairy-tale mermaid. She was so happy. She was so cold. . . . She felt her way, in the dim bedroom upstairs. . . . She felt for the dressing-table in the dark, brushed at damp hair. (152, 154, 155)

Chapter Six

From Agon to "Héros Fatale"

Pre-Raphaelite Transformations of Male
Modernism/Modernity

Even as Freud compelled H.D. to rediscover the daughter's love for the mother, he also brought about a necessary redefinition of the father: Loving the mother enabled H.D. to imagine a marginalized male culture of sympathetic fathers and brothers ouside the punitive Law of the Father that seemed everywhere in male modernism/modernity.[1] If the later H.D. refigured the mother after the abject femme fatale – H.D. raved over Swinburne's *Lucretia Borgia* shortly after she began *Helen in Egypt* – she reconceptualized the father/brother as a twin-deject after the Pre-Raphaelite *"héros fatale."* Like H.D.'s Helen, the exiled Achilles of *Helen in Egypt* enters the Egyptian scene similarly attired in abjection. "The Body, / wounded, stricken," lamed by the arrow that lodged in "the bruised and swollen flesh" of his vulnerable heel, Achilles limps after "the bereft" femme fatale.[2] She then proceeds, as DuPlessis succinctly observes, "to perform a rescue operation" on Achilles, releasing him from the "iron ring" of a proto-Fascism and accommodating him back to the mother Thetis ("Romantic Thralldom" 417). H.D. specifically linked the "Achilles of the Helen sequence" with what she described as *"the héros fatale"* of her Pre-Raphaelite novels, which included "The Sword Went Out to Sea" and "White Rose and the Red" (*Compassionate Friendship* 30). No longer poising herself as boy in relation to a Greek homoerotic continuum of her male contemporaries, H.D. pronounced the Pre-Raphaelite woman's feminine (male) double, "Le *Prince Lointain*," to be her latest "personification of the lost companion, the twin" that had appeared with "each turn of [her life's] spiral" ("The Sword" 119). In *Trilogy,* composed before "White Rose and the Red," but after H.D.'s "revival" had begun, H.D.'s "straggling company" of artist-dejects and survivors of Fascism include both women and men scriptors of the feminine who voyage through war-torn cities toward epoch-shattering visions of female prophets. H.D.'s reabsorption of her male contemporaries back into the Pre-Raphaelite cult of womanhood in "White Rose and the Red," *End to Torment,* and other works, involved a dramatic reconstitution of the father/brother agon depicted in such narratives of gender anxiety as *HER, Paint It Today,* and *Murex.*

Indeed, H.D. now adopted William Morris as her "guardian spirit" and associated him with the feminine side of the art/science binary that had earlier divided *HER's* remote, forbidding, Professor from the Swinburnian myth of mother/sister love. "This 'William Morris' father might have sent me to an art school," she wrote in an entry of her "Hirslanden Notebooks" (February 3, 1957), "but the Professor of Astronomy and Mathematics . . . wanted . . . to make a higher-mathematician of me, a research worker or scientist" (26). H.D.'s fantasy of Pre-Raphaelite reparenting extended back to her childhood in Pennsylvania, reconstituting *HER's* divisive sex/gender affiliations. Hermione had "disproved science" by opting out of the conspiratorial Law of the Father that aligns the Doctor, Lowndes-Pound, and brother, Bertrand-Gilbert, against the mother, Eugenia-Helen, and the "sister," Fayne-Gregg. H.D. continues to "disprove science" (patriarchy), but her Pre-Raphaelite locution of "origins" relocates the early "Ezra" and father on the side of art and the feminine under the protective auspices of the spirit-father, Morris: "This is my guardian, the god-father that I never had. But I did have him. I was ten when he died. . . . a little later Ezra Pound read the poetry to me. . . . my father had made a bench for my room, some book-cases downstairs, from William Morris designs" ("Hirslanden Notebooks" 26). Similarly, in H.D's Pre-Raphaelite scripts – "White Rose," *End to Torment,* and other works – the paternal/fraternal agon no longer opposes Romanticism in the charged Romantic-versus-modern configuration, but masks variously as the "feminine" Morris (Lawrence), Rossetti (Aldington), Pound (Swinburne), and the "*héros fatale*" of a "brother" tradition. (It must be remembered, however, that H.D.'s characters – including herself – are of course fictions and therefore do not correspond exactly to their "real" prototypes or may be composites of several people or personal identities. I am concerned here with H.D.'s enabling or disabling transformations of the principal living sources of her acute poetic and sexual anxiety.)

As a narrative of authorship anxiety, H.D.'s circular histories appear to trace a Bloomian triad of personal identities from the earliest "H.D," young protégé to the Romantic Pound,[3] turned his rebel antagonist (*HER*, *Paint It Today*), and finally his conciliatory twin-quester for the mother muse ("White Rose and the Red"). H.D.'s scripts thus proceed through the Bloomian, basically tripartite grouping of phases from youthful admiration through misprision/rejection, to reabsorption of the "father" – which translates for H.D. as male modernity.

However, H.D.'s regrouping of her male contemporaries around the nineteenth-century cult of womanhood also represents an ambitious scheme for a continuous feminine tradition rooted in the Pre-Raphaelite past. H.D.'s scheme appears to have been facilitated by her new conviction that only a collective return of both male and female modernists to the subversive feminine masks of Pre-Raphaelitism would provide the antidote to a fallen male modernism/modernity. Indeed, after living with the male modernist consensus on the "tragic generation" of "lost Romantics" for much of her career, H.D. arrived at the same – albeit more compassionate – conclusion regarding her male modernist contemporaries. The advent of World War II, Pound's Fascist sympathies, and other misdeeds of male modernism affirmed H.D.'s lifelong belief that the male modernist "swerve" from Romanticism had been tragically misdirected. H.D.'s literary transposition of her male contemporaries from agon to Romantic "*héros fatale*," however, conveyed her growing faith that despite past mistakes, the entire "straggling company of the brush and quill" became allied dejects under the inhumanity of the "new heresy," and that it remained for the long-desecrated woman artist to lead her dispossessed brother across the divide of changing epochs (*CP* 568, 517).

Notably, H.D.'s new myth of origins continues to counter male, anti-Romantic cultural schemes of modernism. We recall that *HER*, H.D.'s earlier contending feminine script of Romantic origins, pits a nostalgic account of a former self under the empathic influence of Swinburne against Eliot's contemptuous tale of adolescent surrender to a demonic Shelley. Similarly, H.D.'s later elision of male modernism for a cultural return to

Pre-Raphaelitism in "White Rose and the Red" continues to challenge the grand schemes of later male modernism that focus conversely on eliminating the Romantic movement as an aberration in modern memory. And as we shall see, the Pre-Raphaelite cult of the femme fatale that informs H.D.'s late epics continues to guard against the anti-Romantic myth of manhood typified by male epics such as the earlier *The Waste Land*. In Eliot's war epic, World War I further debilitates a modern Europe still languishing from the sexually degenerate past imaged by such fatal "Waste Land" inhabitants as the femme fatale in "A Game of Chess": "Unstoppered, lurked her strange synthetic perfumes, / Unguent, powdered, or liquid – troubled, confused / And drowned the sense in odors . . ." (*The Waste Land*, II, lines 87–9). H.D.'s World War II strategy to encourage a cultural revival of Romanticism and simultaneously save the male modernists from themselves by offering them the gift of their former Romantic personae, takes several forms in the later prose and poetry. Apart from the poetic rescue operations performed on Achilles-Aldington, Paris-Pound, and others, conciliatory gestures toward Aldington, Lawrence, and Pound abound in H.D.'s later notebooks and novels in the form of "open letters," tributes, and various written admissions of "compassionate friendship" – often openly urging them toward the feminine (sometimes termed as the "*gloire*" or "fiery moment").[4] Stamped " 'nonutilitarian' " (*CP* 517) by the World War II sensibility they had mistakenly facilitated, H.D. now considered her contemporaries to be disarmed and abandoned on the margins with the exiled woman writer. H.D. rejected the demon father/brother of her early work for the array of more complex and "wounded" paternal/ fraternal personae of the 1940s and 1950s, which would include the mysteriously wounded "Papa" of H.D.'s autobiographical *The Gift* (composed, 1941, 1943, 1944), the revised Christos of *Trilogy*, and the imprisoned Ezra Pound of her later works.

Ezra Pound, who was living in exile for his Fascist sympathies, best exemplified H.D.'s present specter of the ruined, outcast modernist she strove to recruit back into the feminine (Romantic) fold. The remainder of this chapter therefore focuses particularly on H.D.'s later Pre-Raphaelite rescriptings of Pound. Critics have often noted that Pound plays a pivotal role in *Winter Love, Helen in Egypt*, and *End to Torment* as the nonhierarchical "brother" lover to a type of H.D.[5] I will suggest that H.D.'s newly

equal brother–sister pairings of herself and her modernist contemporaries
as Helen–Achilles, Helen–Paris, and others, may be traced back to her
Romantic twinship of Pre-Raphaelite misfits, Swinburne (Pound) and Sid-
dal (H.D.) in "White Rose and the Red." Derived directly from Hunt's
Wife of Rossetti and the Romantic tradition of incestuous, rebel twins,
H.D.'s Romantic pairings resemble such famous renegade twins as Brontë's
Cathy and Heathcliff. It is particularly fitting that H.D. chose Swinburne,
her lifelong "brother" – precursor as a Pre-Raphaelite mask for Pound.
Like their Romantic precursors, H.D.'s Pound–H.D. doublings are often
physical twins, both possessing red hair and other transgressive or horrific,
Pre-Raphaelite body tropes that H.D. adapts to "speak" their shared feminine and monstrous, sexual/textual powers. Both Violet Hunt and later,
H.D., are thus among those modern women writers who draw upon Romantic abjection to articulate the subversive energies of the feminine male
as well as the female scriptor. I conclude this discussion by demonstrating
that the "fiery" sometime red-haired Child (Esperance) that proceeds from
H.D.'s imagined couplings of herself and Pound in a network of texts,
including *Winter Love, Helen in Egypt,* and *End to Torment,* is a figure for
the apocalyptic Romantic modernity of H.D.'s World War II cultural mythos. However, before moving to a discussion of Pound, I begin by briefly
surveying H.D.'s Pre-Raphaelite revisions of her contemporaries in "White
Rose and the Red."

I   *The "Feminization" of Male Modernism*

H.D.'s Pre-Raphaelite enterprise to rehabilitate her contemporaries' lost
Romanticism involved, among other things, reverting to the Romantic
literary personae recreated by the first phase of their own gendered scripts
of modernism – minus the crucial rupture with the Romantic foremother.
Indeed, "White Rose and the Red" reabsorbs male modernism back into
an edited and regressed version of the early modernist case histories. H.D.'s
Pre-Raphaelite versions of Pound, Aldington, and Lawrence therefore sus-
piciously resemble the early Romantic Yeats of "The Tragic Generation"
section of *Autobiographies,* for whom "Woman herself was still in our
eyes . . . romantic and mysterious, still the priestess of her shrine, our emo-

tions remembering the *Lilith* and the *Sybilla Palmifera* of Rossetti" (201). Both in his paintings and writings, H.D.'s Rossetti-Aldington ("White Rose and the Red") is not lost to a brutish war sensibility, but seeks the sympathetic female double of his (Rossetti's) short story, *Hand and Soul* (169). Further, Rossetti–Aldington's and Swinburne–Pound's "writings" of Elizabeth Siddal's body constitute an extraordinary articulation of feminine erotic and linguistic potentiality in which, as Auerbach observes of Rossetti's *Beata Beatrix,* "A woman's trance is the single medium of radical and magical change" (Auerbach 41). H.D. quotes approvingly and repeatedly from a source in her "Notes on Pre-Raphaelites" that *Beata Beatrix* is a " 'masterpiece' " – a " 'spiritual devotional,' " a " 'disembodied vision' " that is the " 'swan song of his [Rossetti's] own delicacy & depth of feeling' " (8). Similarly, "White Rose's" William Morris (a composite of Freud and Lawrence) finds solace and visionary self-realization in a feminine aesthetic of intricacy and detail. Contemplating the landscape, he regards "the strange flowers" as his "familiars." H.D.'s Morris "knew" "the foam of meadow-sweet, the flat pads of the elder-berry, the briar-blossom, . . . and the blue bergamot" the way the early beloved Aldington and Lawrence "knew" every flower of the English countryside (248).[6] At privileged moments, H.D.'s Morris shares in the woman's trance of Pre-Raphaelite painting – "That was his first great moment. Every leaf, every hedge-rose, every blue-bell stalk took form. A cluster of blossom detached itself from the maze of the thorn and became stylized, a theme for decoration" (208) – just as H.D.'s Julia in a parallel passage of *Bid Me to Live* is "see-r, 'priestess,' . . . wise-woman with her witch-ball, the world" reading the "Pre-Raphaelite" landscape at Corfu (147): "Here [the landscape was sketched] as minutely as a pattern on a leaf" (147). "There was a strange static quality, the ivy was cut out for a stencil, each leaf was separate and moisture settled symmetrically like raindrops in a pre-Raphaelite painting" (151).

Accordingly, H.D. rewrites her mentors' poetic program so that "make it new" applies (somewhat fantastically) to the feminization rather than the masculinization of art. Ironically, H.D.'s mentors now glibly denounce the *post*-Raphaelites' implicitly masculinist hard, scientific, precision in favor of the intricate play of color and embroidered line that so infuriated *Murex*'s Freddie-Aldington and his modernist prototypes for its resemblance to "wall-paper patterns." In the service of a feminine Aesthetic, Rossetti-Aldington sounds curiously like the modernist Pound energetically BLASTing the "effeminate" Victorian successors of early Romanticism: "Not that I don't like Raphael, it's them that followed after. And them that followed them that followed after," Rossetti complains. "Mechanical rules laid down by Reynolds," he scoffs, " 'block in your pyramid formation, regard your color and proportion it discreetly' " (55). Confronting Ruskin, Rossetti erupts, "Your damned professorial attitude," "[your way] of drawing precise lines before the application of color." "Let them have their fun with color. . . . was there any line in the firmament when heaven and earth created He them?" ("White Rose" 156).

H.D.'s reconception of her male contemporaries as Pre-Raphaelite scriptors of the feminine enabled her to implicate them in her own experience of the anxiety of authorship provoked by gender-biased critical attacks. Her research into the horrifying story of the devastation wrought by Robert Buchanon's censoring *Fleshly School of Poetry* on the Pre-Raphaelite poets not only affirmed H.D.'s own experiences of anxiety, but led her to a "brother" tradition of sex/gender anxiety of authorship which she would project on her male contemporaries. Thaïs Morgan has described Buchanon's attack on the Pre-Raphaelites as "perhaps the most famous and the most injurious case of the identification of mixed metaphor with immorality and sexual perversion"; and indeed it represents a male case study of authorship anxiety inflicted by patriarchal sex/gender socialization.[7] For as H.D. appears to have recognized, the Pre-Raphaelites reacted to the sexual/textual attack on their "effeminacy" with a classic bout of feminine anxiety of authorship, replete with its symptomatic self-projections of the writer as monstrous, unnatural, and diseased.

H.D.'s notes on the Pre-Raphaelites, mined from her mass reading of every biography she could uncover, and guided by a hunt for Pre-Raphaelite analogues to her own experience, carefully record Buchanon's characterization of the Pre-Raphaelites as sexual misfits: "[Buchanon's] attack aimed at Swinburne, R. [ossetti] & Morris. Compared to Baudelaire's *Fleurs du Mal* and Marquis de Sade's *Justine*," H.D. notes, quoting immediately afterward Buchanon's seething judgment of their writing as the repository for " 'abnormal types of diseased lust and lustful disease' " (11). (Indeed H.D. might have recognized Buchanon's accusations against the

Pre-Raphaelite's "morbid deviation from healthy forms of life" (Buchanon 34) in Eliot's identical moral assault on Swinburne's "departure from language in a healthy state," or even Douglas Bush's recent tirade against H.D.'s own "waxen," "unhuman" textual "world of the feminine eye and the feminine heart" (Bush 501).) H.D.'s subsequent catalogue of Rossetti's various maladies reconstructs a parallel case history or worst-case scenario that more than affirms the writing blocks and neurotic symptoms inflicted upon H.D. by her critics. Observing that Buchanon's "attack" took place in "Autumn, 1871" and "circulated later with additions, in pamphlet form," H.D.'s notes on Rossetti continue in an inevitable tone: "Now follow delusions, paranoia, stamina shaken by *chloral* & alcohol." By "June, 1872," H.D. quotes from a source, Rossetti is judged " 'not entirely sane' " and "attempted suicide" at Roehampton "by laudanum" (11). Further detailing Rossetti's slow decline, H.D. notes that "in the last phase" of his life Rossetti's "persecution mania" results from the " 'ignorant [critical] abuse of 1850 & malicious abuse of 1872.' " The notes on Rossetti conclude succinctly, "romantic 'ruined greatness' – lives in seclusion at Chelsea" (13). Similarly, in H.D.'s notes on Swinburne she writes, "July 1 – 1866 – *Poems and Ballads* were printed & withdrawn almost immediately, *vendetta* to suppress poems" ("vendetta" is underscored angrily in red). "From 1866," she notes, Swinburne's "semi-epileptic" "attacks . . . occur fairly regularly" (27). H.D. was also well aware that like her, the Pre-Raphaelites were still submitted – posthumously – to what Rossetti's niece described to H.D. in a letter as the " 'muck-raking' " " 'fiction' " published about them during "the thirties."[8]

Finally, H.D.'s imagined scenarios of her male mentors hotly defending Romanticism appear less extraordinary beside the real-life irony of Aldington's own Bloomian reconciliation with the Romantic past in the midforties. Although H.D. had already been rereading the Pre-Raphaelites for several years, Aldington's fervent return to Morris, Wilde, Pater, Swinburne, and others in 1945 coincided with the height of H.D.'s Pre-Raphaelite research project. When they began corresponding regularly in 1947, Aldington had so completely dropped his anti-Romantic rhetoric that it is hard to reconcile him with the cavalier modernist of H.D.'s *Murex* and *HER*. The Aldington of 1947, who was reverently working on an edition of Pater and another on Wilde, is a sensitive Aesthete. "They do

so hate beauty," he complains to H.D. of his publishers who won't agree
to an edition of Symonds. "These brutes," he continues, "I want to make
them take Oscar, Pater, J.A.S., the Nineties and realize what they have
destroyed, how inferior they are" (Aldington to H.D., May 14, 1947). (Is
this the Aldington who kicked the volume of Browning?) In another letter
to H.D. he describes his recent rereading of William Morris's quest romances "with intense gratitude." "Morris was a lovely person," he adds
(Aldington to H.D., June 7, 1947). The tone of intimacy that develops
between H.D. and Aldington during these exchanges on the Pre-
Raphaelites begins to resemble that of Aldington's moving letters from the
front during World War I.[9] Now assuming the Pre-Raphaelite masks of
Morris's heroic quester, Hallblithe – whom Aldington often mentions –
and Elizabeth Siddal – H.D.'s frequent subject of discussion – H.D. and
Aldington relive something of their old romance. Apart from affirming
H.D.'s mask of the *"héros fatale"* for her newly conceived male contemporaries and suggesting to her important Pre-Raphaelite symbols for her
prose such as "gold wings,"[10] Aldington's renewed enthusiasm also represented a relaxation in the strictures against Romanticism that had inhibited
her for much of her career. As critics such as Bloom, Bornstein, and others
observe, Yeats and even Eliot reconciled with their Romantic precursors
in the final phases of their careers.[11] In terms of the woman–centered model
of modernist influence anxiety I have been developing, this "opening" may
have indicated a new (male) orientation to the feminine that Elizabeth
Cullingford has suggested occurred in the later Yeats. However, for H.D.,
Aldington's reversal must have provided some recompense for her anxiety
and helped to reforge her severed ties with the London literary circle.
When H.D., in a 1952 letter to Pearson (August 8), exclaimed joyously
upon reading *Lesbia Brandon* that " 'the romantics' " had "come really back
... so now I can just get caught up in the tide, no more swimming against
the breakers," she had reason to believe it was true.

II Pound

Curious lies
have Filled your Heart,

and in My Eyes
Sorrow has Writ
that I am Wise (*CP* 178)[12]

H.D. had written Pound-Lowndes out of her early myth of Swinburnian androgyny in *HER*, but she very deliberately wrote him back into the Pre-Raphaelite mythos of her later poetry. Critics have observed that Pound's more favorable and frequent appearance in later works such as *End to Torment, Winter Love,* and *Helen in Egypt* may have arisen, in part, from their reconciliation during the period of his incarceration outside Pisa and subsequent confinement in Saint Elizabeth's (1945–58) (for pro-Mussolini radio scripts and broadcasts made from late 1940 to 1944) (*PW* 357). H.D. was among the few friends to remain loyal to Pound throughout his imprisonment. At his release, H.D. wrote in *End to Torment,* "It is the *feel* of things rather than what people do. It runs through all the poets, really, of the world. One of *us* had been trapped. Now, one of *us* is free" (44). In *HER, Paint It Today,* and *Asphodel,* Pound had been the type of anti-Romantic male modernity and the target of her greatest "anxiety." By the 1940s, H.D. regarded him as the prototype of the modernist-gone-wrong, and in spite of himself, the victim of a self-destructive war sensibility that turned everything – particularly poetry – to detritus. Writing of their early relationship and subsequent estrangement in *Winter Love,* H.D. allowed that, "true, there were others and you were ruthless / and too familiar – you married your Princess," ". . . afterwards, you left Ithaca for another, *Helen,* / Fate, Fortune, Defamation, / Treachery, Adultery, War."[13] His misbegotten odyssey ended in exile, "poor Ezra," as H.D. often referred to him in her letters, became the perfect type of the feminine deject, the "woman in the man" of her post-Freudian affections. Always a kind of twin brother from their shared adolescence in Pennsylvania, to Imagist fame, expatriation, and later their mutual composition of modern, epic war poems (in which each figured), Pound best exemplifies H.D.'s refiguration of the father/brother as the feminine, Romantic "instigator" of a New Age.

Like much of her later prose, the impassioned memoir/tribute H.D. wrote to Pound while she waited anxiously for his release from St. Elizabeth's, *End to Torment,* contained a political/sexual agenda for reconnection with the Romantic feminine past. H.D. was not alone in her belief that Pound's incarceration emblematized the plight of all artists during the World War II era. His status as poet and political exile moved several famous writers and artists to intercede on his behalf; and an article entitled "Ezra Pound 'Ressuscité' " in *Le Figaro Littéraire* (April 12) apparently strengthened H.D.'s conviction that "a great deal will be resurrected or reborn once Ezra is free. Consciously or unconsciously," she added, "it seems that we have been bound with him, bound up with him and his fate" (37). However, H.D. embedded a solution in her hopeful tribute to the best part of her modernist contemporary, and thus of her generation, by eliding the Imagist and post-Imagist Pound for the early Romantic Pound who exuberantly triumphs over all "torments" that may have motivated H.D.'s memoir. The title, "End to Torment," may therefore be interpreted both as a reference to H.D.'s fervent hope for Pound's release and to the curative for a war-tormented generation enacted by the text itself in its studious remembering of the Romantic past. "One esteems Ezra's Gaudier-Brzeska, Wyndham Lewis, Brancusi enthusiasms," H.D. nods fleetingly to Pound's Vorticist experiments, "but this is something different," she exclaims over an art book found among his possessions that recalls a more treasured Pound (and H.D.): "This seems a return to the early D. G. Rossetti and the *Vita Nuova* translation and the Pre-Raphaelite pictures that Ezra brought me. Concern with 'The Blessed Damozel' [by Rossetti]! Surely Ezra read it to me" (*End to Torment* 39). Released from her anxiety, H.D. gleefully acknowledges her early debt to Pound's Romantic influence, "It was Ezra who really introduced me to William Morris. He literally shouted 'the Gilliflower of Gold' in the orchard" (22, 23). This Romantic myth of poetic origins reinstates the agon of *HER* as the *"héros fatale"* of the early Romantic cult H.D also formed with Frances Gregg.

The graceless Lowndes-Pound embodied in *HER* exists largely to press down on Hermione with the weight of patriarchal Law as she struggles toward Fayne, the ethereal boy/girl, and white sister. However the Poundian body vigorously inscribed throughout *End to Torment* deliberately clones the *"héros fatale,"* George Lowndes "spoke" himself aesthetically through nasal parodies of Longfellow. Seeking to catch the boisterous cadences of the early Ezra Pound in *End to Torment*, H.D. chooses to "hear" him raucously quoting Morris's "Gilliflower of Gold" – "How did it go?

Hah! hah! la belle jaune giroflee" (23). This Pound is seen through familiar Romantic body images that dwell on the "sheaf" of his Swinburnian red hair and his likeness to William Morris and other Romantic poet questers. Although "there are very few left who know what he looked like" during their adolescence in Pennsylvania, H.D. likens him to a "tawny Swinburne," and repeatedly calls up the image of his striking "tawny" hair as a contrast to the aging prisoner: "He shakes his tawny head (wheat-colored, I have written and Ezra has written, 'a sheaf of hair / Thick like a wheat swath'), gone grey now, they say . . ." (36). Even Pound's daughter, Mary, inherits his Pre-Raphaelite hair: A photograph of Mary resembles the "girl in . . . [Rossetti's] 'Sister Helen,' " "with her hair, wheat-gold, flowing down over her shoulders" (35). Similarly, a recent "*radiophoto*" of Pound "reminds" H.D. "of William Morris" (40), and elsewhere Pound is described variously as "a composite" including "the victorious and defeated heros of the William Morris poems and stories" (23), and as "a synthesis of William Morris ['of the London period'] and Mark Twain ['of my early American background'] . . . *as I am*" (emphasis mine). Significantly, within the associative and circular patterns of *End to Torment*'s narrative, the Romantic Pound emerges as its hero redeemer, and H.D., remembering "myself then," as his *epipsyche*.

H.D.'s earlier "White Rose and the Red" more specifically identifies its composite Swinburne-Pound and Elizabeth Siddal-H.D. as brother-sister loves, further emphasizing the striking Pre-Raphaelite trope for transgression, red hair, and Swinburne's and Siddal's shared bodily "freakishness" to exemplify a communal, feminine sexuality/textuality. However, before discussing H.D.'s Romantic prototypes for her feminist mythos, I must stress the profound influence of Violet Hunt's initial pairing of Siddal and Swinburne in a cult of abjection (*Wife of Rossetti*), which very probably first alerted H.D. to the feminist possibilities of the grotesque femme fatale and her male twin.

As I mentioned earlier, H.D. proudly acknowledged that she considered her "White Rose and the Red" to have "taken right over from Violet Hunt, whom I knew." "She knew all of [the Pre-Raphaelites]," H.D. continued in a letter to Pearson, "and I give tribute to Violet in a note [the dedication], as I felt myself part and parcel of her own book *Wife of Rossetti* – the title of which I gave her" (August 27, 1948). As I observed earlier, despite Violet Hunt's clear intention to recount the physical "un-raveling" of Elizabeth Siddal at the hands of the neglectful, adulterous Rossetti and the Brotherhood, the progressively deteriorating and grotesque body of the Pre-Raphaelite woman she meticulously inscribes in *Wife of Rossetti* eclipses her tragic history of the tubercular "Lizzie" Siddal.

Like so many feminist writers and their critics, Hunt and, later, H.D. were attracted to Elizabeth Siddal because the myths surrounding her epito-mized the feminist paradoxes and authorship anxieties experienced by talented women among artistic "supermen." Although Hunt was a self-described New Woman, a successful author, and a social bridge be-tween the Pre-Raphaelite painters of her ancestry and the London literary circle, she perceived in Siddal an image of her own woman's body, battered by illness and her tormented relationship to Ford Madox Ford.[14] Similarly, H.D., who gave *Wife of Rossetti* its demeaned title, claimed that she ap-prehended in the conflicted Siddal both "something of [her] early search, [her] first expression or urge toward expression in art," and also of "[her] own emotional starvation" among the artists of the early London literary circle ("Delia Alton" 194). For many women writers then, Rossetti's ex-ploited model/muse, a failed artist whose painting and writing were triv-ialized by the famed Brotherhood, formed the perfect type of the gifted woman writer/writing silenced into art by the male artistic community. However, at the same time, Siddal, the original prototype of the garish Pre-Raphaelite woman, remains for many modern women writers and crit-ics the agent of a female sexual and creative energy that both feeds and somehow exceeds the Pre-Raphaelites' male text.[15] As I mentioned earlier, Gilbert and Gubar point to her body in portraits such as "The Blessed Damozel," and in the fables that grew up around her, as exemplifying the "unhealthy energies, powerful and dangerous arts" emitting from the "monstrous" woman writer's "very freakishness" (*Madwoman* 29).

Hunt invests this energy in the feminine male scriptor Swinburne, who, she takes pains to prove, formed a physical, spiritual, and writerly twinship with the similarly outcast Siddal during her illness. "She was the only woman in his life – ever," Hunt declares, "And it is odd that he, so violent, so emphatic, so really cold-blooded, should be anyone's hope and joy as he was hers" (*Wife of Rossetti* 258). Hunt bonds them in a feminine pact of dejection, which similarly invests Swinburne with the "energies, powerful and dangerous arts" of Siddal, the "monstrous" woman writer and her abject text. Hunt is particularly attentive to the red hair and bodily "deformity" that identifies them as spiritual twins in persecution, exile, and writerly transgression:

> Both Lizzy and he [Swinburne] were red-haired, both mined by diseases of the digestion, both poets, and both of ancient lineage. . . . The common disgrace of their hair was a bond, for, in those days, the shade entailed a certain mild degree of persecution, for was not the betrayer of Our Lord a red-headed Jew called Iscariot? Once a year, in Algernon's part of the world, the villagers turn out to stone the squirrels, bringing in so many head of "nasty Judases," and Fanny, the North-country woman on whom Lizzy had hardly set her eyes, . . . called her the "Cyprus Cat" while to Swinburne she alluded as "The Freak." (257, 258)

Textually as well as sexually they are body doubles: Both "worked up" their "poems," similarly, Hunt observes, "inserting and erasing . . . on long sheets of blue post paper, altering and re-altering them" (65). And bodily alteration – abjection – is the text of their song. The subjects of Siddal's poems are equated with those of the Decadent Poe, and Hunt makes a point of attributing Swinburne's (horrific) poem "The Leper" (in which a lowly scribe, formerly scorned by a high-born lady, finally possesses her as she degenerates from leprosy) to the poet's careful tending of Siddal "in illness": "He [Swinburne] settled down . . . to his pious task [of reading to the bedridden Siddal] with a kind of exaltation." Hunt glosses, "[he was] like Swinburne's lover tending his leprous mistress, 'Changed with disease, her body sweet, / The body of love wherein she abode . . . ' " (237). Hunt's own *Wife of Rossetti* may be described as an ode on feminine bodily/ writerly abjection, articulating the "monstrous" energies of its author through the agency of the Pre-Raphaelite woman and her misfit brother – also a composer of love songs to the abject female body.

H.D. was clearly struck by Hunt's abject twinship of Siddal-Swinburne, which influenced H.D.'s Pre-Raphaelite masks for herself and Pound in "White Rose and the Red" and *End to Torment* and, I am suggesting, formed the prototype for the modernist bands of brother–sister exiles in her late poems. H.D.'s debt to Hunt's biography is evident everywhere in her "Notes on Pre-Raphaelites," which liberally copy directly from *Wife of Rossetti.* H.D. notes, for example, that "Lizzie worked up her poems like S," that "S reads to Lizzie" during her illness (23, 24). Indeed, H.D.'s notes reveal her own search for further evidence of the erotic, creative "twinship." Referring to a series of Rossetti's large "face studies" of Siddal, she writes in parenthesis, "(effect on A.C.S.?)" (13). H.D.'s Elizabeth Siddal in "White Rose" is also the type of the silenced woman poet killed into art who, red-haired and grotesque in her Pre-Raphaelite beauty, wears her abjection like a badge. Further, H.D. recreates Pound-Swinburne as Siddal's "freakish" body/spirit double, borrowing directly from Hunt's twinning of the pair's red-hair and physical "deformities" down to Hunt's references to the exiled Judas and Siddal's defamatory nickname, "the cyprus-cat" (which H.D. alters to "civet-cat"; and we recall that H.D. was called "cat" by Bryher et al.): H.D.'s improvised scene in "White Rose" of a conversation between Morris and Siddal in which he reluctantly acquaints her with Swinburne's deformity, associates him with the childlike, arrested image of the woman writer as well as the freak. "He's hardly grown up yet. He was in Oxford with his tutor. . . . But he's – how shall I say? . . . His head grew but his body didn't: he's a . . ." (ellipses H.D.'s). "You need not say it," Siddal interrupts, "I can see him." While both visualize the apparently unspeakably grotesque misshapen body of Swinburne, they simultaneously arrive at his affinity to Siddal. Morris observes, "Algernon – he has hair like yours. . . ." To which Siddal, a clairvoyant, replies, "Yes, we might be related . . . they called him the fox, like they called me the civet-cat. Judas had red hair and they threw stones at Swinburne of Capheaton in Northumbria" (382, 383).

Moreover, H.D.'s notes seize upon Hunt's suggestion that Swinburne's "The Leper" was inspired by "Siddall [sic] in illness," "as suggested by V.T." – a repeated entry in her notes. The portion of the scribe's lament that H.D. records from this horrific poem about two deviants in exile, the one "leprous" in his necrophile desire/language and the other in her necrobiotic body – his text – may be seen both as an articulation of abject textuality and as an ode on female modernist anxiety:

Yea, though God always hated me.
It may be all my love went wrong –
a scribe's work writ awry and blurred,

scrawled after the blind evensong –
spoilt music with no perfect world. (H.D.'s quotation, "notes on
    Pre-Raphaelites" 25)

H.D.'s and Hunt's fascination with "The Leper" as evidence of Swinburne's and Siddal's pact of dejection reveals their preoccupation with the
abject body of the femme fatale. Kristeva includes the wounded, sickly,
and disintegrating body in her epistemology of horror, describing the
corpse as "the utmost of abjection"; and we recall that the Decadent cult
of the femme fatale frequently centers on the corpse as well as on sick,
dying, twisted, and languishing women.[16] Swinburne's ode to the leprous
siren focuses on the body's disfiguration and decay:

Her hair, half gray, half ruined gold,
Thrills me and burns me in kissing it;
Love bites and stings me through, to see
Her keen face made of sunken bones.
Her worn-off eyelids madden me,
That were shot through with purple once. (*P&B* I, 138)

Although Swinburne's poetry influenced H.D. throughout her career,
she began to perceive Swinburne himself as a twin or poet brother during
her Pre-Raphaelite period. H.D.'s discovery of his fictional autobiography,
Lesbia Brandon, and her comprehensive research into his life provided her
with analogues to her own career. Even as H.D. appeared to see her brief
celebrity as Imagist in Swinburne's "first startling and violent unexpected
success" (30) following publication of *Atalanta in Calydon,* H.D. bitterly
identified with the critical "vendetta" against the *Poems and Ballads* she
noted and underscored in her "Notes." H.D. found relief in the knowledge
that "apparently A.C.S. had some of the same sort of ideas and [writing]
delays" (letter to Pearson, August 8, 1952). It was at this time that H.D.
noted his implicit association with the H.D. of *Sea Garden*'s embattled
mythology of the elements (to which I alluded to in Chapters Two and
Five): "Buffeted by sea, swimming, bruises, struggle, salt-sting caused
young S. sensuous pleasure. Cruelty & beauty in S. as in sea. S. stoic in
face of elements. His own mythology . . ." ("Notes on Pre-Raphaelites,"
28). Further, H.D. encountered the Victorian fascination with the transgressive body troping of male–female doubles in Swinburne's fictional au-

tobiography, Swinburne's posthumously published *Lesbia Brandon* (1952). The book, which H.D. claimed in a letter to Norman Pearson had sent her into "an electric coma," was characterized by several sets of actual and figurative brother–sister twinnings and appears to have influenced H.D.'s *Helen in Egypt* begun just weeks later. Compared by critics to the first half of *Wuthering Heights,* Swinburne's sexual history casts himself as an actual twin desperately in love with his sister, Lady Whariston. The book opens with an erotic, pages-long description of their resemblance, which hovers over the rest of the narrative and includes the familiar red, "golden flame" hair. Notably, references to Swinburne's "Fragoletta" and "Hermaphroditus" are conspicuously absent from H.D.'s Pre-Raphaelite writings; her new emphasis on Swinburne's works such as the "The Leper" and *Lesbia Brandon* point toward her current interest in abjection, the fatal woman, and her male twin.

Finally, the striking Romantic trope of red hair, which forms a typology of transgression in H.D.'s *End to Torment* and "White Rose and the Red," extends to the "spirit Child," fathered by a recuperated Romantic Pound and H.D. in a series of her later works. If Pound's actual daughter Mary becomes a type of Rossetti's Pre-Raphaelite woman, "with her hair, wheat-gold, flowing down over her shoulders," in *End to Torment,* the recurring phantasm of Pound's and H.D.'s fiery, red-haired "Child" at the center of the narrative bears the genetic trace of a new Romanticism that H.D. would pass on to the future. A narrative of Romantic projections as well as origins, H.D.'s memoir/address to a lost generation inscribes the future apotheosis in the form of the imagined "Child" whose body articulates its Romantic inheritance in his wild red hair (like the "tawny Swinburne," like Pound). H.D. apprehends "a small, delicate yet sturdy male object. . . . His curls are short and red and gold. He is the 'fiery moment' incarnate" (*Torment* 33). Predating the later *End to Torment, Helen in Egypt,* and *Winter Love,* "White Rose and the Red" introduces the Pound-H.D.-child triad in their originary Romantic masks. Upon waking from the life-threatening stillbirth of her child, H.D.'s autobiographical Siddal sees Swinburne-Pound as a spiritual "double" and phantasmagoria of the child she lost: "opening her eyes on what she thought was death, she saw like a Child [Algernon], standing with a fiery halo . . . the child they had taken away was not dead. It was Algernon" ("White Rose" 545). Although this scene of Romantic primogeniture bypasses direct mention of the red hair so prominent elsewhere in the novel, the trope has progressed to the orange nimbus of a "fiery halo," later echoed by *End to Torment*'s reference to Pound's and H.D.'s imagined red-haired Child as "the 'fiery moment' incarnate." Indeed, a trace of the transgressive "red" yet remains in the flaming associative chain formed by each text's Pound-Child-H.D. trinity from the "fiery halo" ("White Rose"), become " 'fiery moment' " (*End to Torment*), become "wild moment" in Helen's "fantasy of Paris and a Child / or a wild moment that begot a Child," "Euphorian, *Esperance*" (*Winter Love* 112).

III "*Apophrades*": The Return of the Dead

First love and the poetic initiation mythologized by *HER* had not shielded H.D. from subsequent romantic losses, writing delays, minor and serious psychological incidents, and the critical enmity of modernist anti-Romanticism. H.D.'s Pre-Raphaelite myth of origins therefore spins a further, perhaps necessarily cultural rather than personal tale of survival. In terms of other recently suggested, advanced, feminist evolutionary schemes, H.D.'s Pre-Raphaelite script accomplishes Kristeva's third stage of feminism in Europe, "*insertion* into history," and would apply to DuPlessis's definition of the more enlightened feminist "exploration not in service of reconciling self to world [as in *HER*], but [of] creating a new world for the new self" ("For the Etruscans" 152).[17] H.D.'s tale of survival may therefore be said to have successfully written "beyond the ending"[18] of her earlier feminist text, surmounting the death wish that often follows inevitably upon the "awakening" in a patriarchal world. During her writing block of the 1930s, H.D. may have felt that her critics were killing her, another reason for the death wish that Friedman detects at the end of *Nights*, in which the heroine ice skates into oblivion – like Kate Chopin's Edna surrendering to the sea.

However, H.D. succeeded in generating another script and completing a feminist revisionary circle. The psychodynamics of H.D.'s Romantic refiguration of the father may be said to resemble Bloom's Freudian final phase, "*Apophrades*" ("the return of the dead"), in which the (male) poet

welcomes the agon, the dead spirits of (his) Oedipal desire to which love
always returns:

> The later poet, in his own final phase . . . holds his own poem so open
> again to the [agon's][19] work that at first we might believe the wheel has
> come full circle, and that we are back in the later poet's flooded appren-
> ticeship, before his strength began to assert itself in the revisionary ratios.
> But the poem is now *held* open to the [agon] where it once *was* open, and
> the uncanny effect is that the new poem's achievement makes it seem to
> us . . . as though the later poet himself had written the [agon's] characteristic
> work. (*Anxiety* 15, 16)

H.D.'s similar absorption of the father into her feminine canon through a
seeming rewriting of the father's work, however, involves a different theater of desire, I suggest, dependent upon the continued presence of the
pre-Oedipal mother. Whereas the success of Bloom's isolated father–son
face-off requires the mother's early exclusion from the arena in accord with
theories of male gender identity formation, H.D.'s discovery of the
"mother" in the "father" replicates Chodorow's theory of female identity
formation. According to Chodorow's model, the daughter's erotic attachment to the father is always experienced as a bisexual oscillation between
the daughter's primary and persistent love object, the mother, and the lately
discovered father.[20] Related to this, H.D. cannot summon the dead spirit-
father until she has deciphered the somatic "mother" in the "father," without which he is, culturally, only disembodied Law. H.D.'s rediscovery of
the Romantic twin and body double in her male contemporaries thus
achieves one of the "main projects in a reconstructive feminist criticism"
according to Patricia Yaeger (*Refiguring the Father*): to relieve the father
from his cultural symptom of "*asomnia*" or "bodilessness" by inscribing
him with both pre-Oedipal and Oedipal "plots" – in short, by mapping
the mother's body on the father.[21]

The progression of H.D.'s poetic/sexual anxiety from early dismissal of
"the father as Law" to reacceptance of the "woman" in the "man," may
also describe a general pattern in the lifelong gender narratives of other
twentieth-century women writers. Adrienne Rich's own refiguring of the
father does not occur until the later phase of the lengthy mother–daughter
quest narrative created by her several volumes of poems. In the volume

that purports to be a "re-vision" of past and present psychic landscape, "Your Native Land Your Life" (1986), Rich finally rediscovers her father in "the alien stamp" of the Jewish heritage they share. Looking back in "Sources," the poet admits to the earlier necessity of seeing the father through "an ideology. . . . which let me dispose of you . . . the Kingdom of the Fathers." "It is only now, under a powerful womanly lens," Rich's narrator emphasizes, that she can "decipher" "the suffering of the Jew" and "deny no part of my own."[22]

Despite H.D.'s more conventional inscription of male–female twinning, her transformed brother/father companion merely rejoins the woman poet in her unchanged aspiration toward a mother muse whose abjection spells a range of active and forbidden desires. Poetically, the maternal mythos of the abject femme fatale is most powerfully realized in H.D.'s World War II epic, *Trilogy* (composed 1942–4). Although *Trilogy* was written a few years before H.D.'s "White Rose and the Red," her myth of origins need not have been scripted in prose form before finding its way into her poetry. Indeed, H.D. had been thinking about Elizabeth Siddal and the Pre-Raphaelites for ten years before the poem's composition, just as she had mulled over her psychoanalysis with Freud for a decade before writing *Tribute to Freud*. And as we have seen, *HER* rescripts the sexual agenda of the earlier *Sea Garden*.

Trilogy's designation of the Venusian femme fatale as the leader of a Woman's Age most dramatically distinguishes it from her contemporaries' mythologies of abjection. Eliot's nightmare vision of bodily/cultural abjection in *The Waste Land* is, of course, attributed to the decadence of World War I and the (feminine) cultural legacy of the fin de siècle. H.D. returns to the female image of male modernism's greatest anxiety, while as we have seen in Kermode's *Romantic Image,* many male modernist (and New Critical) theories of the female body focused on "purging" the Romantic foremother of her threatening somatic/semiotic extravagances. I conclude this study with a discussion of *Trilogy*'s full-blown feminist poetic of the abject Venusian body.

Chapter Seven

Feminine Abjection and Trilogy

Recent postmodernist critiques of Yeats, Eliot, and others have explored male modernist deployments of the abject body in an attempt to reclaim poetic modernism from the closed conservative discourse of New Criticism. In *The Failure of Modernism,* Andrew Ross links the modernist "desire to reject old languages and create new ones" with the "response to the abject" he perceives in modern writers such as Pound, Joyce, Stein, Williams, and others. "Governed by a formal imperative to 'make it new,'" these artists "confront the body in new ways" (Ross 87). Enumerating T. S. Eliot's abounding poetic incidences of corpses, "female smells in shuttered rooms," and "subtle effluence[s]" and other bodily wastes, Ross claims that he could write an additional chapter on Eliot's female abjection alone (Ross 81). Similarly, Maud Ellmann (*The Poetics of Impersonality*) jubilantly tracks through the "wastes" of *The Waste Land,* cataloguing all the half-dead, liminal, dejected bodies that swarm through the poem. If waste is what a culture throws away in order to define itself, then the "dead" literary "echoes," cast-off butt-ends of the city's days and ways, and the female abjection of "abortions, broken fingernails, and carious teeth," spread like "contagion" through the poem to "the collapse of boundaries . . . be they sexual, national, linguistic or authorial" (Maud Ellmann 93, 94). Despite the postmodernist methodology, however, these skillful critiques do not argue that in Eliot's poetry, at least, such decentering activity is liberating or revolutionary. Maud Ellmann concludes that abjection in *The Waste Land* "signif[ies] the culture's decadence, as well as bodily decrepitude" and identifies it with "any ravaged center of a dying world," thereby confirming the modernist narrative of crisis and alienation long familiar to the New Critics (Maud Ellmann 93). Ross argues brilliantly that despite its struggle with issues of subjectivity and language, *The Waste Land* ultimately reasserts "purification" through religious authority.[1] As I will demonstrate, H.D.'s epic war poem, *Trilogy,* does not yield the same modernist narrative of despair. Unlike Eliot's collection of misfits from another war, H.D.'s "straggling company" of artist-dejects cannot be said to herald a dying modern world.

A poem of the explosive and exploded body, *Trilogy* is neither a lament for the dilapidation of culture nor a celebration of fascistic violence. Rather the World War II epic adheres to the resurgent power of the expelled, excluded "mat(t)er" that survives its militaristic purge.[2] *Trilogy's* burned out, sliced, and spewing bodies come crowding back from their attempted negation – littering, infesting, ingesting, and at the least, boldly exhibiting their splayed contents throughout the hostile body politic. The trajectory of this quest through abjection may be said to follow "the jettisoned object" – defined by Kristeva as that which "is radically excluded and draws me toward the place where meaning collapses" – across the heady divide of changing epochs (*Powers of Horror* 2). However, *Trilogy's* siege of abject bodies is powered specifically by the violent crossing into female signification, as the "dismembered" bodily "husks," "reviled" worm, and other variously feeding, ingested, and spewed out bodies of *The Walls Do Not Fall* implode into the female, blood-infused "bitter jewel" of the crucible (*Tribute to the Angels*) that conjures "venerous" and now "venerated" legendary femmes fatales – Venus, Bona Dea, and finally Mary Magdalene, in *The Flowering of the Rod.*

I   Abject Bodies

Beginning in Section One of *The Walls Do Not Fall,* the decapitated body of a bombed-out building displays its underbelly as "ruin / opens the tomb, the temple . . . the shrine lies open to the sky"; and in another "sliced" building, "poor utensils show / like rare objects in a museum." The body itself is laid open: "The flesh? it was melted away, / the heart burnt out, dead ember, / tendons, muscles shattered, outer husk dismembered, / / yet the frame held" (*CP* 1; 509, 510, 511). Unlike Eliot's listless inhabitants of *The Waste Land*, *Trilogy*'s dejects do not succumb to the virulent atmosphere, although noxious gas, *"dust and powder fill our lungs / our bodies blunder / . . . / we walk continually / / on thin air that thickens to a blind fog, / . . . . / and the ether / is heavier than the floor"* (43; 543; emphasis H.D.'s). But like Adrienne Rich's diver into the "wreck" of history ("Diving into the Wreck"), they learn to "breathe differently down here."[3] Rapt *"discoverers / of the not-known. / / the unrecorded,"* H.D.'s toxic bodies rove the sloping pavements, "drunk / with a new bewilderment, / sorcery, / bedevilment" (43; 543, 1; 510). Nor can the artist dejects be assimilated, even for the war effort: compared literally to litter, "crumpled rags," they're "no good for banner-stuff, / / no fit length for a bandage" (12; 520).

In the tutorial section of *The Walls Do Not Fall* (4–6), ingested, feeding, and disgorging bodies illustrate the narrator's lesson on the deject's powers of survival, desire, and language: "Be indigestible, hard, ungiving," "be firm in your own small, static, limited / / orbit and the shark-jaws / of outer circumstance / / will *spit* you forth" (4; 514; emphasis mine). Compassion and passionate self-sufficiency are evoked in the burgeoning bod(ies) of the oyster and its waste-product, the pearl: "Living within, / you beget, self-out-of-self, / / selfless, / that pearl-of-great-price" (4; 514). Vomited matter gives way to the parable of the parasitic worm, who escapes "spider-snare," "bird-claw," "scavenger bird-beak," by ruthlessly eating its way "out of" "every calamity": "Gorged on vine-leaf and mulberry, / / parasite. I find nourishment: / when you cry in disgust, / . . . / I am yet unrepentant" (6; 515, 516). Feeding and fed upon, bodies[4] reminiscent of Bakhtin's grotesques in the act of "becoming" – "the body swallows the world and is itself swallowed by the world" (Bakhtin 317) – also encompass desire; the narrator, "pale as the worm in the grass," envisions ecstatic sexual union with the devouring Aries the Ram (Amen-Ra): "Crop me up with the new-grass; / / let your teeth devour me, / let me be warm in your belly . . ." (22; 527). This eros of mutually immured and devouring bodies recalls the female desire imaged by Wittig's passionate consumption of the loved body or by Sappho's plea in Swinburne's "Anactoria": "That I could drink thy veins as wine, and eat

/ Thy breasts like honey! that . . . / Thy body were abolished and consumed, / And in my flesh thy very flesh entombed!" (*P&B* I, 68).

As *The Walls Do Not Fall* turns from desire to language, an implicitly feminine *textual* body hurls itself against the prevailing, critical discourse in the form of unassimilable, vomited matter. In spite of its critics, the narrator exults, writing "spews" unchecked from the unconscious producing the reviled yet precious waste of "shell, pearl": "Depth of the subconscious spews forth / too many incongruent *monsters* / / and fixed *indigestible matter* / such as shell, pearl" (32; 534, emphasis mine). In the subsequent, cynical list of writing "don'ts" pronounced by an adversarial "you," H.D. would seem to be parodying modernist attempts to "purge" the offenses of feminine writing. The list bears a remarkable resemblance to modernist attacks on effeminate Romanticism (and H.D.) in its diatribe against overworked imagery, overreliance on sound, preoccupation with words, vagueness, meaninglessness, inexactness, emotionality, uninventiveness, and sterility:

> . . . imagery
> done to death; perilous ascent,
> ridiculous descent; rhyme, jingle,
>
> overworked assonance, nonsense,
> juxtaposition of words for words' sake,
>
> without meaning, undefined; imposition,
> deception, indecisive weather-vane;
>
> disagreeable, inconsequent syllables,
> too malleable, too brittle.
>
> over-sensitive, under-definitive,
> clash of opposites, fight of emotion
>
> and sterile invention –
> you find all this? (32; 535)

Still, the narrator asserts, the expelled writerly body remains projectile: "We noted that even the erratic burnt-out comet / has its peculiar orbit" (32; 535).

II   The Femme Fatale: Venus, Bona Dea, Mary Magdalene

Indeed the drunken, pestering, and spewing bodies of *The Walls Do Not Fall* seem to rush toward the gap occupied by the "madwomen" prophets of *Tribute to the Angels* and *The Flowering of the Rod*. The poems' ungendered batteries of abjection thus pour into the rift of a female desire/language opened by the wild invaded or exploded bodies of its femmes fatales. Section Twelve of *The Flowering of the Rod* introduces its tale of Mary Magdalene and Kaspar, proclaiming,

So the first – it is written,
will be the twisted or the tortured individuals,

out of line, out of step with world so-called progress:
. . .
the first actually to witness His life-after-death,
was an unbalanced, neurotic woman. (2; 586)

Deborah Kelly Kloepfer notes that the pivotal mother muses of *Trilogy* are sexual dejects, "whores" rather than "Madonnas"; Kloepfer argues that contrary to patriarchal conversion narratives,[5] H.D. makes her approach to the erotic discourse of a maternal (lesbian) desire by way of desecrated rather than redeemed representations of women, "through the whore . . . H.D. finally claims the mother."[6] I would add that through the Decadent femme fatale H.D. achieves the somatic overkill she requires to force the feminine into representation. From the "bitter jewel" body hatching nocturnal visions of a dark Venus, to the innumerable, "Pre-Raphaelite" masks of the Bona Dea, to Mary Magdalene's "extraordinary" visionary hair in *The Flowering of the Rod,* H.D. would appear to bring the feminine more and more viscerally alive with each Decadent narration of the female body.

The consuming "bitter jewel" in the crucible signifies *Trilogy*'s en-trance into the Venusian mat(t)er of a reclaimed Venus, among other femmes fatales. Kloepfer observes that the fragrant, breathing "jewel" offers a "sensuous, linguistic medium" that conducts the narrator into the eroticized maternal discourse (Kloepfer 139). One may also regard the jewel as a transitional sexual/textual body, signaling the movement from the earlier crystalline youth toward the later mother muse, or in H.D.'s words, his "crystallization" into "the mother/matrix." A white pulsing, rose-veined shape-all-light that "breathes" and "gives off – fragrance?" the jewel coalesces various effects of Decadent Romantic/disfiguration suggested by Pater's crystal man, Shelley's amorphous "shape," and the crimson-flushed white body of Swinburne's Fragoletta (113; 554; see Chapters Three and Four). When asked to "name" the jewel and its "color," H.D.'s narrator draws upon Aesthetic codes for the male androgyne; and we are reminded that both "Fragoletta" and H.D.'s "Eurydice" respond similarly to questions about the "naming" of sex/gender otherness – "How should [Love] greet thee?" ("Fragoletta") and "What had my face to offer" ("Eurydice") – with recitations of Romantic *diaphaneitè*. In the narrator's response – "green-white, opalescent / / with under-layer of changing blue, / with rose-vein; a white agate / / with a pulse uncooled that beats yet, / faint, blue-violet" – we recognize the iridescent play of colors (*diaphaneitè*) induced by the sensitivity of "opalescent" white surface to "underlayer of changing" blue/rose venation.

However, the narrator's envisioned self-implosion into the jewel-body's interior refuses the disembodied gaze maintained both by Kermode's stationary figures and the Decadent scene of beautiful youth and admiring male artist. Indeed, this visionary en-trance recalls the devouring (with a touch of the vampiric) Medusan body that changes the viewer from voyeur to participant, "in my flesh thy very flesh entombed." Enchanted, H.D.'s poet recites, "I want to watch its faint / / heart-beat, pulse-beat / as it quivers . . . / / . . . I want to minimize thought, / / concentrate on it / till I shrink . . . and am drawn into it" (14; 555). The narrator's desire suddenly involves the "uncooled," veined, mass of the "bitter jewel" in a sensuous "blood revel" that would not have been possible for the faintly tinted, blushingly transparent Fragoletta or Hyacinth's "white hands inviolate," violet-tinctured though they may be. Perhaps the jewel's blood-infused clash of affected tints – green, rose, violet – might take us to that more garish "place" of apotheosis that Wittig's narrator ardently awaits in the depths of her female lover's body, "where the primary colors are not lacking"; "*I* tremble before the bright red efflux from your arteries, . . . *I* see the dark blood emerge from the blue of our veins, in places it is congealed, violet . . ." (Wittig 21). And it is not unusual for the subtle effluences of the blush to mingle with the more substantive blood-revel in appreciations of the femme fatale. Swinburne's Sappho ("Anactoria") dwells as lovingly on her beloved's "flower-sweet fingers . . . / / roseleaf-colored shells, / And blood like purple blossom at the tips / Quivering" as on "the sweet blood" that flows from "thy sweet small wounds" (*P&B* I, 68).

The bitter jewel's sudden eruption into a vision of the "desecrated" Venusian femme fatale leaves no question about the ferocity of the narrator's crossing. In a move resembling the rend(er)ings performed by Wittig's bisected "I"/lesbian body or Swinburne's Sappho, the narrator forces the Venusian body from its reviled "venerous" position in patriarchal history to that of "venerated" prophet.

> for suddenly we say your name
> desecrated; knaves and fools
>
> have done you impious wrong,
> Venus, for venery stands for impurity
>
> And Venus as desire is venerous, lascivious,
> . . .
> return O holiest one,
> Venus whose name is kin
>
> to venerate,
> venerator. (11, 12; 553, 554)

The narrator's manipulation of the Latin root for Venus, "vener," to accomplish the transition from the Venus of patriarchal desecration to one "whose name is kin / / to venerate, / venerator," requires a searing passage across the symbolic. Far from purgative, the resulting rift in signification leaks abjection, just as "foul witches" uprooting the shrieking sexual/textual body of the mandrake harvest "poisonous" mandragora.

> While the very root of the word shrieks
> like a mandrake when foul witches pull
>
> its stem at midnight,
> and rare mandragora itself

is full, they say, of poison,
food for the witches' den. (11; 554)

Like Faustine's kiss, mixing "milk and blood and passion," the dismembered root's ichor (mandragora) is "poison" to the uninitiated, but "rare" nurture for its sorceress plunderers.

Tribute to the Angels' gallery of female portraits, mapping the narrator's approach to the Bona Dea, shifts from abjection to the language of female "portraiture in movement" H.D. discovered in the film siren and in Rossetti's pictures of Siddal. H.D.'s fluid array of faces, gestures, and hooded, flamboyant, haloed women ostensibly describing the Venuses and madonnas created by "the masters," reminds us that H.D.'s articulation of "her" no longer depends on *diaphaneitè*, but on the thronging visual narrative of the Decadent female face and body: H.D.'s lifelong poetic search for the mother-lover ("she") has switched tracks from the vanishing traces of the white androgyne to *Trilogy*'s galaxy of femmes fatales. Although the narrator disclaims the painterly representations of "her" – "none of these / none of these / suggest her as I saw her" – the pages-long gallery (*CP* II, sections 29–31) speaks eloquently for itself. Indeed, H.D.'s later pronouncement that the Bona Dea's "tale" of a "Fisherman / a tale of . . . jars," is "the same-different – the same attributes, / different yet the same as before" (39; 571), might apply to the galaxy of male-authored paintings now viewed "differently" by the female narrator:

we have seen her,
an empress,
magnificent in pomp and grace,
  . . .
we have seen her snood
drawn over her hair,
  . . .
we have seen her head bowed down
with the weight of a domed crown,

or we have seen her, a wisp of a girl
trapped in a golden halo;

we have seen her with arrow, with doves
and a heart like a valentine;

we have seen her in fine silks imported
from all over the Levant,

. . .

we have seen her sleeve
of every imaginable shade

of damask and figured brocade;
it is true,

the painters did very well by her;
it is true, they missed never a line.
. . . (29; 564, 565)

Not only is the panoply of female frames reminiscent of Rossetti's Pre-Raphaelite paintings – the wan, burdened Mary of his *Annunciation*, the valentines and arrow of *Venus Verticordia*, or the luxuriant brocade of *Monna Vanna* – but the entire passage resembles Christina Rossetti's similar gallery of painterly masks for a Pre-Raphaelite "she" (probably Siddal) in her then unpublished but circulated poem, "In an Artist's Studio"[7]:

One face looks out from all his canvases,
One selfsame figure sits or walks or leans:
We found her hidden just behind those screens,
That mirror gave back all her loveliness.
A queen in opal or in ruby dress,
A nameless girl in freshest summer greens,
A saint, an angel . . .

H.D. had read excerpts from C. Rossetti's poems in Violet Hunt's *Wife of Rossetti*, and she would later copy several of Rossetti's compositions in her "Notes on Pre-Raphaelites" (40–1).[8] However, even if H.D. was not acquainted with the poem, she and her Victorian precursor both strove to articulate an evasive female "I" or "she" through a gallery of Pre-Raphaelite women.[9] Twenty "portraits" or more fill these sections of *Tribute to the Angels*, recalling the unrolling frames of H.D.'s Pre-Raphaelite Screen Beauty, by turns a "hooded woman," Demeter, Proserpine, or Venus in a "tapestried" garden. The narrators' own description of the Bona Dea as "a cluster of garden-pinks" or as a humble and slight-statured woman (43; 574, 38; 569) merely offers a brief metonymy for the earlier, fleshed-out assembly – many of whom show humility and one of whom poses with "a cluster of garden pinks / in a glass beside her." The gallery's sensuous, synecdochical dance of hands alone, as Michie comments on the Victorians' "intricate choreography of tropes" for the female body "itself bespeaks physicality"[10]:

> We see her hand in her lap,
> smoothing the apple-green
>
> or the apple-russet silk;
> we see her hand at her throat,
>
> fingering a talisman
> brought by a crusader from Jerusalem;
>
> we see her hand unknot a Syrian veil
> or lay down a Venetian shawl
>
> on a polished table that reflects
> half a miniature broken column; (30; 565, 566)

III   *The Flowering of the Rod*

> lo, her wonderfully woven hair!
>
> – Swinburne, "Laus Veneris"

Kaspar's induction into a feminist vision of prehistory and a "paradise" of the new Eve, turns on a central (male) Romantic and modern trope for the stranglehold of female sexuality – the Pre-Raphaelite femme fatale's luxuriant, overflowing hair. *The Flowering of the Rod*'s femme fatale, Mary Magdalene, popularly believed to be a prostitute cast out for adultery and an exiled wanderer in the desert, forms the heroic prototype of *Trilogy*'s female deject-prophets. H.D.'s "other Mary" retains rather than expels Magdalene's legendary "demons," renamed "*daemons*,"[11] who are revised to include the reclaimed Venusian femme fatale – "Venus/in a star" (*CP* 25; 595, 596). However, as the narrative makes clear, Magdalene's transforming *daemons* reside in her "extraordinary hair," whose visionary depths provide a luminous gateway into Kaspar's final vision of a prophesied feminine world. Kaspar's seduction begins with the provocation of Magdalene's unveiled, untamed hair, which excites him to brand her variously as "unseemly," "disheveled," "unmaidenly," and "disordered." Although her pale face and luminous eyes command attention, her hair irritates and diverts him: "But eyes? he had known many women – / it was her hair – un-maidenly – / / it was hardly decent of her to stand there, / unveiled, in the house of a stranger" (16; 590). The fantastic lure of Magdalene's glowing hair, however, soon resurfaces in his desperate longings and hallucinatory images "as of moon-light on a lost river / or a sunken stream, seen in a dream / / by a parched, dying man, lost in the desert . . . / or a mirage . . . It was her hair" (17; 591; ellipses H.D.'s). Reverently, he later watches Magdalene at a social gathering "deftly un-weaving / / the long, carefully-braided tresses / of her extraordinary hair" (21; 594). Simon, the host, warns him to resist the spell of her hair, comparing her to a "siren" he had seen in "a heathen picture, / / or a carved stone-portal entrance / to a forbidden sea temple":

> they called the creature,
> depicted like this
>
> seated on the sea-shore
> or on a rock, a Siren,
>
> a maid-of-the sea, a mermaid;
> some said, this mermaid sang
>
> and that a Siren-song was fatal
> and wrecks followed the wake of such hair

Kaspar, nevertheless, is drawn more deeply into the siren discourse, until he yields, entirely en-tranced: Reflected light on Magdalene's hair recasts it as a visionary body that draws him into an infinite regress of mirrors and "flecks" of light, "through spiral upon spiral of the shell / of memory that yet connects us / / with the drowned cities of pre-history" to a "Paradise / before Eve" (32, 33; 603, 602).

Magdalene's wild hair joins *Trilogy*'s cascade of writhing, devouring, imploding bodies even as it draws directly on the famous Pre-Raphaelite trope. Its revised Medusan affect – Magdalene's hair inspires rather than stymies vision – once more reclaims the sexual, creative powers of the Pre-

Raphaelite femme fatale, known for her magic hair. Indeed, H.D.'s por-
trayal of Magdalene's hair may have derived directly from Rossetti's portrait
of the "other" Eve, *Lady Lilith,* combing her magnificent swath of hair.
While the marbled androgynous boys and Artemisian women of H.D.'s
earlier work were not notable for their hair, references to the "mermaid
on the rocks" combing her hair or to "Venus in the looking glass" emerge
frequently following H.D.'s Pre-Raphaelite revival.[12] Elizabeth Gitter's description of the Pre-Raphaelite origin of this powerful Victorian trope for
female, art, sexuality, and narrative, for which Lady Lilith forms a type,
might apply to H.D.'s Mary Magdalene:

> Silent, the larger-than-life woman who dominated the literature and art of
> the [Victorian] period used her hair to weave her discourse . . . at times to
> shelter her lovers [and] at times to strangle them. But always, as Rossetti's
> *Lady Lilith* painting suggests, the grand woman achieved her transcendent
> vitality partly through her magic hair, which was invested with independent
> energy: enchanting – and enchanted – her gleaming tresses both expressed
> her mythic power and were its source.[13]

Notably the most obsessive, Pre-Raphaelite trope of Yeats's early poetry,
the femme fatale's devastating "hair-tent," disappears from his later poetry
along with the victimized Aesthete.[14] However, neither Eliot or Yeats really
abandoned the richly Decadent trope. Yeats's 1917 series of poems to the
dying Mabel Beardsley, sister of the sometime Pre-Raphaelite artist, Aubrey
Beardsley, pays tribute to her Pre-Raphaelite, androgynous beauty – characterized by her hair and former dress. He asks that artists bring her draw-
ings,

> . . . maybe showing
> Her features when a tress
> Of dull red hair was flowing
> Over some silken dress
> Cut in the Turkish fashion,
> Or, it may be, like a boy's. (*VP* 363)

(Yeats's reference to "her lovely piteous head amid dull red hair / Propped
upon pillows," curiously, recalls Hunt's dying Siddal.) And the "talking

hair" of Eliot's female hysteric in "A Game of Chess" elegantly conjures the luminous medium of feminine words and savagery,

> Under the firelight, under the brush, her hair
> Spread out in fiery points
> Glowed into words, then would be savagely still.
> (*The Waste Land* II, lines 108–10)

H.D., of course, would have encountered the Pre-Raphaelite trope in her favorite poems by Swinburne. Faustine's "shapely silver shoulder stoops. / Weighed overclean / with state of splendid hair." Sappho cries to Anactoria, "thy tresses burn me," and the Knight of "Laus Veneris" is drawn into eternal hell by the proverbial sexual snare – "But lo her wonderfully woven hair!":

> Ah, with blind lips I felt for you, and found
> About my neck your hands and hair enwound,
>   The hands that stifle and the hair that stings,
> I felt thee fasten sharply without sound.
> (*P&B* I, 26)

However, H.D. was probably recalled to the Pre-Raphaelite trope by Hunt's *Wife of Rossetti,* whose subtly nuanced and changing portrait of Siddal's abject body focuses as well on the elaborate effects of Siddal's famous hair – braided, "ragged," "luxuriant," "dull," "spread" in "opulent bows" on her deathbed. The "torn edges" of the Siddal Hunt strives to represent, "flesh unhemmed as it were," by illness and suffering, include the doings and undoings of Siddal's magnificent hair (Hunt 124). And we recall, H.D. would later incorporate in her own "White Rose and the Red" Hunt's reference to Siddal's and Swinburne's red hair as a singular mark of transgression and exile.

These last chapters have only begun to inquire into the significance of H.D.'s Pre-Raphaelite revival. There is, as yet, no in-depth scholarship on H.D.'s lengthy, Pre-Raphaelite novels, "The Sword Went Out to Sea" or "White Rose and the Red"; and H.D.'s consuming interest in William Morris has yet to be explored.

Here I focused on the implications of Decadent Romanticism and its sexual poetic for a twentieth-century woman writer attempting to shape a female modernism within the masculinist, anti-Romantic climate of high modernism. As we have seen, H.D. was particularly loyal to Swinburne, whom she repeatedly "rediscovered" with ever deepening admiration as she read more widely into his work. However, H.D.'s tenacious fidelity to Swinburne and the Decadents may also reveal something about the concealed desires of her male contemporaries. Although excluded by her gender, H.D. (among other women writers) was often in daily contact with her male contemporaries, sharing her ideas and enthusiasms. As important, H.D. was, perhaps, more honest about her attachment to the fluid sexualities of the Decadents than Yeats, Eliot, or Pound because as a woman poet she was already guilty by association of "effeminate" writing and constitutionally unfit to participate in the fervid modernist "masculinization" of poets, poetry, and poetics.

And yet, like H.D., Eliot was also haunted by the echo of Philomel's call to the swallow sister in Swinburne's "Itylus" – "O swallow swallow" – which occurs in the prominent last lines of *The Waste Land*. Pound and H.D. clearly discussed their common belief that Yeats would provide a bridge between Pre-Raphaelitism and modernism. And like H.D., Yeats and the Rhymers were infatuated with the "powerful and musical" cadences of Swinburne's "Faustine" (*Auto* 200) which may have informed Yeats's later fascination with lesbians, androgyny, and "the woman in me." Further, just as H.D.'s relation to the past often replicated the homoerotic "Greek" man–boy continuum she gleaned from Pater and Swinburne, Eliot's and Pound's sometime depiction of "influence" as a man–boy "Apostolic Succession" or romantic "affair" may have issued from Pater's homoerotic tributes to the "crystal" men of history, literature, philosophy, and art. Thus, apart from giving us insight into female strategies for subverting patriarchy, which I have attempted to do here, studying the woman writer may also teach us about the "feminine" desires, subterfuges, and secrets of her male contemporaries.

Postscript

Although it is beyond the scope of this book to map the continuities between anti-Romantic modernism and certain masculinist postmodernisms, at least one feminist critic, Alicia Ostriker, has blamed Eliot's " 'extinction of personality' " and the currently "popular critical fiction" of "the death of the author" for the oppression of the feminine "I" in Anglo/American literary modernity.[1] I suggest further that the implicitly or explicitly gender-biased flight from romantic "selfhood" urged by modern, New Critical, and postmodern critics from Yeats and Eliot to Frank Kermode, Harold Bloom, and Roland Barthes may be traced back, in part, to the crisis in sexual definition provoked by the transgressive "personalities" – female and "effeminate" male – of the last century.

It is therefore, perhaps, no accident that H.D. (and I) dramatize two types of the abject male and female body that are resurfacing again in the personae of the lesbian vampire, femme fatale, Greek male youth, and others in gender (gay/lesbian/feminist) studies.[2] Indeed, Eve Sedgwick includes cross-gender identification with such dissident personae as "feminist men," "drags," and "ladies in tuxedos" in her heady description of "the experimental linguistic, epistemological, representational, political adventures" issuing from "queer" literary practice. I could not have written this book without these criticisms and their attendant assumption that such performances of sexuality and gender (continue to) matter.

H.D. resurrected the Decadent femme fatale and the homoerotic male youth, which positioned her, among other things, against New Critical attempts to sheer away feminine "personality" and "superfluity." Perhaps the postmodern reification of the abject and the material implicit in the reappearance of these transgressive "personalities" may defend similarly against masculinist postmodernisms that kill the fiction of the sexually transgressive "I" in the name of a bodiless "electric materiality" (Brodribb 122).

Notes

INTRODUCTION

1. H.D. referred to the "portrait . . . of the . . . crystalline youth" as the main "theme and center" of *Hippolytus Temporizes* and *Hedylus*, quoted in "H.D. by Delia Alton," *Iowa Review*, 16, no. 3 (Fall 1986), p. 221. (Hereafter cited in text as "Delia Alton.")

2. The gender crises embedded in literary modernism have been attributed variously to all of these. Sandra Gilbert and Susan Gubar locate the origins of the literary "battle of the sexes" in the early modern proliferation of women writers and the New Woman phenomenon, in *No Man's Land*, Vol. I, *The War of the Words* (New Haven: Yale U.P., 1988). Several literary critics treating the lesbian novels of the 1920s trace the movement to the debates sparked by the sexologists, and particularly by Havelock Ellis's "Sexual Inversion" in *Studies in the Psychology of Sex*, 4 vols. (New York: Random House, 1936). See, for example, Catharine Stimpson's "Zero Degree Deviancy: The Lesbian Novel in English," *Critical Inquiry* 8, no. 4 (Winter, 1981), pp. 363–79. For an examination of the impact of both Ellis's theories and the New Woman on a lesbian novelist of the 1920s, see Esther Newton's "The Mythic Mannish Lesbian: Radclyffe Hall and the New Woman," *Signs*, 9 (Summer, 1979), pp. 178–203. Eve Kosofsky Sedgwick's *Epistemology of the Closet* (Berkeley: U. of California P., 1990) first argued extensively that the twentieth-century crisis in homo/heterosexual definition informing male literary modernism (among other discourses) was provoked by the Oscar Wilde trials. (Hereafter cited in text as *Epistemology*.)

3. For a study considering the differing responses to the maternal feminine in modernist men's and women's prose, see Marianne DeKoven's *Rich and Strange: Gender, History and Modernism* (Princeton: Princeton U.P., 1991).

4. Mansfield is quoted in Sydney Janet Kaplan, ' "A Gigantic Mother': Katherine Mansfield's London," in *Women Writers and the City,* ed. Susan Merrill Squier (Knoxville: U. of Tennessee P., 1984), p. 166. (Hereafter cited in text as "K.M.'s London.") See also *Journal of Katherine Mansfield,* ed. J. Middleton Murry (London: Constable, 1954), pp. 13, 11. (Hereafter cited in text as *Journal.*)

5. Richard Dellamora, "Traversing the Feminine in *Salome,*" in *Victorian Sages and Cultural Discourse: Renegotiating Gender and Power,* ed. Thaïs E. Morgan (New Brunswick and London: Rutgers U.P., 1990), p. 264.

6. See Karla Jay's discussion of the Cult of the "Great Mother" that Renée Vivien fashioned from Decadent Aesthetes such as Baudelaire and Swinburne in Jay's chapter four, "Sappho and Other Goddesses," of her book *The Amazon and the Page: Natalie Clifford Barney and Renée Vivien* (Bloomington: Indiana U.P., 1988).

7. Susan Gubar, "Sapphistries," *Signs,* 10 (Autumn, 1984), p. 49.

8. Nina Auerbach, *Woman and the Demon: The Life of a Victorian Myth* (Cambridge, Mass.: Harvard U.P., 1982). Richard Dellamora, *Masculine Desire: The Sexual Politics of Victorian Aestheticism* (Chapel Hill and London: U. of North Carolina P., 1990) (hereafter cited in text as *Masculine Desire*), and *Apocalyptic Overtures: Sexual Politics and the Sense of an Ending* (New Brunswick: Rutgers U.P., 1994) (hereafter cited in text as *Apocalyptic*). Thaïs E. Morgan, "Mixed Metaphor, Mixed Gender: Swinburne and the Victorian Critics," *Victorian Newsletter* (Spring, 1988). Linda Dowling, "Ruskin's Pied Beauty and the Constitution of a 'Homosexual' Code," *Victorian Newsletter,* 75 (Spring, 1989), pp. 1–8, and *Hellenism and Homosexuality in Victorian Oxford* (Ithaca and London: Cornell U.P., 1994).

9. Alan Sinfield, *The Wilde Century: Effeminacy, Oscar Wilde and the Queer Moment* (New York: Columbia U.P., 1994), p. 1.

10. Alicia Ostriker, in "What Do Women (Poets) Want?: H.D. and Marianne Moore as Poetic Ancestresses," *Contemporary Literature,* 27, no. 4 (Winter, 1986), pp. 345–492, argues that despite the proliferation of women writers, past and present, modernist women poets frequently refused to acknowledge their influence.

11. Susan Stanford Friedman, "Modernism of the Scattered Remnant: Race and Politics in the Development of H.D.'s Modernist Vision," in *H.D.: Woman and Poet,* ed. Michael King (Orono, Maine: National Poetry Foundation, 1986), pp. 91–116, and *Penelope's Web: Gender, Modernity, H.D.'s Fiction* (Cambridge, Mass.: Harvard U.P., 1980) (hereafter cited in text as *PW*). Rachel Blau DuPlessis, *Writing beyond the Ending: Narrative Strategies of Twentieth-Century Women Writers* (Bloomington: Indiana U.P., 1985) (hereafter cited in text as *Writing beyond*), and *The Career of That Struggle* (Bloomington: Indiana

U.P., 1986). Sandra Gilbert and Susan Gubar, *No Man's Land,* Vol. I, *The War of the Words,* and Vol. II, *Sexchanges* (New Haven: Yale U.P., 1988, 1989). Shari Benstock, *Women of the Left Bank* (Austin: U. of Texas P., 1986)

12. Frank Kermode, *Romantic Image* (New York: Methuen, 1957).

13. In "Wilde, *Dorian Gray,* and Gross Indecency," *Sexual Sameness: Textual Differences in Gay and Lesbian Writing,* ed. Joseph Bristow (London, New York: Routledge, 1992), p. 55.

14. I use Judith Butler's wonderful phrase, "gender trouble" for all forms of sex/gender debate, in *Gender Trouble: The Subversion of Identity* (New York: Routledge Chapman and Hall, 1990). (Hereafter cited in text as *Gender Trouble.*)

15. I borrow the term from Rachel Blau DuPlessis, who uses it, in *Writing beyond the Ending,* to designate culturally mandated narratives.

16. Harold Bloom, *The Anxiety of Influence: A Theory of Poetry* (New York: Oxford U.P., 1973). (Hereafter cited in text as *Anxiety.*)

17. H.D., *HERmione* (New York: New Directions, 1981). H.D. originally entitled the work *HER,* but her publisher retitled the book to avoid overlap with another publication of the same name. I use H.D.'s original title here. (Hereafter cited in text as *HER.*)

18. H.D., "White Rose and the Red," unpublished manuscript, Beinecke Library, Yale University. (Hereafter cited in text as "White Rose.")

19. Quoted in Anthony Alpers, *The Life of Katherine Mansfield* (New York: Viking P., 1980), p. 91.

20. Lillian Faderman, *Surpassing the Love of Men: Romantic Friendships between Women from the Renaissance to the Present* (New York: William Morrow, 1981), p. 268.

21. Eve Kosofsky Sedgwick's *Between Men: English Literature and Male Homosocial Desire* (New York: Columbia U.P., 1985) draws upon René Girard's theory of "mimetic desire" in *Deceit, Desire and the Novel: Self and Other in Literary Structure,* trans. Yvonne Freccero (Baltimore: Johns Hopkins U.P, 1965) and Gayle Rubin's discovery of the "traffic in women" in "The Traffic in Women: Notes on the Political Economy of Sex," *Towards an Anthropology of Women,* ed. Rayne R. Reiter (New York: Monthly Review P., 1975), in order to demonstrate the implicit misogyny and homoeroticism of cultural, "homosocial," male bonding in a series of literary works including Shakespeare's sonnets. (Hereafter cited in text as *Between Men.*)

22. Walter Pater, "Winckelmann," in *The Renaissance: Studies in Art and Poetry* (London: Macmillan, 1910), pp. 177–232. (Hereafter cited in text as "Winckelmann.") Richard Dellamora argues that Pater's principle of (aesthetic) transparency put forth in "*Diaphaneitè*" prefigures the homoerotic ideal of male statuary depicted in the later essays in *Masculine Desire,* chapter 5, "Arnold, Winckelmann, and Pater," pp. 102–16.

23. Susan Friedman argues that H.D. shifts from male masks of androgyny to female masks of the mother muse, in *Psyche Reborn: The Emergence of H.D.* (Bloomington: Indiana U.P., 1981) and in *Penelope's Web*. Deborah Kelly Kloepfer makes the same argument in *The Unspeakable Mother: Forbidden Discourse in Jean Rhys and H.D.* (Ithaca and London: Cornell U.P., 1989).

24. Both Bloom's *Anxiety of Influence* and Bornstein's *Transformations of Romanticism in Yeats, Eliot and Stevens* (Chicago: U. of Chicago P., 1976) trace a tripartite structure in the pattern of influence from early imitation to rejection and finally reconciliation with the Romantic literary "forefather."

25. Susan Friedman first demonstrated in *Psyche Reborn* this crucial shift in H.D.'s psyche during H.D.'s work with Freud.

26. H.D., "The Sword Went Out to Sea," unpublished manuscript (pp. 175–7), Beinecke Library, Yale University. (Hereafter cited in text as "The Sword.")

27. Julia Kristeva, *Powers of Horror: An Essay on Abjection*, trans. Leon S. Roudiez (New York: Columbia U.P., 1982) (hereafter cited in text as *Powers of Horror*). Monique Wittig, *The Lesbian Body*, trans. David Le Vay (Boston: Beacon, 1986). Mikhail Bakhtin, "The Grotesque Image of the Body," *Rabelais and His World*, trans. Helen Iswolsky (Cambridge, Mass.: MITP, 1965).

28. This phrase juxtaposes Judith Butler's title for her book *Bodies That Matter: On the Discursive Limits of 'Sex'* (New York and London: Routledge, 1993) (hereafter cited in text as *Bodies*) with Somer Brodribb's title, *Nothing Mat(t)ers: A Feminist Critique of Postmodernism* (New York: New York University Press, 1993). Both titles imply the importance of a material female tropology that preserves the power of a gendered sexuality/subjectivity.

29. For studies of Romantic and Victorian influence in the male modernist tradition, see Harold Bloom's *Yeats* (New York: Oxford U.P., 1970); George Bornstein's *Transformations of Romanticism in Yeats, Eliot and Stevens*; Hazard Adams's *Blake and Yeats: The Contrary Vision* (Ithaca: Cornell U.P., 1956); Frank Kermode's *Romantic Image*; Robert Langbaum's *The Poetry of Experience: The Dramatic Monologue in Modern Literary Tradition* (New York: W.W. Norton, 1963); Carol T. Christ's *Victorian and Modern Poetics* (Chicago: U. of Chicago P., 1984) and James Longenbach's *Stone Cottage: Pound, Yeats and Modernism* (New York: Oxford U.P., 1988) and his *Modernist Poetics of History: Pound, Eliot and the Sense of the Past* (Princeton: Princeton U.P., 1987).

30. For example, Joanne Feit Diehl's *Dickinson and the Romantic Imagination* (Princeton: Princeton U.P., 1981) and Susan J. Rosowski's *The Voyage Perilous: Willa Cather's Romanticism* (Lincoln: U. of Nebraska P., 1986).

31. See especially Shari Benstock's references to the impact of the French Decadents on Renée Vivien and Natalie Barney in her chapter eight, "Natalie Barney: Rue Jacob," pp. 277–90. Gilbert and Gubar's first chapter, "Heart of Darkness: The *Agon* of the Femme Fatale," discusses the persona of the femme fatale in male modernist novels such as *She* in *No Man's Land*, Vol. II, *Sex-*

changes. Karla Jay's *The Amazon and the Page* makes reference to the Baudelairean influence on Vivien's Decadent goddesses, and Elyse Blankley's essay on Vivien, "Return to Mytilene: Renée Vivien and the City of Women," in *Women Writers and the City,* also acknowledges Decadent influence. Katherine Mansfield and Oscar Wilde are an integral part of Kaplan's book (Ithaca and London: Cornell U.P., 1991).

32. I am indebted particularly to Dellamora's *Masculine Desire;* Jonathan Dollimore's essay, "Different Desires: Subjectivity and Transgression in Wilde and Gide," *Genders* (Summer, 1988), pp. 24–9, and his subsequent book, *Sexual Dissidence: Augustine to Wilde; Freud to Foucault* (Oxford: Clarendon P., 1991); Thaïs Morgan's several essays, including "Swinburne's Dramatic Monologues, Sex and Ideology," *Victorian Poetry,* 22 (1984), pp. 175–95; and Linda Dowling's essay, "Ruskin's Pied Beauty and the Constitution of a 'Homosexual' Code," as well as her books, *Language and Decadence in the Victorian Fin de Siècle* (Princeton: Princeton U.P., 1986), and *Hellenism and Homosexuality.*

33. Lyndall Gordon, *Eliot's Early Years* (New York: Farrar, Straus and Giroux, 1977) (hereafter cited in text as *Eliot's EE*), and *Eliot's New Life* (New York: Farrar, Straus and Giroux, 1988) (hereafter cited in text as *Eliot's NL*). Gail McDonald, *Learning to Be Modern: Pound, Eliot and the American University* (New York: Oxford, 1993). Andrew Ross, *The Failure of Modernism: Symptoms of American Poetry* (New York: Columbia U.P., 1986). Louis Menand, *Discovering Modernism: T.S. Eliot and His Context* (New York: Oxford U.P., 1987). Elizabeth Butler Cullingford, *Gender and History in Yeats' Love Poetry* (Cambridge: Cambridge U.P., 1993).

CHAPTER ONE

1. Lyndall Gordon's two literary biographies of Eliot, *Eliot's Early Years* and *Eliot's New Life,* demonstrate effectively the extent to which Eliot's insistence on "impersonality" masked not only the personal spiritual quest of his poetry but also his problematic relationships with women. In *The Failure of Modernism,* Andrew Ross notes Eliot's fear of "the feminine" and shifts the focus from "the tired issue of Eliot's body itself" to "the troubled construction of sexuality" in language (p. 54). Further, Ross argues that "sexual . . . failure" in Eliot's poems is "overdetermined as the privileged representation of other forms of ideological crisis" (58).

2. See note 2 of Introduction.

3. See especially Gilbert and Gubar's first chapter, "Heart of Darkness: the *Agon* of the Femme Fatale," in which they assert that to many misogynist male writers, the femme fatale was the New Woman (*No Man's Land,* Vol. II, *Sexchanges,* pp. 3–64). Eve Sedgwick describes, in *Between Men* (217), how the

type of the homosexual became associated with Oscar Wilde's Aesthete persona after his famous trials.

4. W.B. Yeats, *The Autobiography* (New York: Collier Books, 1965), p. 189. (Hereafter cited in text as *Auto*.)

5. T. E. Hulme, *Speculations,* ed. Herbert Read (New York: Harcourt Brace, 1924), p. 131. (Hereafter cited in text as *Speculations*.)

6. In *Literature and the American College: Essays in Defense of the Humanities* (1908), ed. Russell Kirk (Washington, D.C.: National Humanities Institute, 1986).

7. In 1928, Eliot professed that he had "begun as a disciple of Babbitt." *Selected Essays* (New York: Harcourt, Brace and World, 1964), p. 429. (Hereafter cited in text as *SE*.)

8. In "The Metaphysical Poets" (*SE* 241–50)

9. T.S. Eliot, "London Letter," *The Dial*, 71 (Aug. 1921), pp. 216–17.

10. Ezra Pound, "Lionel Johnson," *Literary Essays,* ed. T.S. Eliot (New York: New Directions, 1968), p. 362. (Hereafter cited in text as *LE*.)

11. W.B. Yeats, *The Letters,* ed. Allen Wade (New York: Macmillan, 1955), p. 434. (Hereafter cited in text as *Letters*.) Elizabeth Cullingford notes that he wrote little lyric poetry between 1903 and 1908 (78).

12. T. E. Hulme, *Further Speculations,* ed. Sam Hynes (Minneapolis, 1955), p. 99.

13. Richard Aldington, "Violet Hunt," *The Egoist* (Jan. 1, 1914), p. 17. (Hereafter cited in text as *Egoist*.)

14. Nancy Chodorow, *The Reproduction of Mothering: Psychoanalysis and the Sociology of Gender* (Berkeley: U. of California P., 1978), p. 174.

15. Hélène Cixous's "The Laugh of the Medusa" perhaps best summarizes the French Feminist notion of women's writing, in *New French Feminisms,* ed. Elaine Marks and Isabelle de Courtivron (New York: Schocken Books, 1981), pp. 245–64.

16. Scott's earlier edition, *The Gender of Modernism: A Critical Anthology* (Bloomington, Indiana U.P., 1990) contains selections from Eliot and Pound and introductions by, respectively, Nancy Gish and Ronald Bush, which consider the sexual politics of Eliot's doctrine of "impersonality" and Pound's attitude toward the feminine (pp. 139–54, 363–71). Shari Benstock briefly discusses the masculinist theory of language behind Pound's insistence on the Image's correspondence between the word and its referent in *Women of the Left Bank* (pp. 327–31).

However, modernist critics are in the course of reassessing male poetic modernism in terms of recent critical theories. See Maud Ellmann's *The Poetics of Impersonality,* which demonstrates the simultaneous movements of self-creation and undoing enacted in Eliot's poems that belie his rigid pronouncements about impersonality. In *The Failure of Modernism,* Andrew Ross uncovers debates about language and subjectivity in Eliot's poetry, claiming that language necessarily resists Eliot's "theoretical advances." Studies such as

McDonald's *Learning to Be Modern* or Louis Menand's *Discovering Modernism* view (male) modernist theories such as impersonality as part of Eliot's or Pound's predetermined cultural agenda to enhance the reputation of poetry.

Bonnie Kime Scott's recent book, *Refiguring Modernism*, Volume I, *The Women of 1928* (Bloomington: Indiana U.P., 1996) represents the first significant inquiry into the male modernist poets' relation to gender and sexuality. Although her emphasis is on women modernists, *Refiguring Modernism* contextualizes this study in relation to male modernism in Part Two, "The Men of 1914," which contains chapters on Pound, Wyndham Lewis, and Eliot, among others. Scott cites the need for more scholarship on Eliot in particular whose "complex responses to gender and sexual orientation [have yet to be] sufficiently analyzed" (113).

17. Jessica R. Feldman, *Gender on the Divide: The Dandy in Modernist Literature* (Ithaca and London: Cornell U.P., 1993), p. 16.

18. Ibid., p. 5.

19. Peter Ackroyd, *T. S. Eliot: A Life* (New York: Simon and Schuster, 1984), pp. 136–7.

20. T. S. Eliot, "On the Development of Taste," *The Use of Poetry and the Use of Criticism* (London: Faber & Faber, 1964), pp. 33–4. (Hereafter cited in text as *TUPTUC*.)

21. Richard Ellmann's *The Man and the Masks* (New York: E. P. Dutton, 1948) and George Bornstein's *Transformations of Romanticism* trace this still relevant pattern of gendered phases in Yeats's career. More recently feminist critics such as Cullingford have revalued the "feminine" phases.

22. W. B. Yeats, *Essays and Introductions* (New York: Macmillan, 1961), p. 271. (Hereafter cited in text as *E&I*.) W.B. Yeats, *The Variorum Edition of the Poems*, ed. Peter Allt and Russel Alspach (New York: Macmillan, 1957). (Hereafter cited in text as *VP*.) Yeats first mentioned his "movement downward upon life" in a letter to Florence Farr (*Letters* 469).

23. T. S. Eliot, "Reflections on Contemporary Poetry," *The Egoist* (July, 1919), pp. 39–40. (Hereafter cited in text as "Reflections.")

24. Coleridge's notes for a lecture on dramatic illusion in T. M. Raysor's *Coleridge's Shakespearean Criticism*, 2 vols. (Cambridge: Cambridge U.P., 1939). This edition has been reissued by J. M. Dent, Everyman's Library, nos. 162 and 183. All notes refer to this edition (I, 16–17).

25. Julia Kristeva, *Revolution in Poetic Language*, trans. Margaret Waller (New York: Columbia U.P., 1984). Raysor, I, 18. Raysor, I, 335.

26. See Eve Sedgwick's discussion of the various binaries and triangles of male homosocial desire in Shakespeare's sonnets in chapter two of *Between Men*, "Swan in Love: The Example of Shakespeare's Sonnets," pp. 28–48.

27. Nancy Gish, introduction to T. S. Eliot in *The Gender of Modernism: A Critical Anthology*, p. 141.

28. Ezra Pound, *Personae* (New York: New Directions, 1971). (Hereafter cited in text as *Personae*.)

29. Ezra Pound, *Gaudier-Brzeska* (New York: New Directions, 1970), p. 85.

30. Ezra Pound, "Patria Mia," *Selected Prose: 1909–1965*, edited and with introduction by William Cookson (New York: New Directions, 1973), p. 104. (Hereafter cited in text as *SP*.)

31. *Blast*, no. 2, p. 33.

32. *Blast*, no. 1, p. 18.

33. H.D., *End to Torment: A Memoir of Ezra Pound*, ed. Norman Holmes Pearson and Michael King (New York: New Directions, 1979). (Hereafter cited in text as *End to Torment*.)

34. Ezra Pound, "How I Began," *T.S.'s Weekly*, 21 (June 6, 1913), p. 707.

35. For a discussion of the male–male homoerotic dynamics behind Eliot's and Pound's collaboration on *The Waste Land*, see Wayne Koestenbaum, "*The Waste Land:* T. S. Eliot's and Ezra Pound's Collaboration on Hysteria," in *Double Talk: The Erotics of Male Literary Collaboration* (New York: Routledge, 1989), pp. 112–39.

36. Ezra Pound, *The Spirit of Romance* (New York: New Directions, 1968), p. 91.

37. See note 35.

38. Pound, *The Spirit of Romance*, p. 5.

39. James Longenbach, *Modernist Poetics of History*, p. 30.

40. Ezra Pound, *Ezra Pound and Margaret Cravens: A Tragic Friendship*, ed. Omar Pound and Robert Spoo (Durham and London: Duke U.P., 1988), p. 42.

41. Ellmann, *The Man and the Masks*, pp. 181, 183.

42. Gail McDonald observes that "precision, hardness and clarity are among Pound's and Eliot's premier aesthetic values in their early careers" (71). Eliot admires the "hard coldness" of Hawthorne in "American Literature," *Athenaeum*, 4693 (April 25, 1919), pp. 236–7.

43. Cullingford discusses Yeats's sympathy with homosexuality and Wilde, pp. 268, 269.

44. W. B. Yeats, *A Vision* (New York: Collier Books, 1966), p. 150. (Hereafter cited in text as *Vision*.)

45. W. B. Yeats, *Letters to the New Island*, ed. Horace Reynolds (Cambridge: Cambridge U.P., 1934), p. 147.

46. See George Bornstein's chapter six, "The Epipsyche and the Mask: The Vicissitudes of Imaginative Love," in *Yeats and Shelley*, pp. 141–73.

47. "A First Rough Draft," p. 36, unpublished manuscript, quoted in Bornstein, *Yeats and Shelley*, p. 142.

48. See my essay, "W. B. Yeats and Florence Farr: The Influence of the 'New Woman' Actress on Yeats' Changing Images of Women," *Modern Drama*, 28 (1985), pp. 621–37.

49. See Cullingford's chapters 13 and 14, "Crazy Jane and the Irish Episcopate"

and "A Foolish, Passionate Man" for a discussion of Yeats's return to the feminine in his later years. Yeats suggested to Dorothy Wellesley that her boyish androgyny brought out "the woman in me," in W. B. Yeats, *Letters on Poetry to Dorothy Wellesley,* ed. Dorothy Wellesley (London: Oxford U.P., 1964), p. 108.

50. Pound, *The Spirit of Romance,* p. 14.

51. Wallace Stevens, *Opus Posthumous,* ed. Samuel French Morse (New York: Knopf, 1969), p. 161.

52. Ronald Bush describes New Criticism as "a movement more univocally conservative than modernism ever was," in "The Modernists under Siege," *Yeats: An Annual of Critical and Textual Studies,* Vol. VI (1988), p. 6. And John Henry Raleigh comments in "The New Criticism as an Historical Phenomenon" that "unlike either 'art for art' or science," which the modernists proposed to blend, "New Criticism has been determinedly, sometimes lugubriously moral," *Contemporary Literature,* 11 (Winter, 1959), pp. 22–3. Kermode's *Romantic Image* best sums up Yeats's conservative notion of the female "thinking body" in his paraphrase of Yeats: "In women, as in poems, the body as a whole must be expressive: there should be no question of the mind operating independently of the whole body. In a sense, the body does the thinking" (50). Kermode amasses Yeats's theory from various images and references made in Yeats's work, including his discussion of, respectively, the unified image of a girl playing a guitar and of a contrastingly "shrill" and "abrupt" girl in "A Guitar Player," and "The Looking Glass" sections of "The Cutting of an Agate" (*E&I* 268, 269); his reference to Herodiade "dancing seemingly alone in her narrow luminous circle" as an emblem of Aesthetic purity (*Auto* 215); the dancer in "Michael Robartes and the Dancer," who is instructed to have no thoughts unless "her foot sole think it too"; and the dancer inseparable from the dance in "Among Schoolchildren."

CHAPTER TWO

1. H.D. never published the review, but it has been reproduced in *Agenda,* 25, nos. 3–4 (Autumn/Winter, 1987–8), pp. 51–3.

2. See Lawrence Rainey, "Canon, Gender, and Text: The Case of H.D." in *Representing Modernist Texts: Editing as Interpretation,* ed. George Bornstein (Ann Arbor: U. of Michigan P., 1991). For a response to Rainey's essay, see Robert Spoo's forthcoming essay, "H.D. Prosed" in *The Future of Modernism,* ed. Hugh Witemeyer.

3. Rachel Blau DuPlessis's *Writing beyond the Ending* (Bloomington: Indiana U.P., 1985) demonstrates that many women writers subverted the traditional romance plot by writing beyond the conventional ending in which the heroine often marries.

4. Letter to Amy Lowell, July 19, 1919, Beinecke Library, Yale University. H.D. complained to Amy Lowell about the "cynicism" and undue stress upon "originality and cleverness" of the "modern cult of brutality" she perceived in Joyce and probably in Pound's "Blast" poems (Sept. 1918).

5. Letter to John Cournos, July 9, 1917, Beinecke Library, Yale University.

6. Susan Stanford Friedman and Rachel Blau DuPlessis identify *HER* as essentially a lesbian text whose heroine discovers poetic, prophetic, and erotic power through union with a "twin-self sister," in " 'I Had Two Loves Separate': The Sexualities of H.D.'s *HER*," *Montemora*, 8 (1981), pp. 7–31. Reprinted in *Signets* (Madison: U. of Wisconsin P., 1990), pp. 205–32. (Hereafter cited in text as "Two Loves".)

7. Rachel Blau DuPlessis has demonstrated H.D.'s use of shifting erotic/familial bonds to escape "romantic thralldom" to male power in later works such as *Helen in Egypt*, in chapter 5, "Romantic Thralldom and 'Subtle Genealogies' in H.D.," of her *Writing beyond the Ending*, pp. 66–83.

8. A. C. Swinburne, *Swinburne Replies*, ed. Clyde Kenneth Hyder (New York: Syracuse U.P., 1966), pp. 3, 18.

9. A. C. Swinburne, *Poems and Ballads,* first series (London: Chatto and Windus, 1914). (Hereafter cited in text as *P&B,* I.)

10. Shari Benstock also perceives *HER* as a critique of high modernism and particularly of the Imagist enterprise in *Women of the Left Bank* (pp. 335–49).

11. The English poetic tradition confuses the sisters.

12. Richard Jenkyns discusses the Victorian Hellenists' use of the color white as a code for homoeroticism in *The Victorians and Ancient Greece* (Cambridge, Mass.: Harvard U.P., 1980), pp. 147–53.

13. Barbara Guest, *Herself Defined: The Poet H.D. and Her Work* (New York: Quill Press, 1984), p. 81, n. 1. (Hereafter cited in text as Guest.)

14. Douglas Bush, *Mythology and the Romantic Tradition in English Poetry* (London: Oxford U.P., 1937), pp. 505, 506.

15. Letter to Bryher (April 5, 1936), Beinecke Library, Yale University. See also Friedman's discussion in *Penelope's Web* of the genesis of H.D.'s "Crystalline" poetic and the reaction of H.D.'s critics to the epithet (53).

16. Louis Untermeyer, *American Poetry since 1900* (New York: Henry Holt, 1923), p. 134.

17. For a detailed examination of the quest pattern, from erotic imprisonment to "unity" in the male Romantic tradition, see Harold Bloom's "Internalization of Quest Romance" in *Romanticism and Consciousness: Essays in Criticism* (New York: Norton, 1970).

18. For an analysis of Swinburne's response to the Romantic quest pattern, see David Reide's *Swinburne: A Study of Romantic Mythmaking* (Charlottesville: U. of Virginia P., 1978).

19. Letters to Amy Lowell, Nov. 1915 and Oct. 4, 1916, Beinecke Library, Yale University.

20. H.D., *Collected Poems: 1912–1944*, ed. Louis L. Martz (New York: New Directions, 1983), p. 17. (Hereafter cited as *CP*.)

21. Leslie Brisman, "Swinburne's Semiotics," *Georgia Review*, 31 (1977), p. 582.

22. Adalaide Morris quotes from *The Egoist*, 3 (1916), p. 183, in her article, "The Concept of Projection: H.D.'s Visionary Powers," in *Contemporary Literature*, xxv, no. 4 (1986), pp. 410, 411.

23. Jerome J. McGann, *Swinburne: An Experiment in Criticism* (Chicago and London: U. of Chicago P., 1972), p. 134.

24. Walter Pater, "An English Poet," *Imaginary Portraits*, ed. Eugene J. Brzenk (London, New York, Evanston: Harper and Row, 1964), p. 39.

25. For more on Swinburne's disruptive landscapes, see Pauline Fletcher's *Gardens and Grim Ravines: The Language of Landscape in Victorian Poetry* (Princeton: Princeton U.P., 1983). Fletcher's study of Swinburne's Romantic landscapes notes that "[Swinburne] subverted the traditional associations of the garden, transforming it from a symbol of paradisal innocence to something disturbingly different." Fletcher's analysis of Swinburne's stormy seascapes and stoic sea flowers recalls both H.D.'s desire to mingle with a dangerous and intoxicating sea-mother/lover in poems such as "The Shrine" (*CP* 9) and the stoicism of her embattled sea flowers (Fletcher 192).

26. "Notes on Pre-Raphaelites," p. 28, Beinecke Library, Yale University.

27. Charles Baudelaire, *Les Fleurs Du Mal*, preface by Théophile Gautier (Paris, 1968). The translation is from Patricia Clements's *Baudelaire and the English Tradition* (Princeton: Princeton U.P., 1985), p. 60.

28. Letter to Richard Aldington, Oct. 18, 1953, Beinecke Library, Yale University.

29. H.D. claimed that she had written her first poems for Frances Gregg; and Gregg's careful inscription of Swinburnian love poems – one titled "Hermaphroditus" – on H.D.'s copy of *Sea Garden* appears to claim the Imagist volume as a tribute to the Greek aesthetic of androgyny and homoeroticism they had mutually created from Swinburne (Guest, Illustration).

30. *The Egoist* (May 1, 1915), pp. 65–84.

31. Letter to H.D., April 7, 1918, Beinecke Library, Yale University.

32. In a letter to John Cournos, July 9, 1917, H.D. confessed that she was experimenting with the more personal form of the novel in order to work her way out of "an old emotional tangle" in which her "personal self" had come "between me and my real self," Beinecke Library, Yale University.

33. Edith Sitwell, "Modernist Poets," *Echanges*, p. 82.

34. Letters to Lowell, Sept. 1918 and July 9, 1919, Beinecke Library, Yale University. Aldington referred to H.D.'s comment that she felt "deracinée" in a letter to H.D., April 24, 1918. H.D. called herself "old fashioned" and "not

dans the movement" in a letter to Lowell, July 19, 1919, Beinecke Library, Yale University.

35. This is Rachel DuPlessis's argument in "Romantic Thralldom and 'Subtle Genealogies' in H.D.," in *Writing beyond the Ending*.

36. H.D., *Bid Me to Live* (Redding Ridge: Black Swan Books, 1983), p. 136.

37. Robert Langbaum's *Poetry of Experience* (New York: Random House, 1957) claims that the "extraordinary moral positions and extraordinary emotions" characteristic of the dramatic monologue reached "pathological extremes in Swinburne" (93). For another study of Romanticism and the dramatic monologue in the male tradition, see Carol T. Christ's chapter 2, "Dramatic Monologue, Mask and Persona," in *Victorian and Modern Poetics* (Chicago and London: University of Chicago Press, 1984), pp. 15–52. Christ compares the Victorians' and moderns' reaction against the Romantic focus on the self in what she regards as similar theories of the mask and persona in the monologue. However, Christ singles out Tennyson's and Swinburne's more "confessional" approaches to the monologue as exceptions. Langbaum stresses the continuities between the Romantic lyric "song of the self" and the Victorian monologue's preoccupation with a "poetry which makes its statement not as an idea but as an experience" (35). Langbaum's more Romantic definition of the Victorian monologue resembles H.D.'s.

38. A version of this discussion of H.D.'s "Hyacinth" appeared in my "H.D.'s Romantic Landscapes: The Sexual Politics of the Garden," *Sagetrieb*, H.D. Centennial Issue, 6, no. 2 (1987), pp. 57–75. The essay has also been reprinted in *Signets*.

39. See Rachel DuPlessis's *Writing beyond the Ending* for an examination of how H.D. and other modernist women writers create narrative strategies to disrupt the traditional romance plot of nineteenth-century fictions. These strategies include "fraternal-sororal ties," emotional attachments to women in bisexual love plots, female bonding, and lesbianism (xi).

40. William A. Ulmer, *Shelleyan Eros: The Rhetoric of Romantic Love* (Princeton: Princeton U.P., 1990), p. 138.

41. Susan Gubar, "Sapphistries," *Signs*, 10, no. 1 (1984), pp. 43–62.

42. H.D., *Hipparchia*, in *Palimpsest* (Carbondale: Southern Illinois U.P.), pp. 29–31.

CHAPTER THREE

1. Walter Pater, "*Diaphaneitè*," in *Imaginary Portraits: A New Collection*, ed. Eugene J. Brzenk (New York, Evanston and London: Harper and Row, 1964). (Hereafter cited in text as *Diaphaneitè*.)

2. As I mentioned in Chapter Two, Richard Jenkyns's *The Victorians and Ancient Greece* first began to uncover "the complex pattern of imagery" that Aesthetes

such as Pater associated with a Hellenic homoeroticism. More recently Richard Dellamora's *Masculine Desire* explores the codes and tropes of male–male transgressive desire in several Victorians. See particularly chapter three, "Pater at Oxford in 1864: Old Morality and *Diaphaneitè*," pp. 58–68. Linda Dowling's essay, "Ruskin's Pied Beauty and the Constitution of a 'Homosexual' Code," discusses the term *poikilos* as part of the Aesthetes' homosexual vocabulary. Both this essay and Dowling's subsequent *Hellenism and Homosexuality in Victorian Oxford* discuss the code of "Dorianism." Dellamora's most recent book, *Apocalyptic Overtures,* contains a chapter on Dorianism (chapter 2) that focuses on the code as a means to "mobilize male–male libidinal energies in service of the nation-state" (43). I am indebted to these works in my discussion of Aesthetic codes for the transgressive male body.

3. Walter Pater, *Plato and Platonists* (London: Macmillan, 1910), p. 41.

4. Quoted in Linda Dowling's essay, "Esthetes and Effeminati," p. 52.

5. Oscar Wilde, *Dorian Gray, The Complete Works of Oscar Wilde,* with introduction by Vyvyan Holland (London and Glasgow: Collins, 1973), p. 32. (Hereafter cited in text as *Dorian Gray.*)

6. Walter Pater, "Winckelmann," in *The Renaissance: Studies in Art and Poetry,* (London: Macmillan, 1910), p. 222. (Hereafter cited in text as "Winckelmann.")

7. This may have governed his choice of the more masculine Athena rather than Venus to be the marble goddess.

8. Richard Ellmann, *Oscar Wilde* (New York: Alfred A. Knopf, 1988), pp. 141–2.

9. See Sydney Janet Kaplan's chapter four, "The Strange Longing for the Artificial," in *Katherine Mansfield and the Origins of Modernist Fiction.* Kaplan uses this quote to illustrate the female/nature, male/artifice dyad that lies behind Pater's homoerotic Aestheticism. She demonstrates that Mansfield mixed the natural with the artificial in her writing as a means of escaping the conventional equation nature = female.

10. Although the speaker's gender is not specified, there is strong evidence to suggest "he" is male, as I demonstrate at the conclusion of Chapter Four.

11. See also William Ulmer's discussion of transparency in Shelley's "veiled maid" of *Alastor* (38).

12. Quoted in the entry to "diaphanous" in *The Compact Edition of the Oxford English Dictionary* (New York: Oxford U.P., 1971), p. 717.

13. Paul de Man, "Shelley Disfigured," in *The Rhetoric of Romanticism* (New York: Columbia U.P., 1984), p. 109.

14. In *Aestheticism and Deconstruction: Pater, Derrida and de Man* (Princeton: Princeton U.P., 1991), Jonathan Loesberg argues that Pater's famous "Conclusion" encompasses the "multiplicity" of the deconstructive process: like Derrida's philosophical analysis, Pater accepts "the contradiction within the foundation

of knowledge" and uses Aestheticism as "a central mode of interpreting and engaging a range of discourses" (6, 4).

15. Quoted in Harold Bloom's Introduction to *Selected Writings of Walter Pater*, ed. Bloom (New York: Columbia U.P., 1974), p. xxvii.

16. Naomi Schor, *Reading in Detail: Aesthetics and the Feminine* (New York, London: Methuen, 1987). See especially chapter three, "Decadence: Wey, Loos, Lukács" (pp. 42–64).

17. Quoted in Naomi Schor, *Reading in Detail*, p. 43.

18. Linda Dowling, "Ruskin's Pied Beauty and the Constitution of a 'Homosexual' Code," p. 1. Barbara Hughes Fowler describes the word's significance as the play of light and texture, in "The Archaic Aesthete," *American Journal of Philology*, 105 (1984), p. 119.

19. Linda Dowling, "Ruskin's Pied Beauty and the Constitution of a 'Homosexual' Code," p. 6.

20. Mary Russo's essay was first published in *Feminist Studies / Critical Studies*, ed. Teresa de Lauretis (Bloomington: Indiana U.P., 1986), p. 214, and later incorporated into her book, *The Female Grotesque: Risk, Excess, and Modernity* (New York and London: Routledge, 1994).

21. Eileen Gregory discusses the liminality or "in-betweenness" articulated by H.D.'s white erotic body in "Virginity and Erotic Liminality: H.D.'s *Hippolytus Temporizes*," pp. 140, 141.

22. See particularly William Ulmer's discussion of Shelley's *Epipsychidion* (138) in *Shelleyan Eros*.

23. See Karla Jay's chapters three and four in *The Amazon and the Page*, "Gynocentricity" and "Sappho and other Goddesses," for more on Vivien's and Barney's Decadent Romantic cult of the Great Mother.

24. Karla Jay explores Vivien's and Barney's philosophy of lesbian love in chapter five, in her book *The Amazon and the Page*, "The Religion of Love."

25. Muriel Ciolkowska, "A Pagan Poet," p. 149. H.D. exclaimed over the article in a letter to John Cournos (Oct. 16, 1916), "Did you read the article in the *Egoist* about Renée Vivien? You must get Frank to tell you of her. Isn't it curious that she should have come from America?"

26. H.D., *Notes on Thought & Vision & The Wise Sappho* (San Francisco: City Lights Books, 1982), p. 32.

27. I am indebted to Wendy Kolmar for pointing out to me certain details of this poem.

CHAPTER FOUR

1. Oscar Wilde, *The Soul of Man under Socialism* (1891), reprinted in Richard Ellmann, ed., *The Artist as Critic: Critical Writings of Oscar Wilde* (Lon-

don: W. H. Allen P., 1970) p. 272. Jonathan Dollimore, "Different Desires: Subjectivity and Transgression in Wilde and Gide," *Genders*, 2 (1988), p. 27.

2. Sharon O'Brien, "The Thing Not Named: Willa Cather as a Lesbian Writer," *Signs* (Summer, 1984), p. 575.

3. Oscar Wilde, *The Letters of Oscar Wilde*, ed. Rupert Hart-Davis (New York: Harcourt Brace, 1962), p. 252. Barbara C. Gelpi, *Dark Passages: The Decadent Consciousness in Victorian Literature* (Madison: U. of Wisconsin P., 1965), p. 54.

4. Wilde, *Complete Works of Oscar Wilde*, with introduction by Vyvyan Holland (London and Glasgow: Collins, 1973), p. 709.

5. Rachel Blau DuPlessis theorizes about the possibility of a female aesthetic in her important essay, "For the Etruscans: Sexual Difference and Artistic Production – the Debate over a Female Aesthetic," *The Future of Difference*, ed. Hester Eisenstein and Alice Jardine (New Brunswick, N.J.: Rutgers U.P., 1985), pp. 128–56.

6. Marilyn Farwell particularly equates the "Romantic Aesthetic relationship" with the woman–woman connection between a "lesbian community" of poet readers in "Toward a Definition of the Lesbian Literary Tradition," *Signs* (Autumn, 1988), p. 117.

7. O'Brien, *Willa Cather: The Emerging Voice* (New York: Oxford U.P., 1987), p. 147.

8. See Richard Ellmann's discussion in *Oscar Wilde*, p. 29.

9. Linda Dowling, "Ruskin's Pied Beauty and the Constitution of a 'Homosexual' Code," p. 2.

10. Quoted in Richard Ellmann, *Oscar Wilde*, p. 29.

11. Dellamora theorizes that Swinburne's *Poems and Ballads* did encourage Pater's relatively overt discussion of homoeroticism in his subsequent essay on Winckelmann in *Masculine Desire*, p. 69.

12. Dellamora makes this connection in another context in *Masculine Desire*, p. 196.

13. Adrienne Rich, "Compulsory Heterosexuality and Lesbian Existence," *Signs*, 5 (Summer, 1980), p. 650.

14. Kaplan, *Katherine Mansfield and the Origins of Modernist Fiction*, pp. 54, 39–40.

15. Phyllis Wachter, unpublished essay, "Surname: Arnold's Description: Spinster; Avocation: New Woman."

16. See my introduction to H.D.'s *Paint It Today*, "Lesbian Romanticism: H.D.'s Fictional Representations of Frances Gregg and Bryher," pp. xv–xli.

17. Barbara C. Gelpi discusses Swinburne's allusion to Cathy's pronouncement in *Dark Passages*, p. 181.

18. Claire Tomalin, *Katherine Mansfield: A Secret Life* (New York: Knopf, 1988), p. 37. Tomalin reproduces "Leves Amores" in Appendix I, pp. 259–69.

19. Thaïs E. Morgan, "Male Lesbian Bodies: The Construction of Alternative

Masculinities in Courbet, Baudelaire, and Swinburne," *Genders*, 15 (Winter, 1992), p. 40.

20. Martha Vicinus, "The Adolescent Boy: *Fin de Siècle* Femme Fatale," *Journal of the History of Sexuality*, 5, no. 1 (1994), pp. 90–114.

21. Among the many functions of women writers' masking practices, Cheryl Walker includes the use of masking as a "deconstructionist strategy" for undoing the conventional male subject; see Walker's "Feminist Criticism and the Author," *Critical Inquiry* (Spring, 1990), pp. 551–71.

22. I use Ann Herrmann's term, sexual "indifference," which she applies to a female character who undergoes a sex change in Christa Wolf's "Self Experiment." Herrmann asserts that Wolf's impersonation of a sex change trades in sexual difference for "indifference," and "deconstructs gender as an epistemological category," in "The Transsexual as Anders in Christa Wolf's 'Self-Experiment,'" *Genders*, 3 (Fall, 1988), p. 53.

23. H.D., *Hippolytus Temporizes* (New York: New Directions, 1985), p. 7.

24. John Walsh, "Afterword: The Flash of Sun on the Snow," in *Hippolytus Temporizes*, p. 144.

25. Walter Pater, *Hippolytus Veiled: A Study from Euripides* in *Greek Studies*, reprinted in *Selected Writings of Walter Pater*, ed. Harold Bloom (New York: Columbia U.P., 1974), pp. 250, 249. (Hereafter cited in text as *Hippolytus Veiled*.)

26. Eileen Gregory, "Virginity and Erotic Liminality: H.D.'s *Hippolytus Temporizes*," *Contemporary Literature*, 31, no. 2 (Summer, 1990), p. 141.

27. H.D., *Hedylus* (Redding Ridge: Black Swan Books, 1980), p. 68.

28. I am indebted to Eileen Gregory's discussion of the "white" body of the proem in her essay, "Virginity, Erotic Liminality: H.D.'s *Hippolytus Temporizes*," an image she attributed to classical sources. I agree with Gregory's assertion that in *Hippolytus Temporizes* "love of the absent mother" is metaphorically associated with the "white" erotic body, although I place the "white" body in the context of the Decadent Romantic "white" image complex of "forbidden" desires.

29. Lisa M. Steinman, "Shelley's Skepticism: Allegory in 'Alastor'," *ELH*, 45 (1978), pp. 264–65.

30. Rachel Blau DuPlessis, "Seismic Orgasm: Sexual Intercourse, Gender Narratives and Lyric Ideology in Mina Loy," in *Studies in Historical Change*, ed. Ralph Cohen (U. of Virginia P., 1992), pp. 264–91.

31. T. S. Eliot, *On Poetry and Poets* (London: Faber & Faber, 1957), p. 143.

32. Linda Dowling discusses the linguistic implications of Swinburne's preference for the spoken word in *Language and Decadence in the Fin de Siècle*, p. 177.

33. In "Swinburne's Dramatic Monologues: Sex and Ideology," *Victorian Poetry*, 22 (1984), pp. 175–95.

34. Julia Kristeva, "The Semiotic and the Symbolic," in *Revolution in Poetic Language* (New York: Columbia U.P., 1984), pp. 21–106.
35. Ibid., p. 26.
36. H.D., *Tribute to Freud: Writing on the Wall: Advent,* with foreword by Norman Holmes Pearson (New York: New Directions, 1974), p. 51.
37. H.D., *Ion* (Redding Ridge: Black Swan Books, 1987), quoted in the afterword by John Walsh, p. 122.
38. Jacques Lacan, "The Empty Word and the Full Word," in *Speech and Language in Psychoanalysis,* translated with notes and commentary by Anthony Wilden (Baltimore: Johns Hopkins U.P., 1981), p. 9.
39. From René Girard's *Deceit, Desire and the Novel,* and Gayle Rubin's "The Traffic in Women: Notes on the 'Political Economy of Sex'," in *Toward an Anthropology of Women,* ed. Rayne R. Reiter (New York: Monthly Review Press, 1975).
40. Earl Jackson, Jr., *Strategies of Deviance: Studies in Gay Male Representation* (Bloomington: Indiana U.P., 1995), p. 3.
41. See Dale Davis, "Heliodora's Greece," in *H.D.: Woman and Poet,* ed. Michael King (Orono: National Poetry Foundation, 1986), p. 154. Caroline Zilboorg writes in an unpublished manuscript, "H.D.'s Heliodora: Soul of My Soul." " 'Heliodora' and its companion poem 'Nossis' merit close attention as they reveal the intimacy of the Aldingtons' creative relationship, the nature of their early collaboration, their view of translation as a creative art, and their precise and rich use of Hellenic materials" (p. 10).
42. Dale Davis, "Heliodora's Greece," p. 152.
43. Ann Herrmann, "The Transsexual as Anders in Christa Wolf's 'Self-Experiment," p. 54.

CHAPTER FIVE

1. Violet Hunt, *Wife of Rossetti: Her Life and Death* (New York: E. P. Dutton, 1932). In "H.D. by Delia Alton," H.D. referred to her conversations with Hunt, stating that "Violet [Hunt] spoke to [her] almost exclusively of Elizabeth Siddall [sic]" (191). H.D. was proud that she had supplied the title, *Wife of Rossetti,* for Hunt's book. Later, H.D. dedicated her own (fictional) biography of Siddal, "White Rose and the Red," to Hunt and claimed that her book had taken "right over from Violet Hunt" (letter to Pearson, Aug. 27, 1948, Beinecke Library, Yale University).
2. Horace Gregory wrote that when he "met" H.D. in 1934, "she had been reading William Morris with her characteristic enthusiasm." He observed that "those who, even now, associate her solely with Pound's Imagist verse, are wrong." He added, "She had probably reawakened her interest in the Pre-Raphaelites, and therefore in William Morris, through her friendship with

Violet Hunt, for she was among the most extraordinary of H.D.'s London friends" (Guest, 222).

3. H.D. wrote excitedly to Viola Jordan, "I have gone deep into the . . . Pre-Raphaelites," describing how she was having books "sent out from the London Library" to aid her research (letter to Viola Jordan, Jan. 9, 1949, Beinecke Library, Yale University).

4. In "H.D. by Delia Alton," H.D. discusses at length the "continuity" she feels with the Pre-Raphaelites, whom she considers her "familiars" (194). Elsewhere she elaborates on their power to reincarnate "the child," who first learned their legend in the "old woman" ("The Sword Went Out to Sea," pp. 181, 277).

5. This has become a commonplace of H.D. criticism. Susan Friedman in *Psyche Reborn* first explored at length the shift in H.D.'s masks toward the mother muse and the more cultural scope of H.D.'s late, long poems. See also Deborah Kelly Kloepfer's *The Unspeakable Mother* and Rachel Blau DuPlessis's *Writing Beyond the Ending,* chapter seven, "Romantic Thralldom and 'Subtle Genealogies' in H.D." More recently, Donna Hollenberg Kronik shifts the emphasis toward H.D. as mother in her examination of the childbirth metaphor and H.D.'s career (*H.D.: The Poetics of Childbirth and Creativity* (Boston: Northeastern U.P., 1991)). Susan Edmunds also takes a new angle on H.D.'s mother–daughter dyads, which she explores in relation to Melanie Klein's theories about the aggressive, consuming daughter; see Edmunds, *Out of Line: History, Psychoanalysis, and Montage in H.D.'s Long Poems* (Stanford: Stanford U.P., 1994), pp. 21–93.

6. Susan Friedman points out the more "inclusive" nature of H.D.'s later feminist myth making in *Psyche Reborn.* Rachel DuPlessis theorizes in *Writing beyond the Ending* that H.D.'s later narrative strategies to dispel the "romantic thralldom" of her unequal relationships with men include employment of the brother–sister bond.

7. I borrow this phrase from the title of Judith Butler's book, *Bodies That Matter.*

8. King, "H.D. and Her Reputation," conference paper, *H.D. Centennial Conference,* University of Maine, Orono, June 5–7, 1986.

9. *Manchester Guardian,* Dec. 21, 1931.

10. *Oxford Anthology of Modern Literature,* vol. II, ed. William Rose Benet and Norman Holmes Pearson (London: Oxford U.P., 1938), pp. 1287–8.

11. *Winter Roses,* p. 2 (Beinecke Library, Yale University).

12. This phrase combines Judith Butler's title *Bodies That Matter* and Somer Brodribb's *Nothing Mat(t)ers: A Feminist Critique of Postmodernism.* Butler argues that the materiality of the body is reified even in prohibitive discourses, while Brodribb claims specifically that the postmodern prohibition against materiality is motivated by masculinist bias toward the mother's body and the feminine.

13. Thaïs E. Morgan, "Male Lesbian Bodies: The Construction of Alternative Masculinities in Courbet, Baudelaire, and Swinburne," pp., 37–57.

14. Nina Auerbach, *Woman and the Demon: The Life of a Victorian Myth* (Cambridge, Mass. and London: Harvard U.P., 1982), p. 41. Helena Michie, *The Flesh Made Word: Female Figures and Women's Bodies* (New York and Oxford: Oxford U.P., 1987), p. 123.

15. Thaïs E. Morgan, "A Whip of One's Own: Dominatrix Pornography and the Construction of a Post-Modern (Female) Subjectivity," *NLH,* 20, 2 (Winter, 1989), p. 120.

16. See "The Heart of Darkness: The *Agon* of the Femme fatale," chapter one.

17. See Thaïs E. Morgan's "Swinburne's Dramatic Monologues, Sex and Ideology" for a discussion of Swinburne's perversions of biblical language in "Anactoria."

18. Sue-Ellen Case, "Tracking the Vampire," *Differences,* 3 (Summer, 1991), pp. 1, 2.

19. See Susan Edmunds's introduction to *Out of Line,* " 'This Unsatisfied Duality': Reading H.D. for (with) Ambivalence" (pp. 1–19), and also her earlier short article derived from her book, "Stealing from 'Muddies Body' ": H.D. and Melanie Klein, *H.D. Newsletter,* ed. Eileen Gregory, 4, no. 2 (Winter, 1991), pp. 17–30.

20. Helena Michie, *Sororophobia: Differences among Women in Literature and Culture* (New York, Oxford: Oxford U.P., 1992), p. 9.

21. Queer theorists propose that while drawing upon feminist theory, queer theory should create a space for discussions of sexuality that do not center on gender oppression, psychoanalysis, gender identity, female bonding, and other privileged sites of feminist criticism. Gayle S. Rubin, for example, seeks to create a forum for lesbian sexuality that would allow explorations of sexual practice, female–female lust, violence, sadomasochism, etc. See her articles, "Thinking Sex: Notes for a Radical Theory of the Politics of Sexuality," in *The Lesbian and Gay Studies Reader,* ed. Henry Abelove, Michele Aina Barale, and David M. Halperin (New York and London: Routledge, 1993), pp. 3–44; "Toward a Butch-Femme Aesthetic" in the same anthology; and her interview with Judith Butler, "Sexual Traffic," in a special issue of *Differences,* "Feminism Meets Queer Theory" 6 (Summer-Fall), 1994), pp. 62–99.

22. Joyce P. Lindenbaum, "The Shattering of an Illusion: The Problem of Competition in Lesbian Relationships," *Feminist Studies,* 11, no. 1 (Spring, 1985), p. 86.

23. Catharine Stimpson, "Zero Degree Deviancy: The Lesbian Novel in English," in *Writing and Sexual Difference,* ed. Elizabeth Abel (Chicago: U. of Chicago P., 1982), pp. 256, 257.

24. Linda Williams, "When the Woman Looks," *Re-Vision: Essays in Feminist Film Criticism,* ed. Mary Ann Doane, Patricia Mellencamp, and Linda Williams

(Frederick; Md.: U. Publications of America, 1984), pp. 83–99. Williams hyphenates en-tranced in order to emphasize the woman's *entrance* into the gaze as a participant rather than an observer.

25. Deborah Kelly Kloepfer perceives the language of Hermione's disjunctive ravings as an entrance into the empowering, female semiotic modality.

26. H.D., *Narthex*, *The Second American Caravan: A Yearbook of American Literature*, ed. Alfred Kreymborg, Lewis Mumford, and Paul Rosenfeld (New York: Macaulay Company, 1928), p. 231.

27. Ben Jones discusses Powys's sadomasochism and quotes from the poem, "Sadista," which appeared in a letter to Gregg in his introduction to Frances Gregg's *The Mystic Leeway*, edited and with introduction by Ben Jones, with preface by Oliver Marlow Wilkinson (Ontario: Carleton U.P., 1995), p. 65.

28. Silvia Dobson, "Cloud of Memories: Books H.D. Shared with Me, 1934–1960," *H.D. Newsletter*, ed. Eileen Gregory, 1, no. 2 (Winter, 1987), pp. 36, 37.

29. Michie, somewhat surprisingly, does not provide any instances of the mistress in her otherwise varied examples of the "other woman" (*Sororophobia*).

30. H.D. hinted that she had encouraged Patmore to "console" Aldington while H.D. was indisposed following the stillbirth of her child. Also, Patmore was a very loyal friend to H.D. after Aldington abandoned H.D. for Dorothy Yorke. The tangled stories suggest a strongly ambivalent relationship.

31. H.D., "The Cinema and the Classics," "Beauty," *Close Up*, I (July 1927), pp. 22–33. (Hereafter cited in text as "C. and C.")

32. Betsy Erkkila, "Greta Garbo: Sailing beyond the Fame," *Critical Inquiry*, 11 (June 1985), pp. 598, 599, 601.

33. At one point, Astrid repeatedly jabs at her lover with a knife, producing thin jets of blood. The scene is very effective.

34. H.D., *Borderline: A Pool Film with Paul Robeson* (1930). Reprinted in *Sagetrieb*, 7 (Fall, 1987), pp. 29–50. All my quotations are taken from the original copy in the Beinecke Library, Yale University. (Hereafter cited in text as *Borderline*.)

35. Hilary Schorr, " 'Innumerable Pictures of Myself': The Fragmented Female Face in Victorian Fiction," paper read at MLA Convention, New Orleans, Dec. 1988.

36. One is reminded that *Proserpine* is among Rossetti's most striking paintings, and that H.D. often quoted from Swinburne's "Hymn to Proserpina."

CHAPTER SIX

1. Susan Friedman first made this point in her discussions of Freud and H.D. in *Psyche Reborn* and later in *Penelope's Web*.

2. H.D., *Helen in Egypt* (New York: New Directions, 1961), pp. 7, 8.

3. This earliest "H.D." is assumed in the prehistory to *HER* and *Paint It Today*,

which open at the onset of the heroine's disenchantment, but allude to her former admiration. Later H.D. resurrects the admiring "H.D." in *End to Torment* and elsewhere.

4. See, for example, Julia's open letter to Rico (who is believed to be a type of D. H. Lawrence) that concludes *Bid Me to Live,* H.D.'s tribute/memoir to Pound, *End to Torment,* her notebook, *Compassionate Friendship,* and the Hirslanden Notebooks.

5. Rachel DuPlessis notes that in *Winter Love,* Helen-H.D. offers to share a brother–sister bond with Paris-Pound, but instead "Paris emerges as Helen's child by Achilles" ("Romantic Thralldom" 419). However, DuPlessis and Friedman both point out that H.D.'s fictionalized relationships to types of Pound and Aldington in the later poetry more often approximate a brother–sister kinship.

6. H.D. also brings out this side of the young Aldington and Lawrence in *Bid Me to Live.*

7. See Thaïs E. Morgan's "Mixed Metaphor, Mixed Gender: Swinburne and the Victorian Critics," pp. 16–19.

8. Letter to H.D. from Olivia Rossetti Agresti, October 18, 1948, Beinecke Library, Yale University.

9. See *Richard Aldington and H.D.: The Early Years in Letters,* ed. Caroline Zilboorg (Bloomington and Indianapolis: Indiana U.P., 1992), pp. 51–154.

10. Aldington sent her "Gold Wings" and "Two Red Roses across the Moon," among other poems that reappeared in "White Rose and the Red" as important symbols. She also quoted directly from Aldington's letters in passages from "The Sword Went Out to Sea" in which the "*héros fatale*" appears as Hallblithe, among others.

11. George Bornstein traces each poet's return to Romanticism in *Transformations of Romanticism in Yeats, Eliot and Stevens.*

12. Although this poem, "Toward the Piraeus," was published in *Heliodora* in 1924 and therefore some years before Pound's infamous radio broadcasts and his stay at Pisa, it was prophetic. H.D. was already concerned about Pound.

13. H.D., *Hermetic Definition* (New York: New Directions, 1972), p. 89.

14. See Robert and Marie Secors' several essays on Violet Hunt.

15. Nina Auerbach makes this argument particularly about Siddal's image in *Beata Beatrix* in *Woman and the Demon* (39, 40).

16. See Bram Dijkstra's *Idols of Perversity: Fantasies of Feminine Evil in Fin-de-Siècle Culture* (Oxford: Oxford U.P., 1986).

17. Julia Kristeva, "Women's Time," *The Kristeva Reader,* ed. Toril Moi (New York: Columbia U.P., 1986), p. 195.

18. DuPlessis is of course referring to the socially constituted "ending" of romance; however, women writers can evolve beyond their own outworn rescriptings as well.

19. To avoid confusion, I have replaced Bloom's term, "precursor" with another of his terms, "the *agon*," which like *daemon* can apply to any object of "anxiety."

20. See Nancy Chodorow's chapter 7, "Object-Relations and the Female Oedipal Configuration," in *The Reproduction of Mothering*, in which she describes how the girl's "turn" from her father is always "based in a girl's relation to her mother, both as this has become part of her internal object-world and ego defenses and as this relationship continues to be important and to change (129).

21. Yaeger theorizes that the male is culturally constituted as "bodiless" in the same way that the female is associated with anxieties about the body's materiality. She demonstrates the feminist necessity of giving "the father a body" in "The Father's Breasts" (3–21), *Refiguring the Father: New Feminist Readings of Patriarchy*, ed. Patricia Yaeger and Beth Kowaleski-Wallace (Carbondale and Edwardsville, Southern Illinois U.P., 1989), p. xvii.

22. Adrienne Rich, *Your Native Land, Your Life* (New York: Norton, 1986), p. 9.

CHAPTER SEVEN

1. Julie Newman argues in "Back to the Future: Abjection, Apocalypse and the Maternal in Lawrence's *Women in Love*," that for Lawrence "Love and sex become . . . a purification ritual – a response to the horror of gender" and the mother (5). Paper read at International Narrative Conference, Tulane, April 1990. Cullingford, however, finds an exception in Yeats's abject Crazy Jane who, she argues, "disputes through her ballad poetics and carnivalesque insistence on the grotesque body the monologic identity constructed by a celibate clergy and enshrined in law by the State" (227).

2. My reading of *Trilogy* is not intended to be exhaustive or definitive. I use the poem to illustrate my thesis about H.D.'s later fascination with the mask of the abject femme fatale.

3. Adrienne Rich, *Diving into the Wreck* (New York: Norton, 1973), p. 23. For a discussion of *Trilogy*'s impact on Adrienne Rich's "Diving into the Wreck" and other works, see Friedman's " 'I Go Where I Love': An Intertextual Study of H.D. and Adrienne Rich," *Signs*, 9 (Winter, 1983), pp. 22–46.

4. Susan Edmunds's recent book *Out of Line* discusses the feeding and fed upon bodies of *Trilogy* in the context of Melanie Klein's theories of the mother–daughter relation in "Eating a Way Out of It: H.D.'s Hunger Stories," pp. 33–52.

5. By contrast, Susan Gubar's "The Echoing Spell of H.D.'s *Trilogy*" claims that *Trilogy* suggests Eve's redemption through her "mothers" (138).

6. Kloepfer maintains that in *Trilogy* "the pivotal Mary figure [must] first be accepted erotically, be entered as a kind of sensuous, linguistic medium" (139).

7. Christina Rossetti, *The Complete Poems,* edited and with an introduction by R.W. Crump (Baton Rouge and London: Louisiana State U.P., 1990), p. 264.

8. In 1948 H.D. wrote to Christina Rossetti's niece, Olivia Rossetti Agresti, inquiring about the publication of Rossetti's verse (letter to H.D. from Olivia Rossetti Agresti, Beinecke Library, Yale University).

9. Hilary Schorr's "Innumerable Pictures of Myself: The Fragmented Female Face in Victorian Fiction" quotes from this poem in her discussion of Victorian "female" narratives of the woman's face (paper read at MLA Conference, New Orleans, Dec. 1988).

10. Michie discusses "hands" and "arms" particularly in *The Flesh Made Word* (98–9).

11. H.D. follows a traditional, popular association of Mary Magdalene with the biblical "woman taken in adultery" of John, chapter 8.

12. Evident, for example, in *Bid Me to Live* in which both the vision of Venusian Screen Beauty and Julia herself are also mermaids who ascend stairs toward a dressing table where Julia pulls a comb through her hair (see Chapter Five).

13. Elisabeth G. Gitter, "The Power of Victorian Women's Hair in the Victorian Imagination," *PMLA,* 99 (Oct. 1984), p. 936.

14. William Tindall first coined the term "hair-tent" to describe the Yeatsian trope he associates with Pre-Raphaelitism in *W. B. Yeats* (New York: Columbia U.P., 1966). I also discuss the hair-tent as a characteristic of Yeats's early femmes fatales that does not reappear in Yeats's later representation of the New Woman in "W. B. Yeats and Florence Farr."

POSTSCRIPT

1. Alicia Ostriker, *Stealing the Language: The Emergence of Women's Poetry in America* (Boston: Beacon P., 1986), p. 12.

2. A selected list of such recent theories/criticism evoking these male and female "abject" bodies (some of which I have cited and others I have not) might include: Lynda Hart's *Fatal Women: Lesbian Sexuality and the Mark of Aggression* (Princeton: Princeton U.P., 1994); Judith Butler's *Bodies That Matter;* Eve Kosofsky Sedgwick's "White Glasses," which discusses her cross-gender identification with the gay male in her tribute to a friend dying of AIDS, in *Tendencies* (Durham: Duke U.P., 1993); Thaïs Morgan's "A Whip of One's Own"; Sue-Ellen Case's "Tracking the Vampire"; Diana Fuss's "Homospectatorial Fashion Photography" (in which she discusses "vampiric identification"), *Critical Inquiry,* 18, no. 4 (1991); Nina Auerbach's *Our Vampires, Ourselves* (Chicago: U. of Chicago P., 1995); Alan Sinfield's *The Wilde Century,* particularly chapter two, "Uses of Effeminacy"; Earl Jackson, Jr.'s *Strategies of Deviance: Studies in Gay Male Representation;* Richard Dellamora's *Masculine*

Desire and *Apocalyptic Overtures;* David Bristow's "Wilde, Dorian Gray, and Gross Indecency" in *Sexual Sameness;* Jessica R. Feldman's *Gender on the Divide: The Dandy in Modernist Literature;* and essays in the anthologies *The Lesbian and Gay Studies Reader* and *Lesbian Texts and Contexts.*

Index

abjection, in Frank Kermode's *Romantic Image*,
23, 24–6; in Swinburne's "Fragoletta," 74–
7; in H.D.'s *Trilogy*, 172–7; in H.D.'s
Hippolytus Temporizes, 96; in Eliot's *The
Waste Land*, 170–1; *see also* androgyne,
Decadent male; and abjection; *see also*
femme fatale, Decadent; and abjection
Ackroyd, Peter, 6
Aldington, Richard, 3, 19–20, 42, 51, 52, 54,
59, 89, 122–3, 124, 136, 151, 155, 157, 158
Allingham, William, 143
androgyne, Decadent male, in H.D.'s *HER*,
39–40; in H.D.'s "Hyacinth," 58–60; in
Walter Pater, 63; and modern women
writers, 89; and abjection, 72–6;
homoerotic codes for: crystal, xi, 63, 71,
76, 175; *diaphaneitè*, xiv, 63, 65, 70, 72, 76–
9, 80–3, 175, 177; *poikilia*, 73, 74–6, 76–9;
veined human body, 72, 74–6, 76–9;
whiteness, 93–7, 97–102, 102–7; white
statuary, 39, 40, 43, 65–70; *see also* boy–
man erotic dyad, Decadent
Arnold, Ethel, 88
Auerback, Nina, x, 127, 144–5

Babbit, Irving, 3, 124–5
Bakhtin, Mikhail, xvii, 24–5, 73, 75, 127–8
Barnes, Djuna; *Nightwood*, 12
Barney, Natalie, xviii, 79
Barthes, Roland, 185
Baudelaire, Charles, 19, 49; 50, 89, 128, 156
Beardsley, Aubrey, 2
Benstock, Shari, xii, xviii, 42
Bloom, Harold, xiii, xvi, xviii, 4, 119, 152,
158, 167–8, 185n17, 196,

Bornstein, George, xvi, xviii, 158
Benda, Julien, 125
Blast, 14
Botticelli, 146, 147
boy–man erotic dyad, Decadent, xiv; and
Eliot's myth of origins in "Reflections," 9–
10; in Eliot's "Hamlet and His Problems,"
12; and Pound's "Apostolic Succession,"
15–16, 183; in H.D., 67–70, 77–9; and
H.D.'s "Heliodora," 109–12; and H.D.'s
"Hyacinth," 54–9; and Swinburne's
"Fragoletta," 74–6; and the Victorians, 63–
73; *see also* androgyne, Decadent male;
homoerotic codes for
Brancusi, Constantin, 160
Brisman, Leslie, 47
Bristow, David, 209n2
Brobdribb, Somer, 122, 204n12
brother–sister erotic dyad, Decadent, 150,
152, 153–4; and Pound's *Mauberly*, 13; and
H.D.'s fictionalizations of Pound, 159–167;
and H.D.'s fictionalizations of Elizabeth
Siddal and Swinburne, 167
Browning, Robert, 124
Buchanon, Robert, 156–7
Burne-Jones, 299
Bush, Douglas, 43, 123, 125, 157
Bush, Ronald, 13
Butler, Judith, 5, 23
Byron, 3, 7

Case, Sue-Ellen, 129, 133–5
Cather, Willa, xviii, xix, 85, 89
Celine, Louis-Ferdinand, 128
Christ, Carol T., 54